Luiz Armando Tavares
Armando Jorge Soares

Portuguese Fighter Colours
1919–1956
Piston engined

STRATUS

Published in Poland in 2016
by STRATUS s.j.
Po. Box 123,
27-600 Sandomierz 1, Poland
e-mail: office@mmpbooks.biz
for
Mushroom Model Publications,
e-mail: rogerw@mmpbooks.biz

http://www.mmpbooks.biz

ISBN
978-83-63678-45-6

Editor in chief
Roger Wallsgrove

Editorial Team
Bartłomiej Belcarz
Robert Pęczkowski
Artur Juszczak
James Kightly

Colour Drawings
Chris Sandham Bailey
Karolina Hołda
Artur Juszczak
Zygmunt Szeremeta
JP Vieira

Printed by
Drukarnia Diecezjalna,
ul. Żeromskiego 4,
27-600 Sandomierz
www.wds.pl
marketing@wds.pl

PRINTED IN POLAND

Table of contents

***Photo on Title page:** Supermarine Spitfire RL+A and+B respectively serial numbers 1 and 2 at Ota Air Base. Of note is the variation in the format of the aircraft code letters mostly noticeable on the design of the letter "R". In the background the remains of the Airacobras from Flight "OK", already being scrapped, can be discerned. (Coll MusAr)*

Acknowledgements

We wish to extend our sincere thanks to all that helped us in this project namely:

Lieutenant General Mimoso e Carvalho (*FAP*), a long time friend and fellow researcher, for his always helpful comments, and for the great assistance in choosing and obtaining the photos used in our work.

To the *AHFA-Arquivo Histórico da Força Aérea* (Air Force Historical Archives) *Museu do Ar* (Air Museum), and *MAIS ALTO* (the Portuguese Air Force magazine), for the use of their photos.

To all the *FAP* (Portuguese Air Force) members mentioned in the text that we interviewed along the years, and which supplied many valuable and interesting memories and photos.

To the *VOA PORTUGAL* site (www.voaportugal.org), his administrators, members and forum users, always an invaluable source of interesting information and photos.

To all friends and fellow enthusiasts that in varied *fora* and through Internet are bringing always new and valuable information to add to the Portuguese Military Aviation History.

And, last but not least, to our understanding wives, Maria Manuela and Maria Laurinda, we wish to dedicate this book as a tribute to their patience and support during the long hours that this enterprise took to accomplish.

To all, our deepest and sincere thanks.

Introduction

Since the beginning of time, man has been obsessed by the idea of flying. From dream to reality there was but one step that the boldest were willing to take. As in every country, Portugal had its share of visionaries, some luckier than others, eager to transform dreams into reality, moved by the vision of liberation from their condition as merely earthly creatures, to traverse the air as birds do.

The first documented reference in the history of aviation in Portugal dates from June 1540 when one João Torto, shoemaker in Viseu, an inner country town, jumped from the tower of the Cathedral with a winged apparatus of his construction. He reportedly glided for a short distance before crash landing on the roof of a Chapel in the vicinity, dying several days later from his injuries. In today's town of Viseu, this failed attempt to reach for the skies is marked with a street named in Torto's honour[1].

In June 1709 Bartolomeu de Gusmão, a Jesuit priest, scientist and scholar, presented a revolutionary invention, a hot-air balloon, to King D.João V and a selected audience of court members. A model of his creation rose in the air to the ceiling of the Royal Palace Audience Room,

1 The feat of João Torto is also remembered in the Portuguese *Museu do Ar* (Air Museum) in Sintra where a winged figure is shown jumping from the Cathedral tower of Viseu.

staying there until a servant destroyed it for "being too close to the curtains...", thus demonstrating to the spectators, well before the Montgolfier Brothers did in 1783, the possibility that man might fly. One month later a full-size model of his *Passarola* ('Little Bird') took to the air from S. Jorge Castle and landed in the Tagus River, on the Lisbon waterfront. Fear of the Inquisition led Gusmão to keep his discovery secret, and he falsified drawings and models to obscure his intention of manned flight. This failed to stop him coming to the attention of the Inquisition, and he fled the country seeking refuge in nearby Spain, where he later died in poverty.

Other Portuguese pioneers tried, with greater or lesser success, to create and fly devices that would liberate them and their fellow humans from the laws that kept them bound to the earth. Some enjoyed a brief success; others saw their dreams and flying machines shattered, when they themselves were lucky enough to survive disaster.

By the beginning of the twentieth century, aviation finally became practical and all European countries were captivated by the idea of heavier-than-air flight. Portugal was no exception, and rapidly the thought of creating an 'air component' to the Army grew among the Portuguese elites. In December 1909 this idea went ahead and a group of Army officers founded the *Aero-Club de Portugal*. The club's statutes claim "...the Institution is destined to promote the development of Aviation in Portugal... as well as... to the foundation of Military Aviation".

Five years later, in 1914, their purpose was finally attained with the creation of the *Escola Militar de Aeronáutica* (Aeronautical Military School) in Vila Nova da Rainha (Azambuja, 60km North East of Lisbon). With this act, the *Aeronáutica Militar Portuguesa* (Portuguese Military Aviation, hereafter referred to as A.M.) was officially created. Although belonging to the Army, the School was also designed to train the first Naval Aviation pilots.

Portuguese Aviation in the Great War[2]

The participation of the Portuguese Armed Forces (Army, Navy and Aviation) in the conflict that prevailed for four years across the World between 1914 and 1918 is not well known or recognised out of the country. In effect, Portugal forced its participation on the Great War against the will of the Allies, notably Great Britain, not only because Portugal overseas territories, notably Northern Mozambique and Southern Angola, were at risk of being invaded by forces of Imperial Germany. Some skirmishes had already taken place between border forces. Portugal also wished to join the conflict because the commercial sea routes and port access were under the threat of submarines and other vessels of the German Navy.

With this in mind, and also with a political desire to assert the young Portuguese Republic on the forum of the Nations involved in the War, the Government declared a state of war against Germany on the 9th March 1916. Orders were given to the Army and Navy Chiefs to put in place the necessary arrangements to send a military force to Mozambique, in which an air component should be included.

This element, the *Esquadrilha Expedicionária a Moçambique* (Expeditionary Flight to Mozambique) was composed of aircraft of French origin, three Farman F40 scouts equipped with Renault 130CV engines, and an accompanying crew of three pilots, three observers/officers and three mechanics. Unfortunately, the first fatal accident occurred straight away, as soon as the aeroplanes were considered fully operational, when *Alferes* Jorge Gorgulho perished as a consequence of fire when his aircraft crashed on 8 October 1917.

Meanwhile in Europe, the *Corpo Expedicionário Português (CEP* – Expeditionary Portuguese Corps) was organising and preparing for departure to France, in its ranks 31 pilot officers and an equal number of mechanics. These personnel, in conformity with the agreement established with British Forces, were to join the British Sector and constituted a mixed Flight Group, one Fighter Group and two more Flights for reconnaissance and artillery spotting. This agreement included the equipment by the British of one Flight with SPAD Fighters and two other with Sopwith observation aeroplanes, although in the event the aircraft were never provided, due to the shortage of material for British Forces.

In response to the British inability to provide the promised equipment, in November 1917 the Portuguese pilots and mechanics were integrated into several French *Escadrilles* by special permission of the General Chief-of-Staff of the French North and Northeast Armies, after a transitional training period on French aeroplanes in Plessis-Belleville. After that instructional phase the pilots and mechanics were distributed among French *Escadrilles* operating at the front, and served there until the end of the conflict.

Among them were individuals who would later became famous, either by their involvement in the conflict (such as *Capitão* Oscar Monteiro Torres, who served in the famous *Escadrille SPAD 65, Les Cigognes* and died in an air combat against a superior number of German fighters) or in the structuring of a future *Aeronautica Militar* upon their return to Portugal (such as *Tenentes* Sousa Leite, António Sousa Maya and Lello Portela of *Escadrille SPAD 124,* La Noblette).

However, it was not until the end of the First World War that the *Aeronáutica Militar* would become a true reality and an entity of itself. The return of the pilots that had fought over Flanders fields brought back the much-needed skills to become instructors for the new generations of aviators. With the purchase and receipt, as a compensation for involvement in the war, of a considerable number of aeroplanes, including trainers, fighters and bombers – enough to create the embryo of a military aerial component– the *Aeronáutica Militar* finally took off. In the meantime, the Navy was in a better position, due to its specific territorial defence commitment during the world conflict – search and rescue, shore surveillance, protection of vessels against submarines and scouting

2 *Os Portugueses na Flandres*, 1914–1918 – General Pedro Cardoso, Brussels 1982. These paragraphs are a summary of a larger chapter of this book under the sub-title A *Aviação Militar na Guerra de '14–'18.*

missions, for example – and therefore already possessed a reasonable number of aeroplanes in its inventory, all of recent design, and a number of pilots judged to be sufficient to its needs.

The aim of this book is not to provide a complete or comprehensive history of both aerial components of the Portuguese Armed Forces since their inception, or give an in-depth description of all their flying materiel. Instead, the reader and enthusiast alike, be they historian or modeller, are offered the most interesting and accurate facts and figures on the aircraft that served the Portuguese Nation from the end of the Great War to the birth, at the beginning of the 1950s, of an independent Air Force, merging the Army and Navy air branches.

As the title of the book suggest, the choice of aircraft fell exclusively on the fighter aeroplanes, powered by piston engines, that served under the Portuguese colours from the first, the SPAD 7 until the last, the Republic F-47 Thunderbolt. Between them lay a considerable variety of aircraft that were predominantly acquired during a dramatic period of European and World history, featuring events that caught a small peripheral country amid the torment, while trying to recover from intense internal turmoil. This would be the period of its recent History in which the Portuguese armed forces were to be provided with the largest quantity of modern equipment, be it in land, sea or air.

This book will follow the story of these aircraft, their arrival on Portuguese shores, be it by means of negotiations inside comfortable offices, by harsh diplomatic discussions or in the trauma of forced landings, some to be interned and serve their new owners, others only good for the scrapyard. Additionally, descriptions of their insignia and markings, camouflage and colours and the system of serial and numbering will be included – the last of which is far from straightforward to explain,

It is to the *Força Aérea Portuguesa*, recently celebrating one hundred years of Military Aviation in Portugal (2014) – the repository of traditions and values of the old Army and Navy components that paved the way – to the Men and Women, anonymous or renowned, who through these decades kept the dream of flight alive in succeeding generations, that the authors would like to dedicate this book.

SPAD S.7 C1

Background

By the end of the Great War, Portugal was the recipient of a certain amount of equipment, civilian and military, as compensation for its contribution to the war effort on the Allied side in Europe and Africa. In aeronautical terms this took the shape of a number of SPAD S.7 fighters and Breguet 14A-2 bombers, destined to equip the newly born Army air component, the *Serviço Aeronáutico Militar*[1].

Even a century after their receipt, a disagreement continues regarding the quantity of SPAD fighters delivered. Some sources mention 12 aircraft, while others suggest there were 22. It is the authors' opinion that the actual quantity was probably higher even than 22, as it will be explained below.

Following a simple procedure, the arriving aircraft were numbered from 1 upwards. (See the chapter on Identification and Numbering Systems). No images have come to light of aircraft with serial numbers* higher than 12. Nevertheless, it is quite possible that lower serials were re-used, as happened later with other aircraft.

**** Serial number, number, s/n are used interchangeably – editor.***

As no formal unit existed to operate the above aircraft, nor those that would be received in 1920, the Army Ministry established, by Decree 5141, dated 7 February 1919, a mixed group of autonomous flights, the *Grupo de Esquadrilhas de Aviação República* – G.E.A.R. (Group of Aircraft Flights "Republica") at Amadora airfield near Lisbon, *Major* António Maya being its first Commanding Officer.

The aeroplanes arrived during February 1920, and later several were transferred to *Esquadrilha Mista de Depósito* (Mixed Depot Flight) at Tancos airfield, roughly 130km northeast of Lisbon.

This *Esquadrilha* came into being at Alverca airfield in June 1918, before relocating to Tancos airfield in October 1919.

In 1924 all remaining SPADs still at Amadora were also transferred to Tancos. The abovementioned unit was later to be renamed *Esquadrilha Independente de Aviação de Caça* (E.I.A.C.) (Independent Fighter Aircraft Flight) or *Esquadrilha nº. 1 de Caça*. For a second time, this unit was

1 Later to become *Arma de Aeronáutica* in 1924.

SPAD S.7 no. 12 of G.E.A.R at Amadora airfield showing the cat in the moon insignia. (FAP/AHFA)

A SPAD S.7 behind a Caudron G.3 at Alverca. (FAP/AHFA)

renamed in 22 October 1927, this time as *Grupo Independente de Aviação de Protecção e Combate* (G.I.A.P.C. – Independent Group of Protection and Combat Aviation).

The SPAD fleet was regularly flown in training operations around the country, with the occasional goodwill visits to nearby Spanish airfields. By 1925, according to an official document, the following distribution was noted:

- Three aircraft at *Escola Militar de Aeronáutica* (Military Aeronautical School) – Sintra;
- One aircraft at *Esquadrilha de Treino e Depósito* (Training and Depot Flight);
- Six aircraft at *Esquadrilha nº 1 de Caça* (Fighter Flight no.1) – Tancos;
- Eleven aircraft at *Depósito de Material Aeronáutico* (Aeronautical Material Depot)

As can be seen, this list amounts to a total of 21 SPADs. Taking into consideration aircraft accidents and losses suffered until that date (as described below), the total number of SPADs would appear to exceed 22.

- 9 April 1921, one SPAD crashed near the town of Leiria, killing its pilot *Tenente Coronel* Castilho Nobre;

SPAD S.7 at Sintra air base. (FAP/AHFA)

Portuguese pilot in France with a SPAD during the Great War. (Coll.MUSAR)

- 15 May 1921 – three SPADs numbered 2, 5 and 6 participated in the town-festivities in Elvas, a Portuguese city close to the Spanish border, performing aerobatic demonstrations. On the return flight to its home base by 23 May, aircraft no. 6 crashed, killing its pilot;
- 15 August 1923 – two SPADs, flown by *Capitão* Ribeiro da Fonseca and *Tenente* Dias Leite, departed Tancos for an air display near the border town of Badajoz, Spain. On the 16th, when *Tenente* Dias Leite was performing aerobatics, the aircraft's engine stopped and it crashed on the roof of a house, being destroyed. The pilot was extracted from the remains alive and sent to hospital, surviving the crash and returning to his home base at Tancos three days after the accident.

All the aforementioned accidents occurred before 1925 and with the total loss of the aircraft, either the official document stating the existence of 21 SPADs is not correct, or more aircraft were received later – the latter hypothesis is the more likely. The last SPADs were finally retired in 1932.

SPAD with French insignia crushed by hangar roof that collapsed at Amadora during very strong winds in 1921. The explanation for the French roundels is not known (aircraft bought from France and not yet painted in Portuguese colours?). (Coll. MUSAR)

Camouflage & Markings

For the first time ever the *Cruz de Cristo* was to be applied to a Portuguese fighter flying over National territory. The SPAD was not, of course, a complete stranger to the Portuguese as during the First World War, some pilots sent to France, as part of the contingent fighting with the Allies, flew the aircraft over the Western Front, bearing British or French markings.

During the conflict, it is known that at least one SPAD pilot, *Tenente* Lello Portela, applied the Portuguese National colours to his aircraft in form of a pennant painted on the fuselage underneath the SPA 124 unit emblem, Jeanne d'Arc's head. The National Coat of Arms was also shown on the fuselage top, just behind the cockpit. Another pilot, *Capitão* Oscar Monteiro Torres, a respected hero to the Portuguese population, was killed while flying a SPAD S.7 during a dogfight with German aircraft.

Apparently all SPADs that were delivered to Portugal maintained the original factory silver-dope colour (See caption under SPAD s/n 8). It seems however, from the few available photographs, that the front fuselage of plywood/metal had another colour tone, possibly a blue-grey ('Battleship Grey?') known to be used on other aircraft and equipment.

The red *Cruz de Cristo*[2] was applied to the upper surface of the upper wing and undersurface of the lower one, over a white disc. The red and green National Flag, with Coat of Arms, divided the rudder in equal parts, with the green portion leading. Serial numbers were painted on the fuselage in black, just behind an insignia if applied to a particular aircraft, a practice commonly followed until the late 1930s by all units of the *Aeronáutica Militar*[3].

Aircraft Characteristics SPAD S.7 C1	
Quantity used:	22+
Crew:	One
Years of Service:	1919–1932
Span:	22.96' (7.00 m)
Length:	19.68' (6.00 m)
Height:	7.22' (2.2 m)
Wing area:	192.14 sq ft (17.85 m^2)
Engine:	One 150 CV *Hispano Suiza 8Aa*
Empty weight:	1,102.3 lb (500 kg)
Loaded weight:	1,554.26 lb (705 kg)
Maximum speed:	111.84 mph (180 km/h) at 9,842.52 feet (3,000 m)
Service ceiling:	18,044.62 feet (5,500 m)
Climb to 3,000 m:	11min 20s
Armament: One	7.7 *Vickers* machine gun and two 10 kg *Anilite* bombs

Lt. (or Capt.) Paiva Simões standing in front of SPAD S.7 s/n 8. (FAP/AHFA)

2 *See Markings and Insignias* Appendix – *Major* A. Maya, first CO of G.E.A.R. and himself a war veteran, was the origin of the adoption of the red *Cruz de Cristo* (Christ Cross) as the insignia of the Portuguese military aviation, replacing the red circle with green centre in use until then by the Army and Navy aviation branches.

3 See photo of aircraft no. 12.

SPAD S.7 C1 serial number 8 in an apparently all silver paint scheme, most probably with* Grupo de Esquadrilhas de Aviação República – *G.E.A.R. at Amadora Airfield near Lisbon, circa 1920.*

SPAD S.7 no. 8. (FAP/AHFA)

** As stated by Messrs. Rimell and Guttman in their opus SPAD S.7, (Windsock Publications volume 8 published by Albatross Productions, Ltd) "...the definitive study of WWI French aeroplane colours and markings has yet to be written..." and "... the subject of the SPAD colours in itself would fill a book many times larger then this one...".*

As described by the above authors, the first SPAD aircraft delivered to the Allied Units had clear-doped surfaces with the metal areas and forward fuselage painted in a protective light yellow colour extending to a vertical line behind the cockpit entrance. They express also that it was a regular practice with French manufacturers to over-paint these colours with a mix of a greasy varnish and linseed oil. This blend had as consequence to shrink and toughen the fabric but also to darken and enhance the colour to a deep yellow look. Later on, in an attempt to protect fabrics against ultra-violet sunrays, aluminium powder was added to the mix. The result of this was not a silvery yellow as could be expected but a rather dense colour which would vary from egg yolk to a near-beige or buff or even to a pale yellow, depending on the age and weathering of the surface.

It is a common assertion with all Portuguese authors referring the colours of the received SPADs as "silver doped". However and to our knowledge, there is no substantial evidence to sustain their claims in the shape of a written official document or other, but only a handful of black and white period photographs to justify their assumption. It is therefore possible that, deceived by the examination of the existing period photos and the contrast between the shades, researchers erroneous concluded on the existence of a silver dope/grey colour scheme for the Portuguese SPADs S.7 instead of the more customary clear-dope/light yellow proposal.

Nevertheless, and if we believe under the light of recent studies that there was no reason for the Arma de Aeronáutica *aeroplanes to have anything other than the usual French* Armée de l'air *colour scheme, we opted for following the widespread belief and show the the Portuguese SPAD S.7 as being silver doped with their engine and cockpit metal surfaces painted grey. Until further and conclusive evidence!*

SPAD S.7 C1 from the Esquadrilha nº 1 de Caça *(Fighter Flight no. 1) based in the Tancos Airfield. Aircraft in all silver paint scheme, showing accordingly the Greyhound insignia used by this Airfield, later Air Base. As explained elsewhere in the book, the Galgo (Greyhound) is the oldest insignia identifying a Portuguese Airfield or Air Base and therefore a source of pride for all the staff that served there.*

SPAD (in the background) and Caudron G.3 (nearest to the camera) at Tancos. (FAP/AHFA)

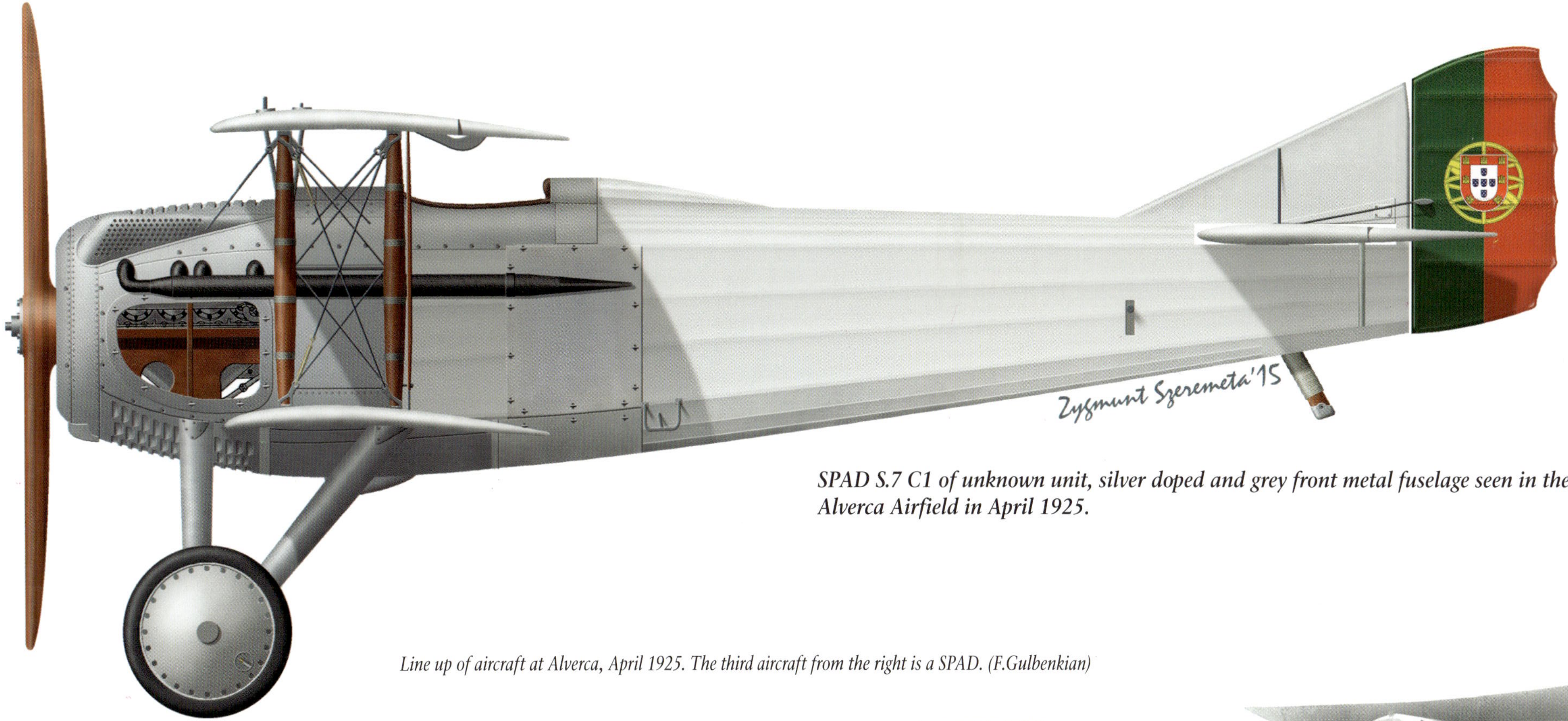

SPAD S.7 C1 of unknown unit, silver doped and grey front metal fuselage seen in the Alverca Airfield in April 1925.

Line up of aircraft at Alverca, April 1925. The third aircraft from the right is a SPAD. (F.Gulbenkian)

SPAD S.7 C1 serial number 12. Aircraft in all silver paint scheme. The origin and meaning of the insignia on the fuselage of this aircraft is unknown, although the character of the "black cat in the moon" is a common subject in the folklore of Central and Northern Europe. It is supposed, without confirmation, that this is a personal insignia and that had its origins on a theme founded on a Great War period postcard, other sources suggesting that it is an emblem of a reconnaissance Unit. We assume that the colours of the insignia depicted on the aircraft are those portrayed on the same period postcard – yellow moon and black cat. Taking into consideration the standard type of photographic film used at the time, with an orthochromatic emulsion, in which the yell ow comes out with a very dark hue we presuppose that the painter of the emblem on the aircraft maintained the colours depicted on the postcard.

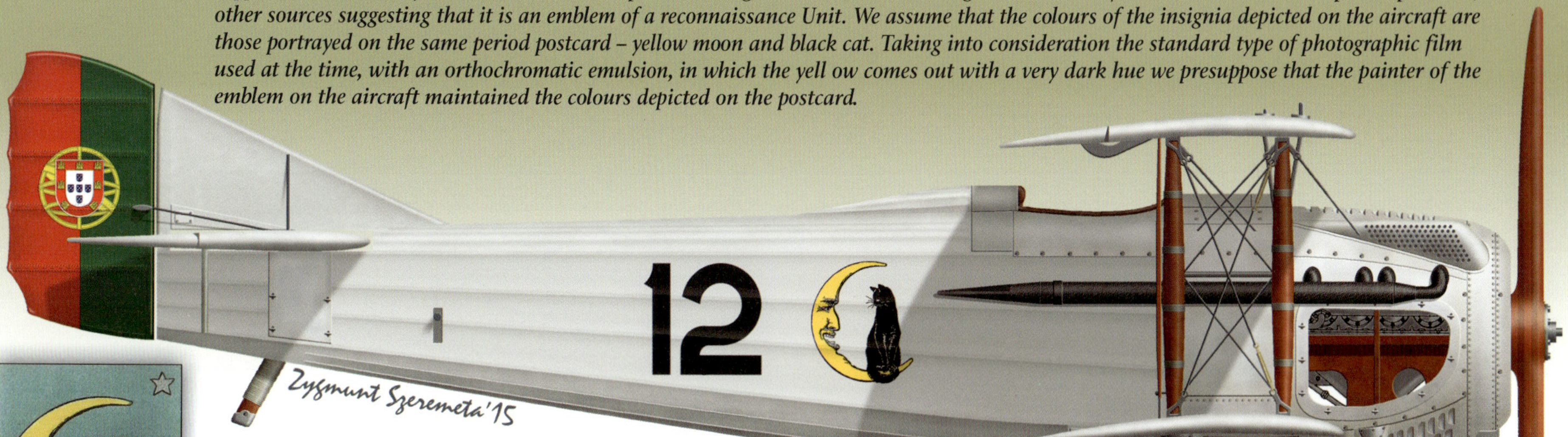

SPAD S.7 no. 12 of G.E.A.R at Amadora airfield. (Coll.MUSAR)

Silver painted upper surface of the upper wing and lower surface of the lower wing showing the arrangement and positioning of the National Insignia for the SPAD S.7 C1.

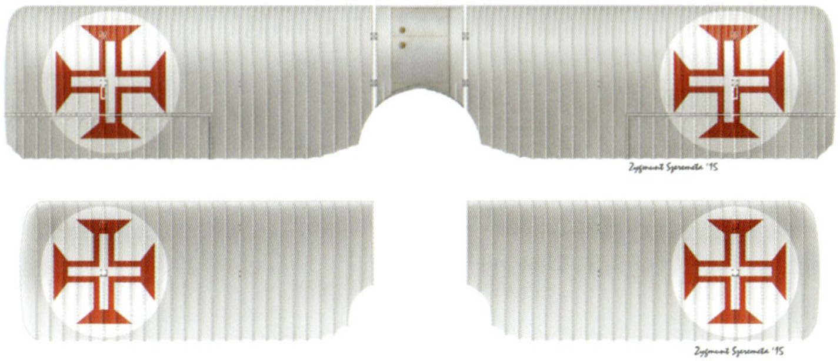

Martinsyde F.4 and F.4A Buzzard

Background

Towards the end of 1917, the British firm Martin & Handasyde Ltd. approached the government with its latest product, the Martinsyde F.3 prototype. Although the performance of the new single-seat fighter biplane was to be considered by everyone involved in the trials, along with other aircraft, to be quite remarkable for the day, the production of the new aeroplane did not go beyond a few aircraft. The main reason behind this was that the Rolls-Royce engine factory could not produce enough of the Falcon engine, which was intended to power the F.3, once all production was absorbed by the Bristol F.2B.

Martin & Handasyde returned to the drawing board, and a few months later returned with a new proposal: the Martinsyde F.4, a revised design derived from its predecessor, but now to accommodate a 300 hp Hispano-Suiza engine.

Unfortunately, the same problem of shortage of engines was repeated and the new prototype ultimately took off powered, ironically, by a Rolls-Royce Falcon. By June 1918 the final model of the F.4, this time in its definitive form with a Hispano-Suiza 300 hp engine, was officially presented to the British authorities. In view of its unquestionably fine qualities, an order was placed for the new aircraft, named in the meantime as the Buzzard.

However, the First World War was reaching its end and the subsequent need for new fighter aircraft was less pressing. Consequently, only around fifty examples of the F.4 were to be constructed during the conflict, destined never to occupy a first-line position in the RAF fighting squadrons, being instead relegated to secondary duties.

Martinsyde F.4 Buzzard production continued in the United Kingdom after the war ended, to meet an anticipated need for over 300 units, a number never attained. On the early stages of its

Although of an indifferent quality, this photo depicts one of the Martinsyde F.4 Buzzard single seat aircraft from Tancos Air Base. (FAP/AHFA)

Partial enlargement of the aircraft line photo clearly showing two airmen standing close to the Buzzard with a pilot onboard. Note the size and location of the cockades. (FAP/AHFA)

development (F.3) the Buzzard aroused the interest of the United States authorities, a contract being placed for some 1,500 airframes to be produced in the US, powered by an indigenous engine. However, this order was soon to be cancelled due, again, to engine availability problems, this time from the US side. Later on, with the emergence of the Martinsyde F.4 Buzzard, interest in the airframe revived, one sample being officially ordered. However, the end of the War and the signing of the Armistice finally led the initiative to be abandoned, thus preventing an 'American Buzzard' from taking the air.

The years after the war were to witness a complete reshuffling of foreign policy across the world. The period would see the emergence of new powers, the signing of new alliances and the surfacing of new countries, mostly born of extinct empires, but eager to be taken seriously in the new world scene. If war surplus materiel was available in large quantities to be distributed to the vanquishers, new weapons could also be presented to the new nations as means of reinforcing their status by force if need it be, inside and outside their borders. This was the reasoning of firms like Martin & Handasyde and others, now in possession of large quantities of unwanted military hardware and hoping to collect a share of the 'peace dividends'.

Two Buzzards and one Breguet 14 at Tancos, date unknown. (FAP/AHFA)

Martinsyde F.4 Buzzard in Portugal

The first Martinsyde F.4 Buzzard to reach the Iberian Peninsula by air was registered G-EANM (c/n E4-500), having been flown from Brooklands to Madrid in October 1919 by the demonstration pilot F.P. Raynham[1].

After a period of display flights in Madrid (Cuatro-Vientos) the aircraft flew the following month to Lisbon, arriving at Alverca by 11 November and at Amadora airfield (near Lisbon) by the 15th of the month. This last leg of the journey concluded the very first air liaison from London to Lisbon. The route and known departure and arrival dates are given below:

- 6 October 1919 – Brooklands – France (unidentified location); France – Spain (Victoria); Victoria – Zaragoza;
- 22 October 1919 – Zaragoza – Madrid;
- 11 November 1919 – Madrid – Portugal (Alverca, near Lisbon) – This last part of the flight, some 360 miles, took 3hrs 5min with a strong headwind.

Although the interest in the new machine and its performance was obvious, especially on the part of the officers of the newly formed *Serviço de Aviação Militar*, (Military Aviation Service) the persistent lack of funds that afflicted the young Portuguese Republic prevented any orders to be placed. In a very common approach for the day, in which military equipment was bought through public subscriptions and presented to the Armed Forces as a token of solidarity, members of the British Colony in Portugal took the initiative to buy the demonstration aircraft with funds raised by their donations and present it to the Portuguese Government. The aircraft was christened *Vasco da Gama* by the British Ambassador's wife[2], Lady Drummond, in a ceremony on 8 December 1919 and was incorporated in the G.E.A.R. *Grupo de Esquadrilhas de Aviação Republica* based at Amadora. At a later date the aeroplane was transferred to the *Esquadrilha Mista de Depósito* (Mixed Flight Depot) at Tancos airfield.

The exhibition Martinsyde F.4 Buzzard thus became the very first Portuguese fighter, as the incorporation of the SPADs into the G.E.A.R. unit occurred only in February 1920.

Subsequently, the sole Buzzard returned to Madrid (Cuatro-Vientos) on May 1922, this time accompanied by two Breguet bombers, in a goodwill visit, which lasted nine days. Captain António

---

1 Upon his return to UK from Spain and Portugal Mr. F.P. Raynham, stated that the Iberian Peninsula was "unsuited for commercial aviation overland, owing to the mountainous nature of the countries...". However "...valuable work could be done...in seaplanes service between coastal towns...(due to the existence of)...many fine harbours suitable for seaplanes and flying-boats". Very soon, time was to prove him wrong! – (From Personals, Flight Magazine, 15 January 1920).

2 The British Ambassador to Portugal was then Sir Lancelot Douglas Carnegie, GCVO, KCMG, PC – 26 December 1861–15 October 1933. (From *Wikipedia*).

Line-up of aircraft, most probably at the Tancos Air Base, showing two types of aeroplanes in service within the Aeronáutica Militar *in the twenties, two Caudron G.3s and one Martinsyde F.4. (FAP/AHFA)*

A Martinsyde Buzzard F.4 single seater. (Coll. Carlos Brazão)

Maya, leading the flight, was piloting the Martinsyde. The return trip to Lisbon (Amadora) was uneventful for the Buzzard while the two Breguets suffered accidents in Cáceres and Badajoz, two Spanish towns visited by the flight. The Martinsyde F.4 Buzzard therefore had the privilege of establishing two 'firsts': the first flight between Madrid and Lisbon in 1919 on its arrival to Portuguese soil and the first Lisbon-Madrid-Lisbon flight, in 1922.

In 1923, when the aircraft was at its new base, Tancos, the commanding officer of the unit, apparently extremely pleased with the performance of 'his' new fighter, bought three more aeroplanes, two single-seaters and one two-seater an in a very unorthodox way even for the day, using unit funds! This operation brought the total number of Martinsyde F.4 Buzzard aircraft in service under Portuguese colours to four. According to an official document consulted in 1979, two F.4 Buzzards were delivered to Tancos on 5 January 1923, the two-seat F.4A being delivered on 29 December 1923[3].

On 9 September, 1923 a new hangar was put into service at Tancos and for the occasion seven aircraft on the unit's charge were officially christened. Among them, two F.4 Buzzards received the names of *Almonda*, after a river in the vicinity of the base, and *Lidador*, after a Portuguese medieval knight. The naming proved to be useful, as some of the aircraft did not display any serial numbers to allow their identification, which was not especially unusual in those times of anomalous regulations. Of their activity after this date, little is known, but it is likely to have consisted of training flights, and the occasional goodwill visit to Spain. For instance, the records shows that one of such flight took place on 14 January 1924 by pilots Ribeiro da Fonseca and Dias Leite, visiting Seville.

Some time later the *Esquadrilha Mista de Depósito* was disbanded and replaced by the *Esquadrilha nº1 de Caça* (Fighter Flight

Single seat Martinsyde with Tancos insignia and the red diagonal band from Amadora. It is evident in the picture that there are no black lines either side of the red band as has been often stated and shown in profile drawings elsewhere. (FAP/AHFA)

3 The aircraft received are quoted as being ex-RAF H7688, civil registration G-EBFA, and ex-RAF H7692, civil registration G-EBDM. These aircraft were sold to the newly constituted firm *Aircraft Disposal Company* (AirDisCo) in January 1923 and June 1922 respectively. (From British Military Aircraft Serials 1878–1987 – compiled by Bruce Robertson).

no. 1) equipped with the four Martynside F.4 Buzzards and SPAD fighters, the number of which is unclear.

By October 1927 the unit had disappeared, to reappear later under the designation of Grupo *Independente de Aviação de Protecção e Combate* – G.I.A.P.C. (Independent Group of Protection and Combat Aviation).

The last Martynside F.4 Buzzard was retired from service in 1933.

Camouflage & Markings

The first aircraft received in Portugal was painted in silver dope (aluminium). As the aircraft came into service in Amadora it received the diagonal red band of the G.E.A.R. on the fuselage. The band should have had a thin black outline, but photographic evidence suggests this was not applied. The national insignia, the *Cruz de Cristo*, was applied in red with a borderless white background disc, in four positions on the upper surfaces of the top wing, and the under surfaces of lower wing. The national flag was painted on the rudder, divided into two equal red/green parts and supporting the full National Coat of Arms. This was placed at mid-height on the rudder on the division between both colours.

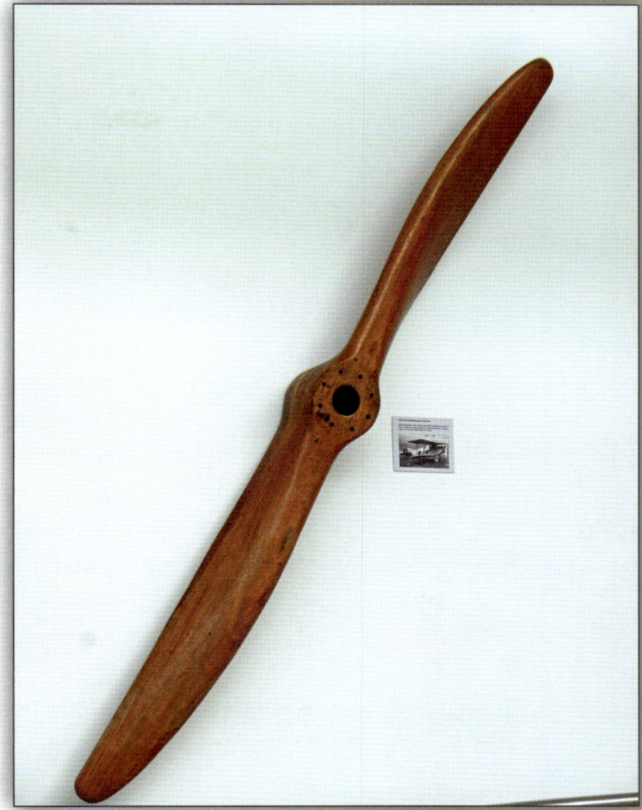

One propeller of a Martinsyde Buzzard survives today and is preserved at Museu do Ar (Sintra). (L. Tavares)

When the Buzzard was transferred to Tancos it retained the original airframe colour and the diagonal red band of its previous

The hub of the same propeller showing the engine designation. (L. Tavares)

unit, in front of which was added the Air Base insignia, a running *Galgo* (greyhound). The greyhound always faced the direction of flight.

Several sources suggested that this insignia was painted red or even brown, which seems unlikely. Published data supports most probable colour for the Tancos *Galgo* emblem, when used on an airframe, as being only ever painted in deep yellow or occasionally black. It is well known how hazardous the identification of colours based on old black and white photographs can be. The use of a photographic film, possibly using orthochromatic emulsion that changed the visible tone of some colours, could easily mislead the judgement of an observer. This being so, and until proof to the contrary appears, the most likely colour of the insignia remains deep yellow.

Until recently it was considered that the three other received aircraft also wore silver dope with a yellow *Galgo* on the fuselage sides. However, the recent emergence of period photos shows three aircraft in a duller colour shade, in contrast to other known pictures that illustrate other aircraft in a brighter hue. This suggests that a colour other then silver dope, possibly a shade closer to mid-grey, was used to cover the surface of the newly arrived F.4 Buzzard. As stated before, no positive identification of the individual aircraft is possible, due to the lack of any serial or code on the airframes and the impossibility of reading the name on the fuselage surface. Concerning the potential grey paint scheme, it has been possible to identify its equivalent under the modern Federal Standard system as close to ref. FS 26132. This was done by matching up a small section of a fuselage at the Portuguese Air Museum with the date of 1921 inscribed on its reverse, which is believed to be from one of the aforementioned aircraft.

The G.E.A.R. red band was, of course, not applied to the airframes of the freshly received aircraft. However, photographic evidence shows that a diagonal white band in a similar position, together with the *Galgo* emblem, was painted on the fuselage of the F.4A two-seater. It is not clear if the diagonal white band adorned the two other purchased aircraft, although they may have done. The insignia of the Tancos Air Base occupied its usual place on both sides of the fuselage.

Two plan views (upper and lower wing), for each scheme (silver and grey) showing the Cross of Christ in two positions on each wing occupying the entire wing chord at wing tip. Other then the variation on the colour, there was no difference between the arrangement and positioning of the National Insignia between the silver doped aircraft and the other three planes that exhibited a grey paint scheme.

The first Martinsyde F.4 Buzzard of Esquadrilha Mista de Depósito *at the beginning of 1923, at the Tancos Airfield. Aircraft in silver dope (aluminium) scheme. Showing already the* Galgo, *emblem of its new home base, it still carries the red diagonal band from its previous service under the* Grupo de Esquadrilhas de Aviação República.

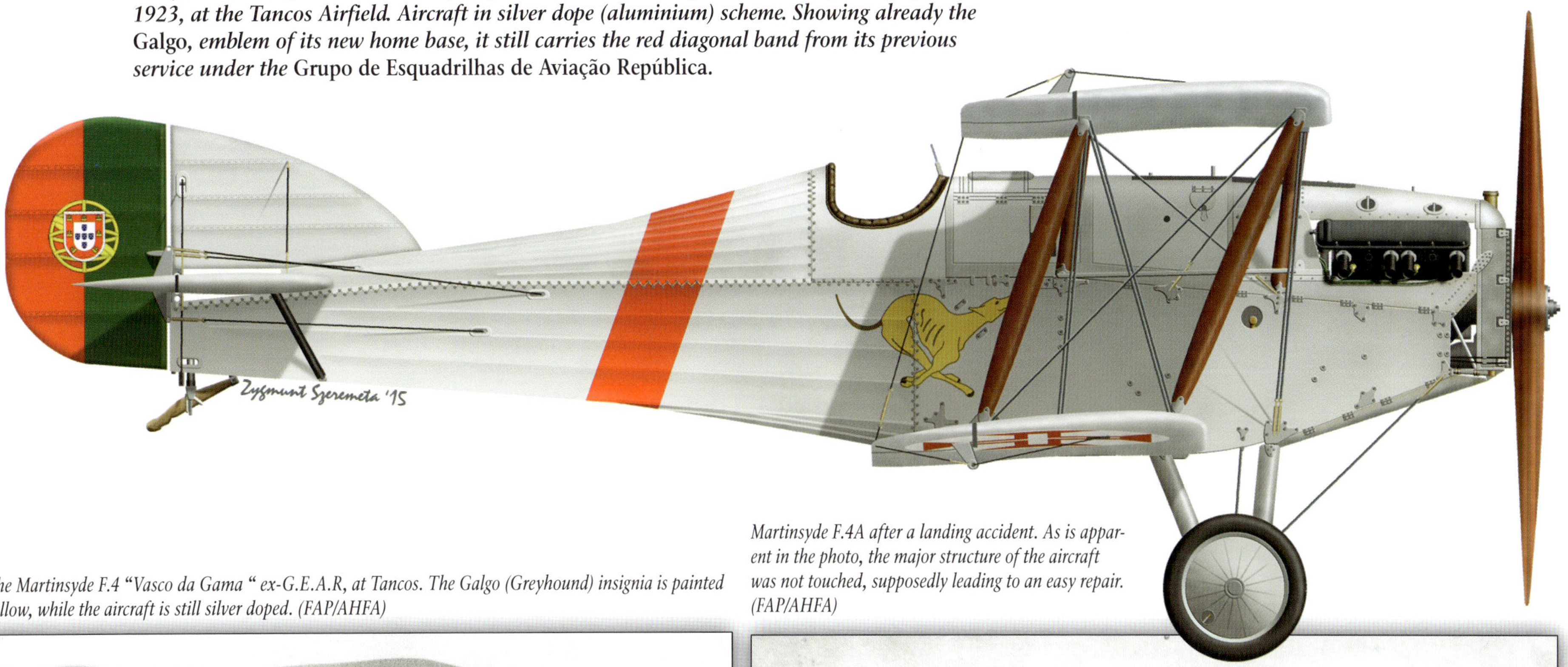

The Martinsyde F.4 "Vasco da Gama " ex-G.E.A.R, at Tancos. The Galgo (Greyhound) insignia is painted yellow, while the aircraft is still silver doped. (FAP/AHFA)

Martinsyde F.4A after a landing accident. As is apparent in the photo, the major structure of the aircraft was not touched, supposedly leading to an easy repair. (FAP/AHFA)

Martinsyde F.4 Buzzard. Aircraft in silver dope (aluminium) scheme, later in the same year (1923) but now without the red band of the Esquadrilha Mista de Depósito. *This one had been removed by then to be replaced by the "*Galgo*" (Greyhound) insignia identifying the Tancos Air Base.*

*Martinsyde F.4 Buzzard from Tancos Air Base clearly showing the "*Galgo*" emblem on the fuselage.* Capitão *Ribeiro da Fonseca, the first CO of the Tancos Air Base and a colourful personality of the period (it was his idea to purchase thre more aircraft with the Air Base funds, instead of following the ordinary and official channels) and famous for defying the then Prime Minister, Dr. Alvaro de Castro, for a duel, is seen proudly standing alongside one of the A.M. aeroplanes. (FAP/AHFA)*

Martinsyde F.4 Buzzard at Tancos Air Base in the mid 1920s. By then the Buzzard fleet – four aircraft – were painted grey overall with a white diagonal band across the fuselage. This band corresponded to the air unit stationed at Tancos, which changed over the years, as explained in the text.

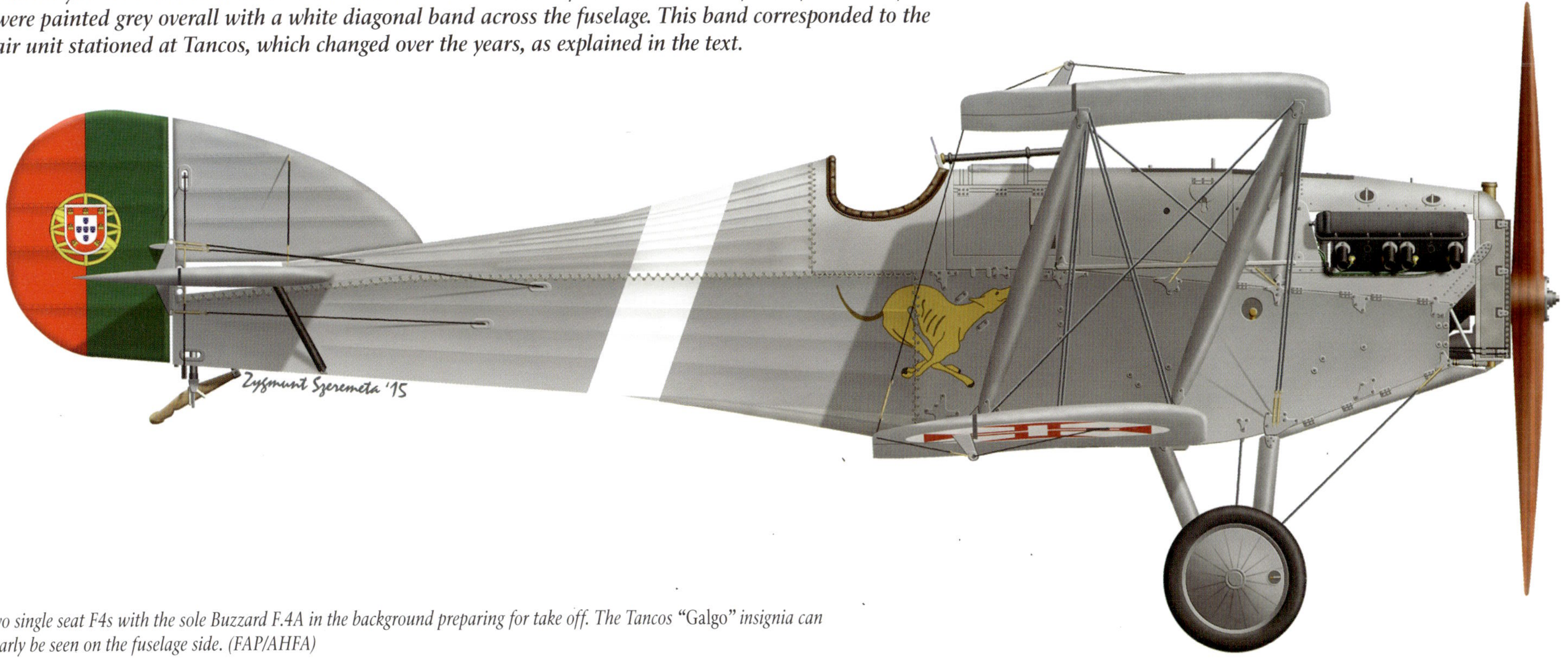

Two single seat F4s with the sole Buzzard F.4A in the background preparing for take off. The Tancos "Galgo" insignia can clearly be seen on the fuselage side. (FAP/AHFA)

The twin-seat Martinsyde F.4A Buzzard equally painted in an overall grey scheme and bearing the white diagonal band across the fuselage as well as the "Galgo" from the Tancos Base.

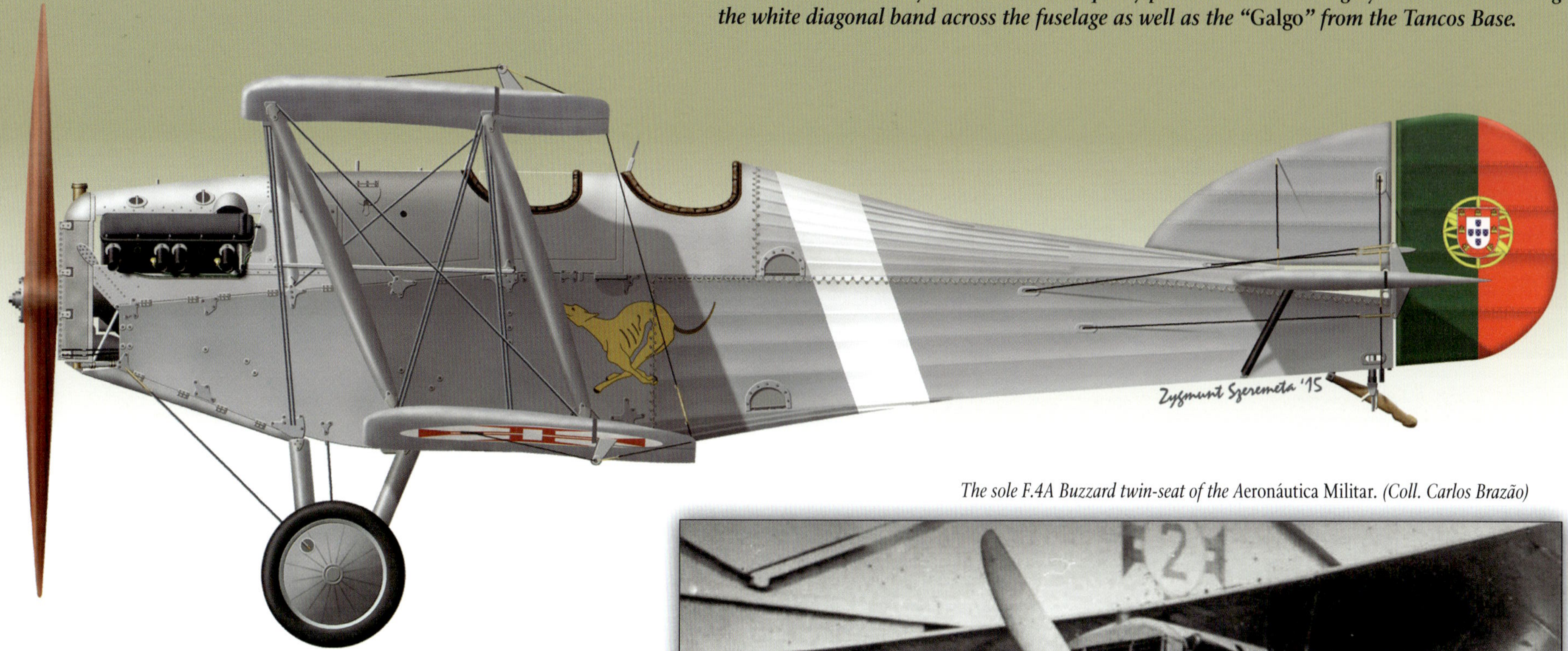

The sole F.4A Buzzard twin-seat of the Aeronáutica Militar. *(Coll. Carlos Brazão)*

Aircraft Characteristics Martinsyde F.4 Buzzard	
Quantity used:	3 single seat (*1 twin seat*)
Crew:	One (*Two*)
Years of Service:	1919–1933 (*1923–1933*)
Span:	32' 9 3/8" (10.99 m) upper wing, 31' 2 3/8" (10.51 m) lower wing
Length:	25' 5 5/8" (7.76 m)
Height:	8' 10" (2.89 m)
Wing area:	320 sq ft (29.76 m²)
Engine:	One *Hispano-Suiza* 305 hp 8Fb water cooled
Empty weight:	1,934 lb (877 kg)
Loaded weight:	2,440 lb (1,107 kg)
Maximum speed:	129.4 mph (208 km/h) at 10,000 feet (3,048 m)
Service ceiling:	19,800 feet (6,035 m)
Climb to 10,000 feet:	8min 09sec
Armament:	Two fixed synchronised .303 (7.7 mm) *Vickers* machine guns

Morane-Saulnier MS.133/MS.230/MS.233

Background

In November 1925 the Morane-Saulnier factory rolled out its Model 120 (Morane-Saulnier MS.120), a high-wing monoplane equipped with a Salmson 9ab radial engine, to fulfil a requirement by the French Air Force for an advanced pilot trainer, that might also be used for observers' and gunners' training.

However, before the aircraft could be presented to the military, Morane-Saulnier decided to revise the single example of the MS.120, and in the process gave it a new designation: Morane-Saulnier MS.130. This new version had a revised wing profile, a bigger tail and the characteristic parasol wing.

In December 1926, under the new designation, the aircraft was put through its paces during an assessment period with the French authorities, drawing enthusiastic comments by the Air Force test pilots. As a result, a large number of this model was ordered by the French military, not only for the *Armée de l'Air* but also for the *Aéronautique Navale*.

Meanwhile, the aviation school owned by Morane-Saulnier (*Compagnie Française d'Aviation*) itself, and several foreign countries (Belgium, China, Guatemala and Turkey) followed the French example and ordered the MS.130. These foreign orders, incorporating certain modifications to the basic airframe required by the customers, led Morane-Saulnier to give different model numbers to each variant ordered (e.g. MS.131, 133, 138, etc.)[1]. In addition, the French Air force issued an official requirement for a two-seat advanced trainer in 1928, the *Services Téchniques of l'Armée de l'Air* testing the resulting MS.133 the next year.

Morane-Saulnier followed its usual practice of modifying and improving the original airframe, and at the end of 1930 issued a new model, the MS.230. This resulted from an evolution of the model MS.130: the wing profile was further improved, as was the wing support structure, while the two legs

An unidentified MS.133 of the batch bought in France, clearly showing its original "French green" painted fuselage. (FAP/AHFA)

1 For instance, the model MS.133 corresponded the installation in the MS.130 airframe of the Gnome et Rhone 5-cylinder engine developing 230 CV. This engine, being a French version of its British counterpart Bristol Titan, was occasionally referred as the Gnome and Rhone Titan.

Three Moranes serial numbers 180, 184 and an unidentified one during a fly-in ceremony in S.Jacinto Naval Air Station on the 4th June 1936. One Tancos Base Tiger Moth no.138 is also visible in the photo as well as personnel from the Naval Station. (FAP/AHFA)

of the landing gear were now separate instead of connected, and were articulated and included pneumatic shock absorbers. The engine was now a Salmson 9ab 9-cylinder radial driving a Chauviére, Levasseur or Ratier two-blade fixed-pitch propeller. The manufacturer also proposed the installation of a synchronised machine-gun on the engine cowling, or a target tug system for gunnery training.

The MS.130 no.54 (n/c 3312) served as a prototype for the MS.230. As with previous models, the MS.230 gave birth to sub-variants, usually corresponding to modifications required by the customer, the most common being an alternative engine.

From the basic model, the MS.230, more than 1,100 examples were built. Other models derived from the original were: the MS.231, MS.232, MS.233, MS.234, MS.234/2, MS.235, MS.235/H, MS.236, MS.237.

Morane-Saulnier MS.133/MS.230/MS.233 in Portugal

By the late 1920s the Portuguese military was looking for an advanced trainer aircraft, and also for the capability to construct aircraft domestically, and the two requirements were combined. The rapidly approaching obsolesence of the country's first combat aircraft (the SPADs, Martynsides and Breguets) also coincided with the creation, at least on paper, of an aircraft construction facility – the *Oficinas Gerais de Material Aeronáutico* (O.G.M.A.)[2].

The advanced trainer to be constructed in the new facility had to be more up-to-date than the existing types in service, while its characteristics would also help to define the specifications for a future fighter as the two would have to be complementary.

The outcome of the tests made by the French military authorities led to an order put forward by the Portuguese military aviation arm for the type. This included four MS.133 already described, plus one MS.230, in view of the possibility of choosing the future aircraft to be built by O.G.M.A., including the engine.

After evaluation of both types, the decision was made in favour of the MS.230, in a specific version for Portugal[3] – the MS.233 Et2 with Gnome & Rhone 5 230CV, 5-cylinder radial engine, the Et2 suffix meaning *Entrainement de Transition Deux Places* (Transition Training Two-Seat). The contract specified that 16 of the 21 aircraft ordered would be built under licence in Portugal. The sixteen O.G.M.A. examples were completed between 1931 and 1932, several aircraft having, according to sources, a machine gun installed above the engine cowling for use as fighters or fighter trainers.

All in all, a grand total of 21 Morane-Saulniers were used by the *Arma de Aeronáutica*, four of them Morane MS.133 Et2, one Morane MS.230 Et2, and 16 Morane 233 Et2.

---

2 When the Portuguese Army's Aeronautical Service was reorganised in 29 July 1918, a facility with the responsibility of storing, repairing, manufacturing and providing aeronautical materiel, as well as training military aeronautical specialists and technicians, was created. Under the name *Parque de Material Aeronáutico* (Aeronautical Material Depot), the new service was activated on 26 August 1918 in Vila Nova da Rainha, to be moved to its current location in Alverca in September the following year. Nine years later, in 1928, the depot was renamed *Oficinas Gerais de Material Aeronáutico* (O.G.M.A.). In the wake of the reorganisation of the military aviation services of the Army and Navy in 1950 and the creation of the Portuguese Air Force in 1952, O.G.M.A. was transferred to this new military branch.

3 The MS.233 prototype originated from Portuguese requirements. The particular changes involving this prototype were to include, among minor changes, a new radial engine, Gnome and Rhone 5ba or 5bc 5-cylinders with 230 CV.

Three Moranes serial numbers 182,183 and 186 flying in formation over a typical Portuguese countryside landscape. (FAP/AHFA)

The operational career of the Morane-Saulnier

The Morane-Saulnier fleet was distributed between two air bases, Sintra and Tancos, the former for advanced training and instruction of the new aviators, and the latter being the home of fighter units. Sintra was the quarters for the *Escola Militar de Aeronáutica* (Military Aeronautics School) while Tancos housed the *Grupo Independente de Aviação de Protecção e Combate* (Independent Group of Protection and Combat Aviation). The operation of the Moranes in Tancos justifies their inclusion in this Portuguese Fighter Colours volume, as, for several years, they were the closest thing to a fighter that the *Aviação Militar* had in its inventory. Together with three Hawker Furies bought in 1934, they served as a stop-gap measure to present a minimal group of fighter aircraft, until the placement of an order for Gloster Gladiators in 1937.

With its introduction into service, the Morane-Saulnier fleet was registered according to the system then in place, in which a group of aircraft of the same type and model received serial numbers starting with no. 1. Moranes 1, 2, 3, etc were therefore distributed between Sintra and Tancos Air Bases.

When the new system of serial numbers by blocks or groups was implemented in 1935, Moranes were issued with new serials, aircraft numbers 2, 3, 4 and 5 at Sintra receiving, respectively, the serials 150, 151, 152 and 153, the 'Morane block' for Sintra being 150-159. The Tancos-based aircraft, 6, 7, 8 and 9 were issued numbers 180, 181, 182 and 183, the block associated with Tancos being 180-189.

An internal document from Sintra Air Base allows also the establishment of a correspondence between the construction number (c/n) and the existing serial. Accordingly Moranes 2, 3, 4, and 5 had respectively the c/n 10, 8, 12 and 15. Regrettably, this document does not allow the identification of the exact type of Morane, as both the 133 and the 233 had the same engine and were treated as the same for the purposes of serial allocation. However, this does indicate that none of the Sintra aircraft above was the single MS.230.

As Sintra Morane no. 1 had probably already been lost by the time of the change of serials (see list of the accidents below), the 20 serial numbers embodied by the two blocks confirm the number of aircraft employed. No more then a year later another change of rules was outlined in Circular

MS.233 serial 153 preparing for take-off. As with all the O.G.M.A manufacture aircraft, this example bears the silver doped/polished aluminium finish. The under wing serial number was painted to be read from the front of the aircraft. (FAP/AHFA)

No. 642 of the *Arma de Aeronáutica*, dated 3 June 1938, giving unique blocks to one or two types of aircraft. In this fashion, for instance, Avro 626 and Morane-Saulnier aircraft would have to be registered in the block 151 to 199.

Movement logs of the two airfields show that aircraft serial numbers 6, 7, 8 and 9 were flying at Tancos in January and February 1934, aircraft 2, 3 and 4 in May 1935 at Sintra and finally Moranes 3 and 8 in Tancos by October 1935, showing that the change of serials ordered in March 1935 had not yet been put into effect.

From 1935 to 1940 regular activity of the Morane fleet was recorded, mainly from Tancos Air Base, operating alongside the Hawker Furies. Most of the missions recorded for the type in the year 1939 were aerobatic training, formation flying and precision landings.

The retirement of the fleet occurred in 1940, the last flights taking place between March and April at Tancos by aircraft 182, 183 and 186, with the very last flight probably being performed by Morane-Saulnier 186 on 4 April 1940.

However, one final task was yet to be reserved to the old Moranes. According to one of their former pilots, the aircraft were used for a time as 'rollers', machines with fuselage and other structures stripped of fabric covering and used as taxiing trainers.

To conclude the Morane-Saulnier chapter, an oddity concerning the use of a single aircraft by Portugal recently surfaced from the archives, in the shape of a photograph showing a Morane-Saulnier MS.233 in Elizabethville, Belgian Congo African territory, in 1930. The aircraft wears the Portuguese Cross of Christ symbol on the fuselage but no visible serial number. The story of this aircraft involves two Portuguese officers, *Major* Alfredo Sintra and *Capitão* Avelino de Andrade, who, in the service of a private company, and assisted by a French mechanic, M. Morin, attempted a flight between Angola and Mozambique, in order to establish the basis for a future airline route connecting these two former Portuguese Colonies. Departing Lourenço Marques, now Maputo, in Mozambique on 20 December 1930 they arrived at Luanda, Angola, by 17 May 1931 with a flight time of 34 hrs and 20 min. with four stops in Mozambique, two in Northern Rhodesia (Zambia), one in the Belgian Congo (Democratic Republic of Congo) and finally four more in Angolan towns before reaching the capital, other sources suggesting different dates for the departure and arrival, none of them coinciding.

The aircraft used for the journey was a Morane-Saulnier MS.233, equipped with a 230 CV Titan engine, directly purchased from the French Morane-Saulnier Company by the *Companhia Portuguesa de Aviação*, or CPA (Portuguese Company of Aviation), a short-lived enterprise specifically founded in order to establish air liaison in the colonial territories.

The MS.233 received Portuguese civil markings CS-AAF being registered as a commercial and photo-reconnaissance aircraft, property of CPA, the use of the *Cruz de Cristo* on the fuselage being not uncommon on Portuguese civilian aircraft at that time.

Accidents / Incidents

The following accidents / incidents were identified involving Moranes:

- 10 February 1934 – Accident involving aircraft no. 10
- 22 February 1934 – Two Moranes collided over Sintra. One of the victims was *Capitão* Brito Pais, an aviator famous for his involvement in flag-showing flights to the Colonies;
- 23 June 1934 – Aircraft no. 9 crashed at Anadia, central Portugal, 200 km from Lisbon, being destroyed. It was flown by *Capitão* Amaro da Cunha and *2º Sargento* J. Lopes;
- 29 November 1935 – Aircraft no. 182 made an emergency landing at Monte de Nossa Senhora de Jerusalém. The propeller of this aircraft is now at the *Museu do Ar*;
- 28 September 1937 – Forced landing of aircraft no. 189 at Caldas da Rainha, 75 km N. of Lisbon, resulting in the destruction of the aircraft. The pilot was *Tenente* Espadanal;
- 8 October 1937 – Forced landing of aircraft no. 188;
- 10 June 1938 – Accident involving aircraft no. 199 (new serial system) at Constância, 109 km. North of Lisbon on the Tagus River.

Contemporary scale model of a MS.233 built at Alverca (OGMA). This model is today under the custody of the Museu do Ar and can be seen at its Sintra facilities. (L.Tavares)

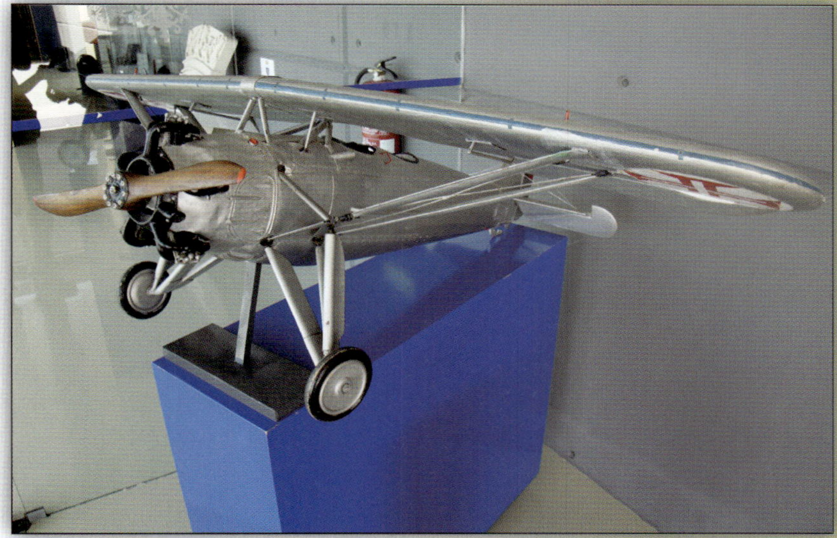

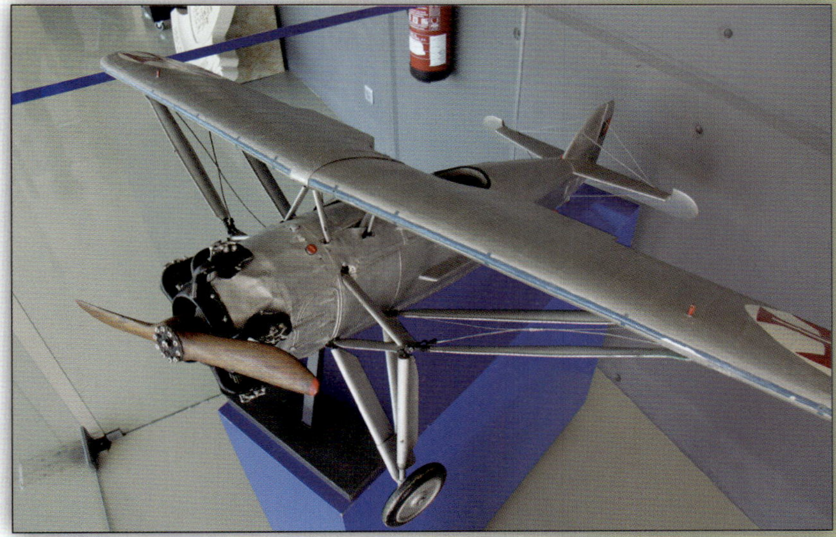

Contemporary scale model of a MS.233 built at Alverca (OGMA). As mentioned elsewhere, of note is the thin blue line segmented painted on the wing leading edge. (L. Tavares)

Camouflage and Markings

Several sources suggest that the Morane-Saulnier aircraft purchased in France (four MS.133 and one MS.230) retained the original French colours for almost the entirety of their service life with the *Arma de Aeronáutica*, (these being green on all fabric surfaces of the fuselage and wings, with the ventral and cowling panels in bare aluminium). The few existing photos would appear to confirm this. At some point during their existence, it seems they received a colour scheme of all-over silver dope, as a photograph of the sole existing MS.230 indicates. The sixteen MS.233 Et2 aircraft manufactured in Portugal by O.G.M.A., however, wore an all-over silver scheme from the beginning.

As usual, national markings of a red *Cruz de Cristo* over a white circle occupied the standard four positions above and below the wing, regardless of the colour of the airframe. The red and green National Flag with Crest including armillary sphere was placed on the rudder only, with green forward.

The aeroplanes based at Tancos had their emblem, the *Galgo* (Greyhound), painted on the fuselage. On those painted green the emblem was to be yellow, while on the silver aircraft this symbol was black. Black was also the colour of the serial numbers, to be painted on both sides of the fuselage and the underside of the wings, reading from the front. On the green aircraft, serial numbers, when carried, were to be painted white. On the fuselage the serial number was applied aft of the *Galgo* emblem on Tancos Air Base aircraft. A thin blue line ran over the leading edge of the wing on the silver aeroplanes, probably in fabric acting as a reinforcement divided by slices of the same colour, separating it in a number of segments.

At least one known photograph represents an all-silver Morane still carrying an old-style serial number – in this case no. 6.

Aircraft Characteristics Morane-Saulnier MS.230	
Quantity used:	21 (4 MS.133Et2+1 MS.230Et2+16 MS.233Et2)
Crew:	Two
Years of Service:	1931–1940
Span:	35' ¼" (10.70 m)
Length:	22' 10 ¾" (6.98 m)
Height:	9' 2 ¼" (2.80 m)
Wing Area:	212.06 sq ft (19.70 m²)
Empty weight:	1,828 lb (829 kg)
Normal loaded:	2,535 lb (1,150 kg)
Maximum speed:	127 mph (205 km/h) at 15,100 feet (4,600 m)
Service ceiling:	16,405 ft (5,000 m)
Armament:	In some MS.233 aircraft one fixed machinegun in front of the cockpit firing synchronized with the propeller
Engine:	(MS.230) 1 Salmson 9AB 230CV

Line-up of MS.233s possibly at Alverca airfield waiting delivery. It is known that the last six aircraft of the Portuguese manufactured batch were handed over to the Tancos Air Base CO, Capitão *António Maya, on 7th November 1933. (FAP/ AHFA)*

Morane-Saulnier MS.133 Et2. Aircraft in original French camouflage. Also stationed at the Tancos airfield and equipped as well with a Gnome et Rhone Titan engine, due to the absence of serial number or other type of identification, it is not known if this is the same aircraft depicted on page 32 at a different time or another airplane.

The MS.133 Et2 again in "French Green", but still without serial. However the Tancos greyhound can be discerned on the fuselage. (FAP/AHFA)

Morane-Saulnier MS.133 Et2 serial number 2, stationed at Tancos airfield. Aircraft in original French camouflage, this aircraft has its serial number on the fuselage only. It was equipped with a Gnome et Rhone Titan 5 cylinder 230 hp engine.

MS.133 serial 2 with Tancos Galgo insignia. The aircraft is still in its original "French green" paint scheme. Of note is the size of the roundel that partially covered the ailerons. At this time, the use of the under-wing serial number was not yet established. (FAP/AHFA)

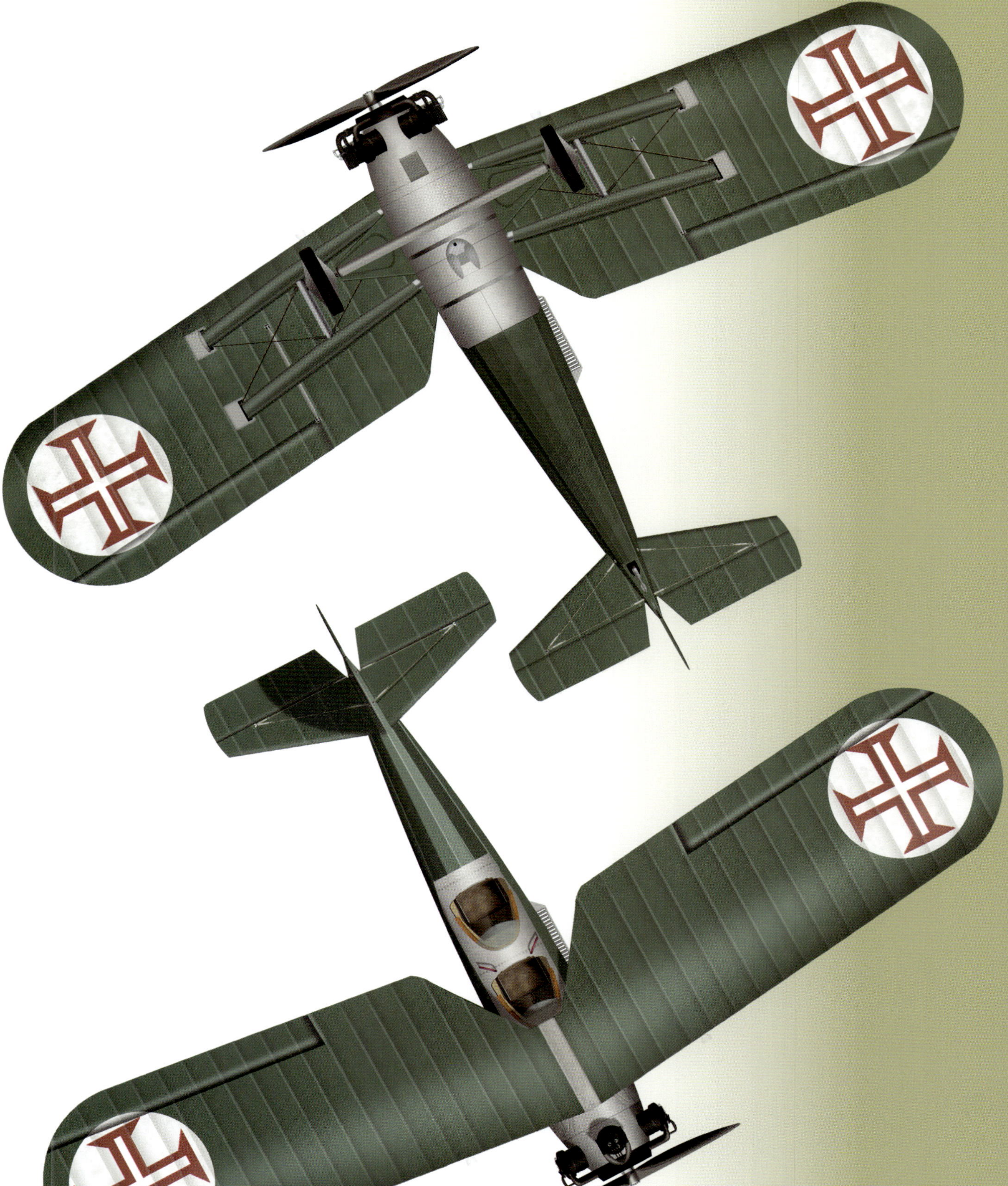

Morane-Saulnier MS.133 Et2, serial number 184. Now in an all silver livery (silver doped) this MS.133 displays, in conformity with the rules established in 1935, its serial number on both sides of the fuselage and under the wings. Also of note is the location of the Morane-Saulnier symbol and aircraft type designation inscribed on the rudder.

Alferes *Barão da Cunha standing in front of MS.133 serial 184. (FAP/AHFA)*

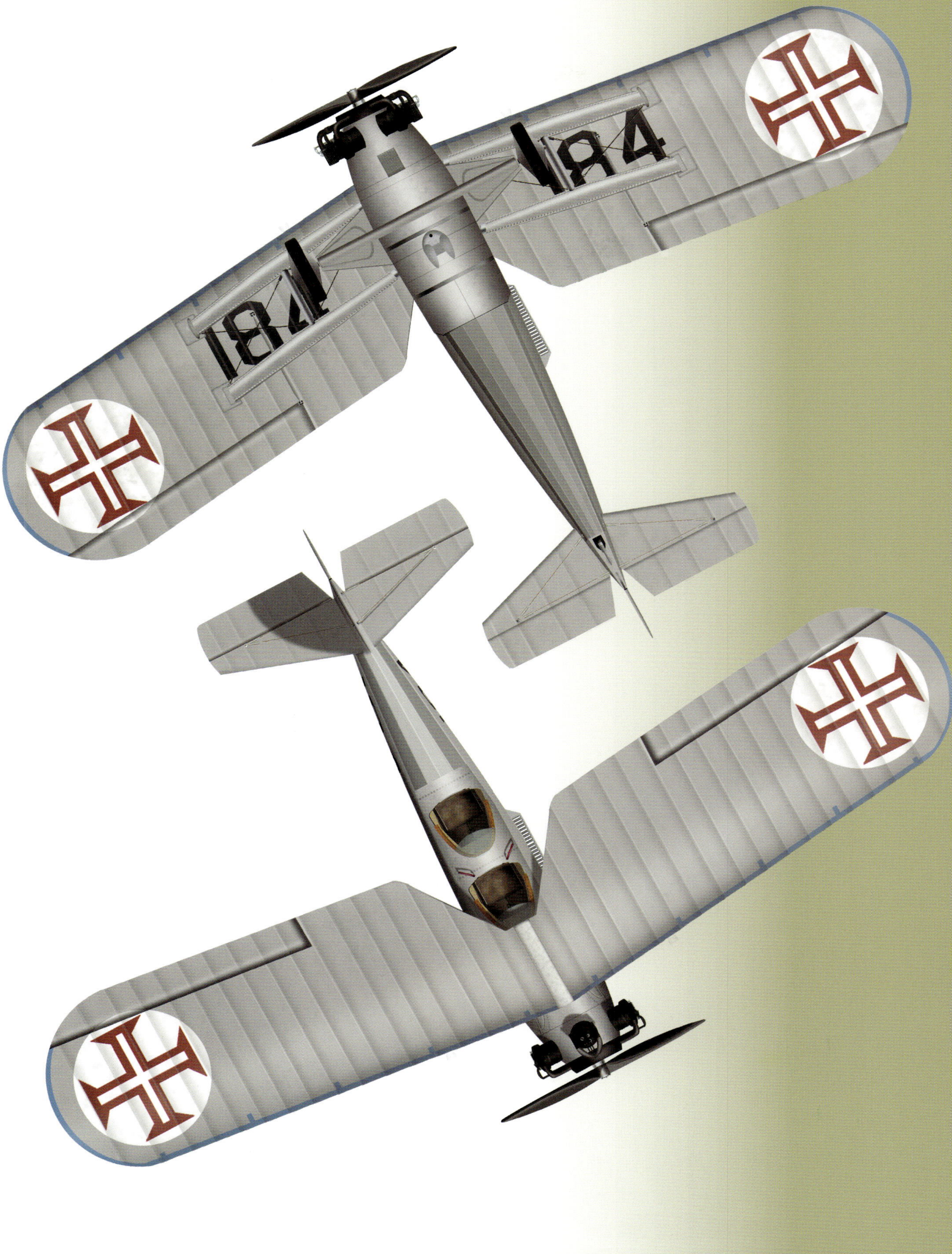
184
184

Morane-Saulnier MS.233 Et2, serial number 194. One of the sixteen O.G.M.A. built aircraft, this MS.233 Et2 is shown here in its silver livery. Again the use of serials is not restricted to the fuselage only but also on the under surface of the wings. In addition, the wing leading edge had a thin blue line applied and separated in sections, the purpose of which is not known. The engine is a Gnome and Rhone Titan.

MS.233 serial 194. Of note are the position and style of the Cruzes de Cristo, *the serial number on fuselage and under the wings only. The National Flag with Crest occupies part of the rudder and the propeller is black with a metallic leading edge protection. (FAP/AHFA)*

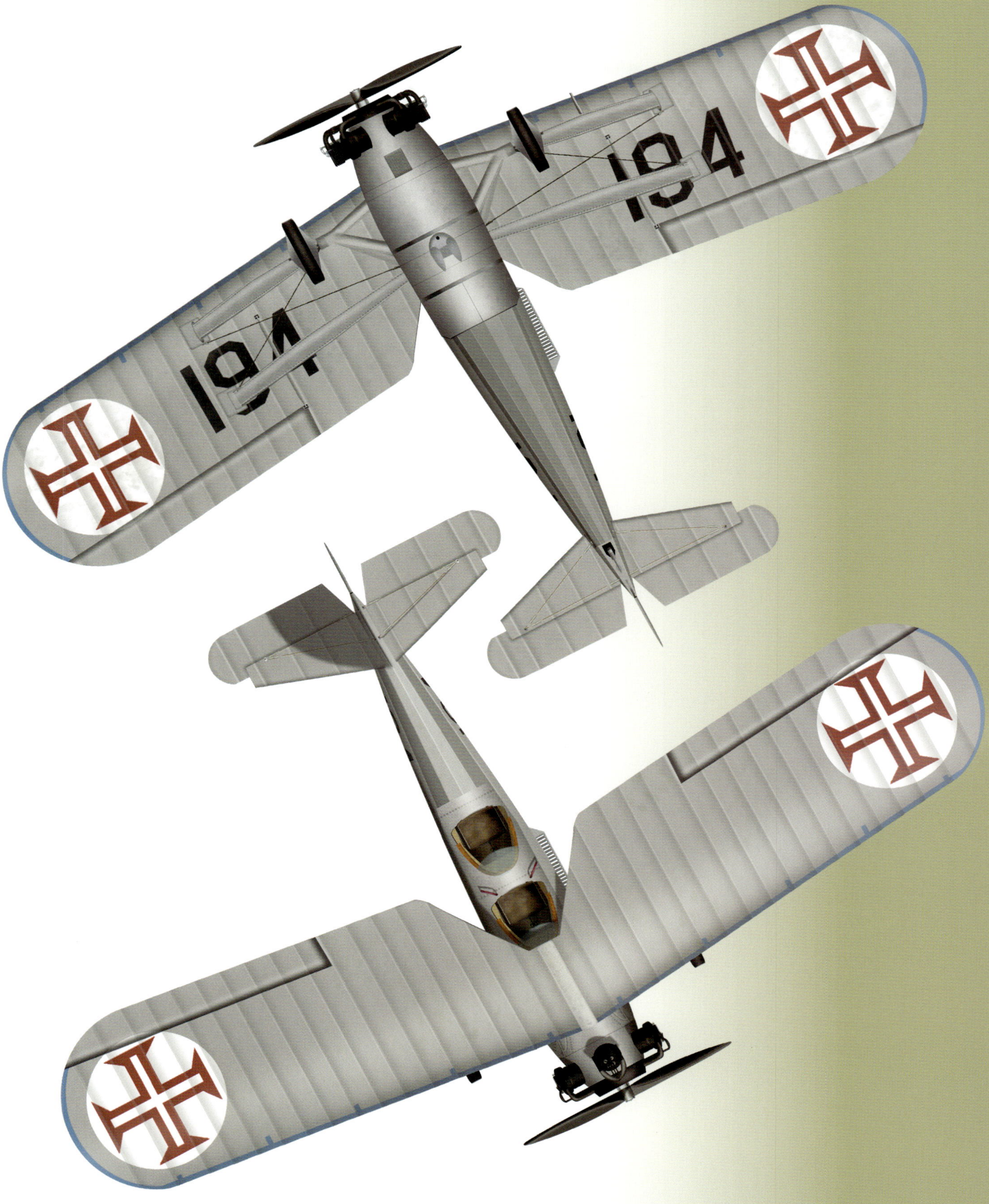
194
194

Morane-Saulnier MS.233 Et2, serial number 185. On this silver doped aircraft the Tancos Galgo (Greyhound) is present on the fuselage, denoting its "home base". The purists will notice also that the axis of the under wing Cruz de Cristo is not parallel to the aircraft fuselage axis. Note in addition that the tail plane of the MS.233 differs from that of the MS.133, as well as its landing gear.

MS.233 serial 185 with the "Galgo" (greyhound) insignia of Tancos airfield painted before the serial number. The leading edge of the wing has a thin blue line divided in several segments as is shown by the model of the aeroplane exhibited at the Museu do Ar, Sintra. (FAP/AHFA)

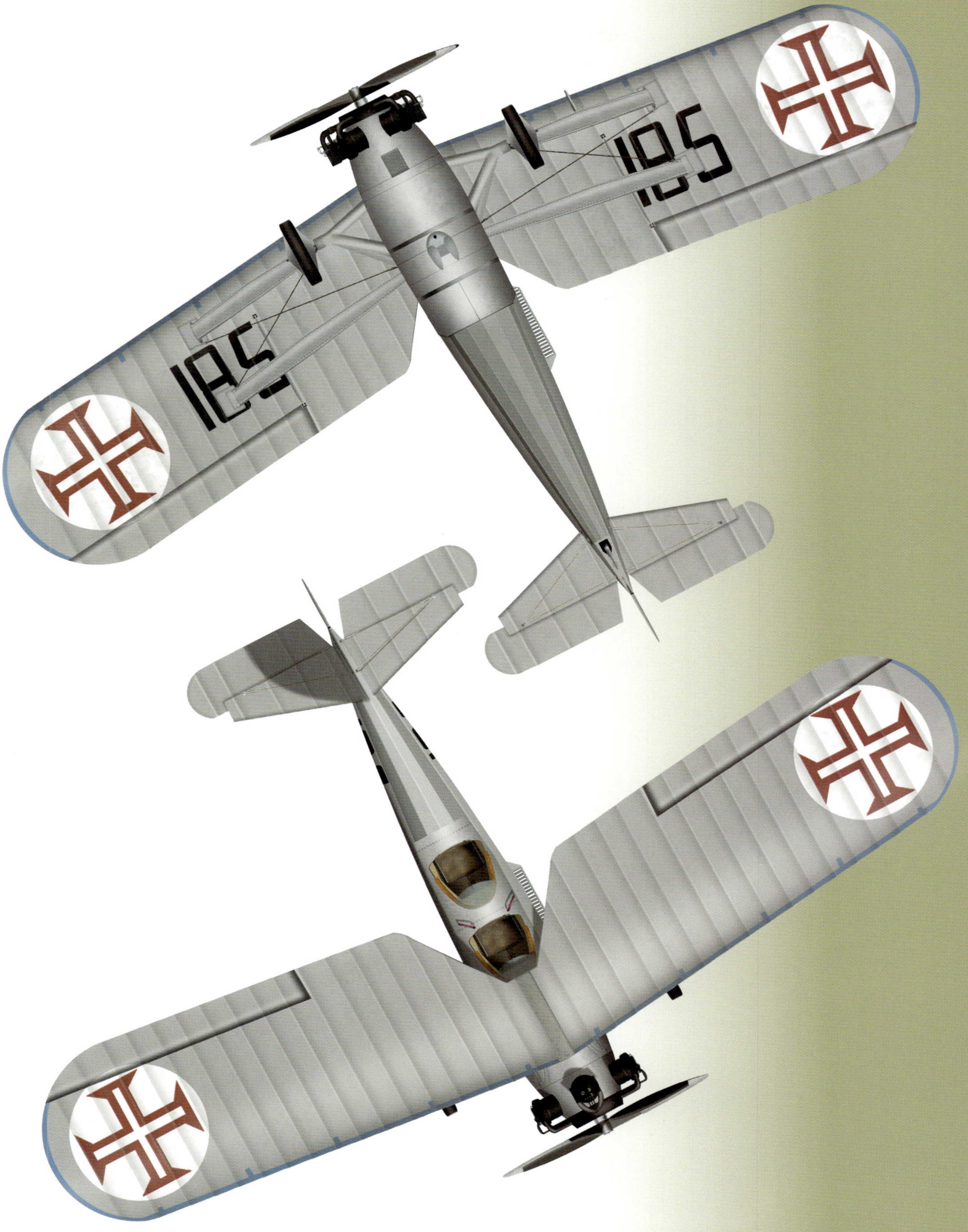
185
185

Morane-Saulnier MS.230. Aircraft silver dope overall. The one and only example of the Morane-Saulnier MS.230 used by the Aeronautica Militar was powered by a Salmson 9ab of 230hp. It was purchased in 1929 by the Portuguese authorities for evaluation of the future type of aircraft to be built by O.G.M.A.

The sole example of the MS.230 of the Aeronáutica Militar. This aircraft was purchased from France together with four MS.133 in order to establish which type would be licence-built by O.G.M.A. (FAP/AHFA)

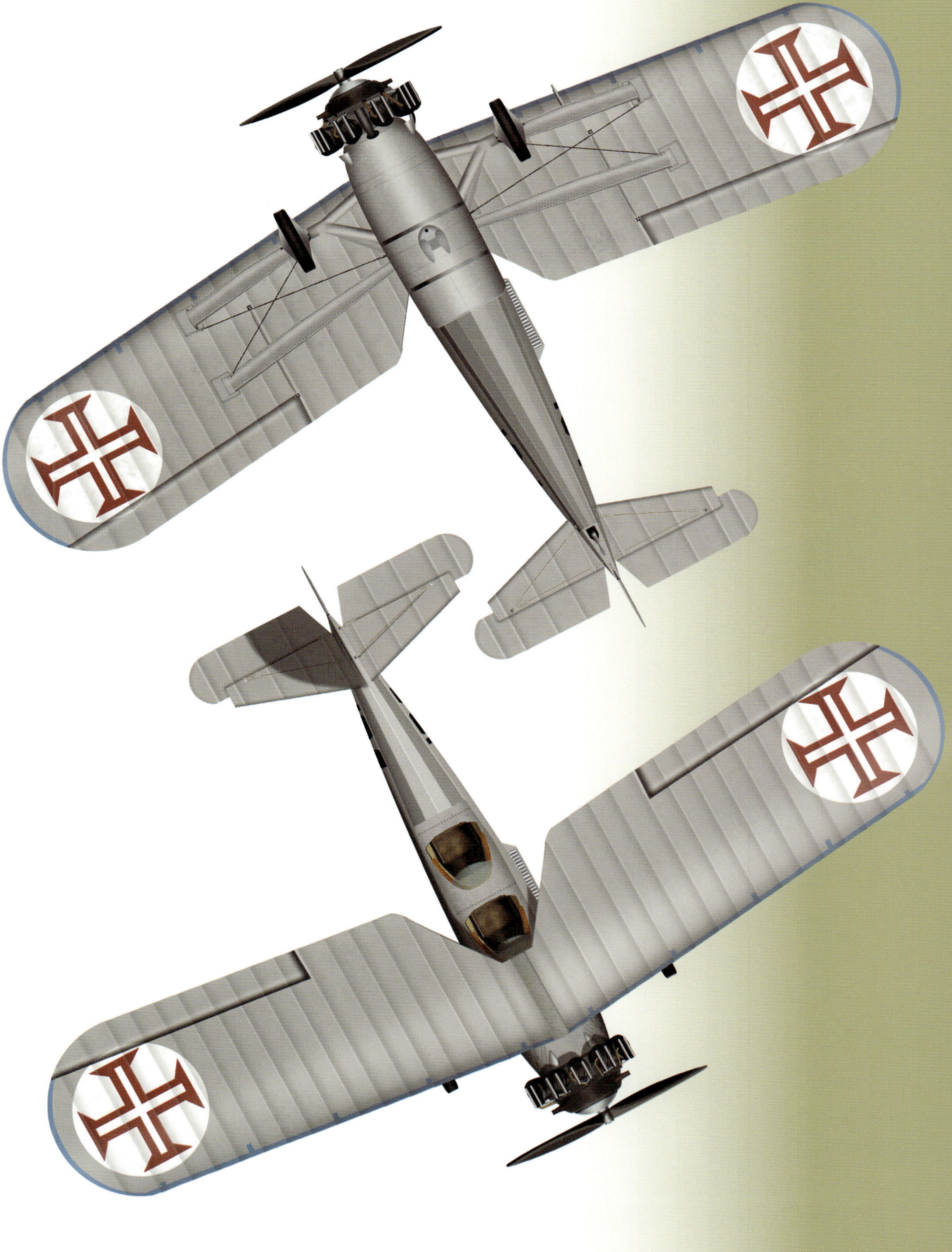

Morane-Saulnier MS.233 civil registration CS-AAF. This aircraft was used for the assessment of an air connection between Angola and Mozambique, in 1930/1931. Although showing the Cruz de Cristo on the fuselage, it was a civil aircraft as denoted by the CS-AAF civil registration on the fuselage side. Many civil aircraft in the Portuguese African Colonies had the Cross of Christ painted in the fuselage, not meaning however that they belonged to the Arma de Aeronautica.

The "African Morane" *used in the test flight between Mozambique and Angola (see text). In the original photo the registration CS-AAF can be seen behind the Cross of Christ. (FAP/AHFA)*

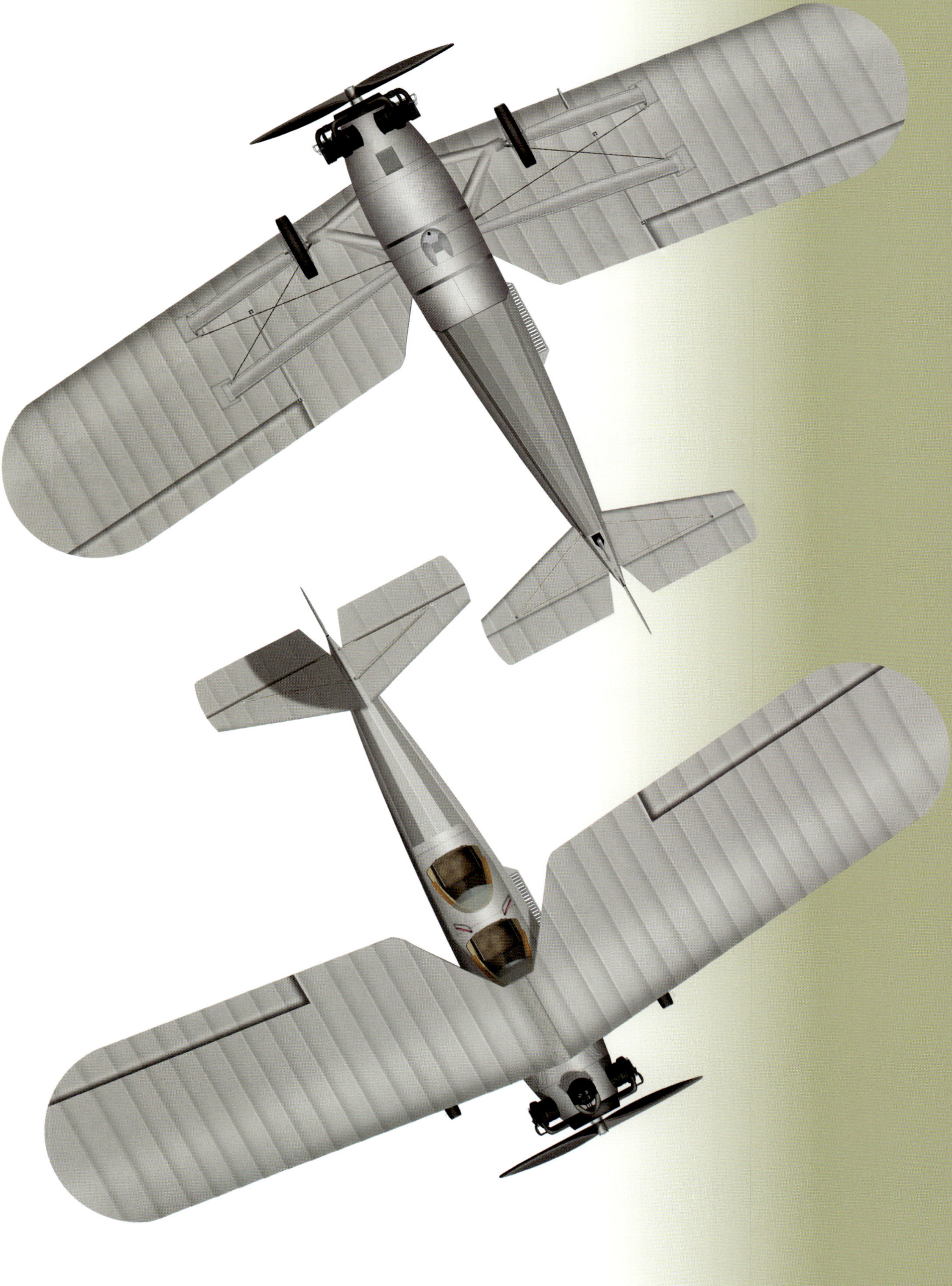

Hawker Fury Mk I

Background

The H.G. Hawker Engineering Co. was one of several companies that responded to Specification F.9/26, issued by the British Air Ministry with the aim of choosing a successor to the RAF's ageing fighters, the Gloster Gamecock and Armstrong Whitworth Siskin. Hawker's entry was the Hawfinch, which was considered by the judges "one of the best of the aircraft evaluated" and a "close runner-up", nonetheless it lost out to the Bristol Bulldog. After the evaluation, the prototype returned to the Hawker works where it eventually was to be used for various experiments, specifically in trials with new engines and floats, and structural experiments.

Hawker's Chief Designer, Sir Sydney Camm, was unhappy with the outcome. He went back to the drawing board, producing a design with the new in-line 420 hp Rolls-Royce F.XIS engine allowing a streamlined forward fuselage, which promised a top speed close to the 'magic' 200 mph, considered at the time to be the maximum possible speed of a fighter aircraft. The new aircraft was regarded as a private venture, although loosely based on another Air Ministry Specification, F.20/27. It was later dubbed Hornet, and made a powerful impression on the public when it made its debut during the 1929 Olympia Air Show in London, flying alongside other examples of the Hawker Company, the Hart and the Tomtit.

Meanwhile, the disastrous performance of the newly adopted Bulldog during the 1930s Air Defence Exercises against "invading bombers", the similarly new Hawker Hart, had created ripples at the Air Ministry. According to a witness "...(the bombers) went ahead to their assigned tasks without any disturbance by the defending fighters..." these proving to be markedly slower then the former. The Air Ministry was therefore required to reassess the position, and consider purchase of another and faster aeroplane to equip the Royal Air Force fighting squadrons. Consequently, he

Portuguese Fury s/n 50 before delivery, flying over the British countryside. (Força Aérea Portuguesa/ AHFA)

Portuguese Fury s/n 50 at Brooklands before delivery. The presence of the support under the fin suggests that it was being prepared for an "official photo session". (Força Aérea Portuguesa /AHFA)

Air Ministry issued a new Specification (F.13/20) in 1930. However, as the funds allocated for acquisitions were small, only 21 fighters were initially ordered and purchased, to equip three squadrons, nos. 1, 25 and 43.

The Hawker Hornet, now renamed Hawker Fury[1] due to a directive from the Air Ministry, that required land-based fighters to bear a name beginning with 'F', entered service in May 1931. The Furies became the first operational RAF aircraft to exceed 200 mph (322 km/h) in level flight. Despite all the received praise, the Hawker Fury was not to be built in large numbers and would see its career as a front line fighter shortened by history, being relegated to secondary tasks due to the rapid progress of aeronautical technology. The type's development would continue, however, with the production of the improved Fury Mk II and a naval relative, the Hawker Nimrod. Between 1930 and 1936 Hawker delivered around 230 aircraft of all marks to the RAF. Another six nations – Norway, Persia, Portugal, South Africa, Spain and Yugoslavia – placed orders, augmenting the domestic production number by 44, with another 40 aircraft being licence built in Yugoslavia by Ikarus (24) and Zmaj (16).

The Fury was very much appreciated by its pilots, as testified by John Nesbitt-Dufort, D.S.O., who relates in his book *Open Cockpit*[2] that the Fury had "...handling characteristics as near perfect as they could be... seeming to have been designed with aerobatics in view."

Hawker Fury Mk I in Portugal

The story of the Hawker Fury in Portuguese colours is an uneventful one, considering it was the first Portuguese modern fighter, and outclassed by far anything flying in Portugal at the time it was received. Over ten years of service, the Fury mostly flew during joint exercises with the Army and advance fighter training sorties, suffering in the interim some minor, and not so minor, mechanical incidents, mostly due to the impetuosity of its pilots, eager to extract the maximum from

1 The Mk I designation was not applied hitherto, only being affected to the earlier aircraft with the emergence of the Hawker Fury Mk II.

2 Speed and Sports Publications, Ltd-1970.

its Rolls-Royce engine and excited by its streamlined racing profile. Much more interesting was the procedure that led to the choice of this aircraft for the *Arma de Aeronáutica*.

At the beginning of the 1930s the lack of a credible air defence in Portugal led the authorities to develop a project for the acquisition of a new fighter. This initiative led to a verbal confrontation by two opposing trends of opinion inside the *Arma de Aeronáutica* itself, where two renowned officers and their followers fiercely debated the subject of "what would be the ideal fighter for the Portuguese Air Defence"... While one side advocated the acquisition of an aeroplane of traditional construction, of wooden or mixed wood-metal structure, the other side believed in the merits of an all-metal construction. This quarrel spilled outside the *Arma de Aeronáutica* and reached the pages of the newspapers and the general public, widening the discussion to the population at large.

The first aeroplane to be examined was not of French or British origin, the usual suppliers of war material to Portugal, but from a Swedish subsidiary of a German company, the Junkers K47. The K47 prototype, Swedish registration SE-ACF, c/n 3355, flown by the factory test pilot Willy Neuenhofen, visited Portugal on a trip through the two Iberian countries, at the end of a European tour in search of customers. It was presented between November 1930 and mid-January 1931 to the Army and Navy authorities. The K47 was not only of all-metal construction, but a monoplane, and the tests confirmed the benefits of both the modernity of its structure and layout, and the advanced nature of German design. Even though the concept and its novelty were excellent, however, the period of tests in Portugal did not lead to a practical conclusion because, as with all the previously visited nations, the high unit cost meant that an order would exceed the allocated funds, even without engines or spare parts.

In March 1932 a small team of *Arma da Aeronáutica* officers, lead by *Major* António Sousa Maya, one of the more prestigious officers of the Portuguese Aviation of the day and of Great War fame, departed Portugal to visit a number of countries that possessed aeronautical industries in order to examine, and if possible, test fly and collect data on the mostly appropriate aircraft to purchase. The visit included Belgium, France, Great Britain and Poland.

Portuguese Fury s/n 50 in flight before delivery. In this very good quality photo the red surround of the "Cruz de Cristo" *disc is quite evident. (Força Aérea Portuguesa /AHFA/ Coll. Museu do Ar)*

Fury serial number 401 after an accident in September 1941. (Força Aérea Portuguesa/AHFA/Coll. Joaquim Barros Prata)

In this latter country, where visit concluded, the team was pleasantly surprised by the development of aeronautical facilities and the excellence of its products, which it found "comparable only to the best in Europe", and had the opportunity to fly another all metal monoplane, the PZL P.11. The flight took place on the 25th April 1932 and, on his report upon arrival back to Lisbon, Major Maya stated that "...the aircraft is much more versatile and manoeuvrable then the Dewoitine[3] recently tested in France...". Similar comments had been made previously to the local press while in Poland, immediately after the test flight.

Meanwhile in Portugal, proposals were being received by the Ministry of War for the supply of aeronautical material, the two major and serious contenders being the Hawker Engineering Co. with its Fury and Państwowe Zakłady Lotnicze presenting the PZL P.11.[4] The other two proposals, the Belgian Fairey Fox and the French Dewoitine, were left outside of the competition because they did not meet the criteria established by the Portuguese authorities.

At the Zurich International Aero Meeting of 1932, the PZL P.11 took second place in the 'pure speed' circuit trial with a time of 71' 10", behind the Fury, which finished first with a time of 68' 38". The Polish team arrived in Portugal on 23 August 1932 to demonstrate its aircraft, thus forcing the conclusion of the purchasing process. The test aeroplane stayed in Portugal for more than a year before its return to Poland. In the interim, the aircraft flew numerous sorties, flown either by national pilots or by Polish ones. The time spent in the country, the lessons learned and all the important data gathered during the flights was not at all wasted and would later be important in the production of manuals for the regular maintenance of the aircraft and its employment,

3 Although no record of the visit exists, it is known that the team of Portuguese officers visited France, as well as the *Societé Aéronautique Dewoitine*, the aero-engine section of Hispano-Suiza and Avions Fairey SA, in Belgium.

4 A very interesting, complete and documented article, in Portuguese only, was published in the Portuguese Air Force magazine *Mais Alto* signed by Rui Aballe Vieira, relating the trials and tribulations of the Fury and PZL in Portugal, that led to the acquisition of the former – see Bibliography.

Portuguese Fury s/n 50 shown again in flight over the UK before delivery. (Força Aérea Portuguesa/ AHFA)

the majority of the conclusions drawn being also used in the development of the Romanian-manufactured PZL P.11b.

Politics and finances being what they were, however, and counter to the pilots' preference for the P.11, the final Portuguese choice of a fighter fell on the Hawker product. Among other considerations noted by the *Arma de Aeronáutica* Purchase Committee, the tag price per unit was more attractive, and, in accordance with the issued specifications, it had been chosen by RAF, having been in service with its home country's air force since 1930. After many tribulations, negotiations for the purchase of a small number of Hawker Fury fighters were finally initiated in 1933.

The initial order (order n° 31709/34) to Hawker (now named Hawker Aircraft Ltd) did not specify more than three aeroplanes, thought it is likely that another 20-23 aircraft would be required, to equip a fighter squadron to be formed in the near future. This consideration is mostly based on A.M. documentation (Circular n° 172, dated 16 March 1935), which reserved a block of 25 numbers (400 to 425) to be allocated to the Fury under its new numbering plan. However, the purchase of further aircraft was never to materialise.

While the Portuguese Fury looked similar to its British counterpart, it differed in several details, particularly an increase of its fuel capacity to make it possible for the aircraft to cover of all of the Portuguese home territory. This was to the detriment of agility, speed and aerobatic capability. For instance, when looping, the aircraft had the tendency to stall making constant vigilance from the pilot necessary. The original concept of 'strategic defence', which the British aircraft was designed for, was consequently replaced by an increase of range much more in accordance with a limited number of fighters that had to cover a large territory. The operating range was thus improved to around 750 km (466 miles) instead of the original 494 km (306 miles), and the top speed decreased to 325 km/h (202 mph) instead of 359 km/h (223 mph) in the case of the British Fury Mk I. Other minor customisation carried out by the factory included the wheels and tyres, the former substituting Dowty solid rims more suitable to the roughness of the Portuguese landing strips, and Palmer-Cord tyres being replaced by low pressure Dunlops.

The first Portuguese Fury flew for the very first time in England on 28 May 1934, proceeding eleven days later, on 8 June, to the A&A.E.E. (Aeroplane and Armament Experimental Establishment) to be submitted there to intensive tests. This was in accordance with orders issued from the Air Ministry due to the changes made to the original design. The first aircraft was followed by two further aeroplanes, already showing the red Portuguese *Cruz de Cristo* on the wings, the yellow *Galgo* on the fuselage and sequential registration (50, 51 and 52). At the conclusion of these tests, the three Furies began the journey to their new home, Tancos, where they arrived by the end of June, to join the GIAPC (*Grupo Independente de Aviação de Protecção e Combate*, or Independent Protection and Combat Aviation Group), where they would form a small combat patrol. Upon their arrival and after a complete technical inspection, the first recorded operational flight of a Hawker Fury over home territory took place on 6 August 1934, being an uneventful 45-minute test flight.

The first quarter of 1935 saw the official replacement of the two-digit serial numbers, in use until then on *Arma de Aeronáutica* airplanes, with the triple digit system mandated by Circular no.172, which reserved a block of numbers for the intended future Furies. In accordance with the new system, Furies numbered 50, 51 and 52 became 400, 401 and 402[5]. This numbering system was not immediately applied, as shown by records existing of Fury no. 50 flying with the old serial as late as mid-October that year. By the end of the year 1935, however, all elements of the combat patrol displayed serials according to the new numbering system.

In 1935 and the following year, the flight operations of the three Furies saw periods of intense activity alternating with quiet intervals in which the aircraft were grounded under strict security measures. The three Hawker Fury fighters, although available only in limited numbers, were the A.M.'s most up-to-date equipment and, until the advent of the Spanish Civil War (July 1936 to April 1939), the fastest aeroplane in the Iberian Peninsula, not to mention the only type equipped with a radio transmitter/receiver. The customary courtesy visits to Spain, previously so frequent, suffered a complete halt for both pilots and aircraft alike, as soon as it was clear there would be a conflict in the neighbouring country[6].

Various incidents, the majority of them fortunately of minor material consequence, punctuated the operational life of the Fury. The most common was the propensity of the large-diameter propeller to break its tips, especially during landing on the bumpy and rocky unprepared airstrips used during exercises. The high cost of the Watts propeller led the authorities to seek an alternative at home within the O.G.M.A. works, which took on the manufacture of a propeller to replace the broken ones. Other incidents recorded included, in one instance, the Rolls-Royce Kestrel engine of Fury no. 401 seizing. This took place when, while returning from a simulated attack on a vehicle convoy and carrying out a 'chandelle', the aircraft's engine abruptly stopped due to the malfunctioning of the cooling system. The pilot, *Alferes* Machado de Barros, was able to maintain control of the powerless aircraft and land it on a recently ploughed field. Three days later, after an in-situ change of engine, the same pilot flew the aeroplane out of the field and returned to his base.

Another incident, with a less happy conclusion, occurred on 6 April 1938, when *Alferes* Vasconcelos de Carvalho, flying Fury no. 400 (ex-50, the first Portuguese Fury) decided to perform aerobatics over his father's estate and farm in the vicinity of Torres Novas, a small country town approximately 100 kilometres from Lisbon. At the end of his performance, while flying very low, the pilot attempted too late to avoid a group of trees, and the left wing hit the ground at the same time

5 Later, Circular 642, dated June 1938, ordered the change of aircraft serial number 400 to 402, an intriguing suggestion as aircraft 400 had been lost in an accident in April 1938.

6 The Spanish Civil War spawned a myth that would prevail until recently, mostly in non-national literature and on the internet, in which it was said that a Portuguese Fury participating in the conflict on the Nationalist side was shot down and lost with its pilot near the border by a Spanish Republican Vickers Vildebeest in a dogfight on 17 August 1937. This event never took place.

Fury no. 401 after its accident in September 1941. Despite the apparent damage, this aircraft was entirely rebuilt and flew again three months later, in December 1941. (Força Aérea Portuguesa/ AHFA/Coll. Joaquim Barros Prata)

that the right wing was ripped off by an olive tree. The outcome of the accident was the complete loss of the airframe, thankfully without harm to the pilot. Elements of the aircraft that could be salvaged, including the Kestrel engine, were returned to the Air Base inventory.

Several months later, on 22 September, Fury no. 401 flown by *Tenente* Ribeiro Ferreira, was, for unknown reasons, obliged to make an emergency landing close to the town of Tomar, 16 km North of Tancos. The airframe, while severely damaged, was considered repairable and was therefore sent to the O.G.M.A. works, where it was completely rebuilt and refurbished, returning to the air in test flights by mid-December, and returning to its base by the end of the year. Once there, it was used most of the time for instruction flights only, predominantly on aerobatics, ending its career after an unexplained accident over the Tancos landing strip that dictated its final withdrawal in February 1942.

The surviving Fury, no. 402 pursued its solitary flying career without any major problems. Its longevity was due mainly to the large number of spare parts still in stock and, oddly enough, to the lack of pilots, the great majority being committed now to the defence of Azores, flying Gloster Gladiators and Curtiss Mohawks. What would be its last flight with a pilot from its home base, Tancos, was recorded on 22 July 1942, during a transit to Alverca, with *Capitão* Jara de Carvalho at the controls. In Alverca the aeroplane stood in a hangar for more than two years, when it was decided, on December 1944, to make a complete overhaul of the airframe and return it to its previous base. At Tancos, the Fury flew three more training sorties in May 1945, only to be grounded again for a further two years, until it was dismantled. The aircraft's fate is confirmed by the *Ordem de Serviço* (Service Order) dated 23 May 1947, when it was finally and sadly stricken from from the inventory of the *Aeronáutica Militar Portuguesa*.

Camouflage & Markings

The Fury sported the original factory livery of fabric surfaces doped silver with highly polished metal parts for the entire period of its service with the *Arma de Aeronáutica*. The National cockade consisting of the red *Cruz de Cristo* superimposed on a white disc were applied to the wings in the usual four positions. A thin outline to the discs, possibly red, was apparently unique to the Fury. The finish was applied while the aeroplanes were still in the factory in England and remained for the service life of the aircraft, as can be seen in a photograph of the scrapped 401 in September 1942.

The yellow *Galgo* emblem of the Tancos air base, was applied on the fuselage ahead of the black registration numbers used at the time the aircraft entered service (50, 51 and 52). As stated earlier, the two digit system serial numbers were replaced by a three-digit system from 1935, when the Furies became then 400, 401 and 402.

Of particular interest is a nickname only used on Fury no. 50 (subsequently no. 400), applied by its usual pilot, *Major* Sousa Maya, the C.O. of Tancos: 'MITA 9°'. Maya always personalised 'his' aircraft with the diminutive name of his wife, Mrs. Maria Clotilde ('Mita') Dantas in a sequence of which the Fury was the ninth aircraft so named. The name and number '9°' were painted in black on both sides of the cockpit while the aircraft was still in England. For more details of this nickname see the Appendix on Markings and Insignia, and Colours and Camouflage.

The red and green National Flag (green leading) was painted on the rudder, in equal width stripes, at the factory, while the Portuguese coat of arms was applied upon arrival in Portugal. Originally, the Furies did not have their serials painted on the lower wing under-surfaces, but these were added when the three-digit system was implemented. The numbers could then be read from the front on both wings, being placed roughly mid-way between the cockades and fuselage.

Aircraft Characteristics Hawker Fury Mk I ("Portuguese Fury")	
Quantity used:	3
Crew:	One
Years of Service:	1934–1947
Span:	30' (9.14 m)
Length:	26' 8" (8.17 m)
Height:	10' 2" (3.10 m)
Wing area:	251.8 sq ft (23.40 m²)
Engine:	One Rolls-Royce Kestrel IIS (S) 515HP (384 kW)
Empty weight:	2,623 lb (1,189.8 kg)
Loaded weight:	3,548 lb (1,609.35 kg)
Maximum speed:	169 mph (272 km/h) at 10,000 feet (3,048 m)
Service ceiling:	26,500 feet (8,077 m)
Climb to 10,000 feet:	5min 42sec
Armament:	Two Vickers .303 in. (7.7 mm) machine guns with 600 rounds per gun

Hawker Fury Mk I, Serial number 50, May/June 1934. Aircraft in original factory livery of fabric surfaces doped silver with highly polished metal parts. The first of the three Fury to be purchased by Portugal was already painted with the National colours, cockades, serial number and the Base emblem, including its nickname "MITA 9º" on both sides of the cockpit entrance, during the tests flights in the UK Of note, however, it is the absence of the National Coat of Arms on the fin flag.

Side view of the Portuguese Fury s/n 50 at Brooklands before delivery. (Força Aérea Portuguesa/AHFA)

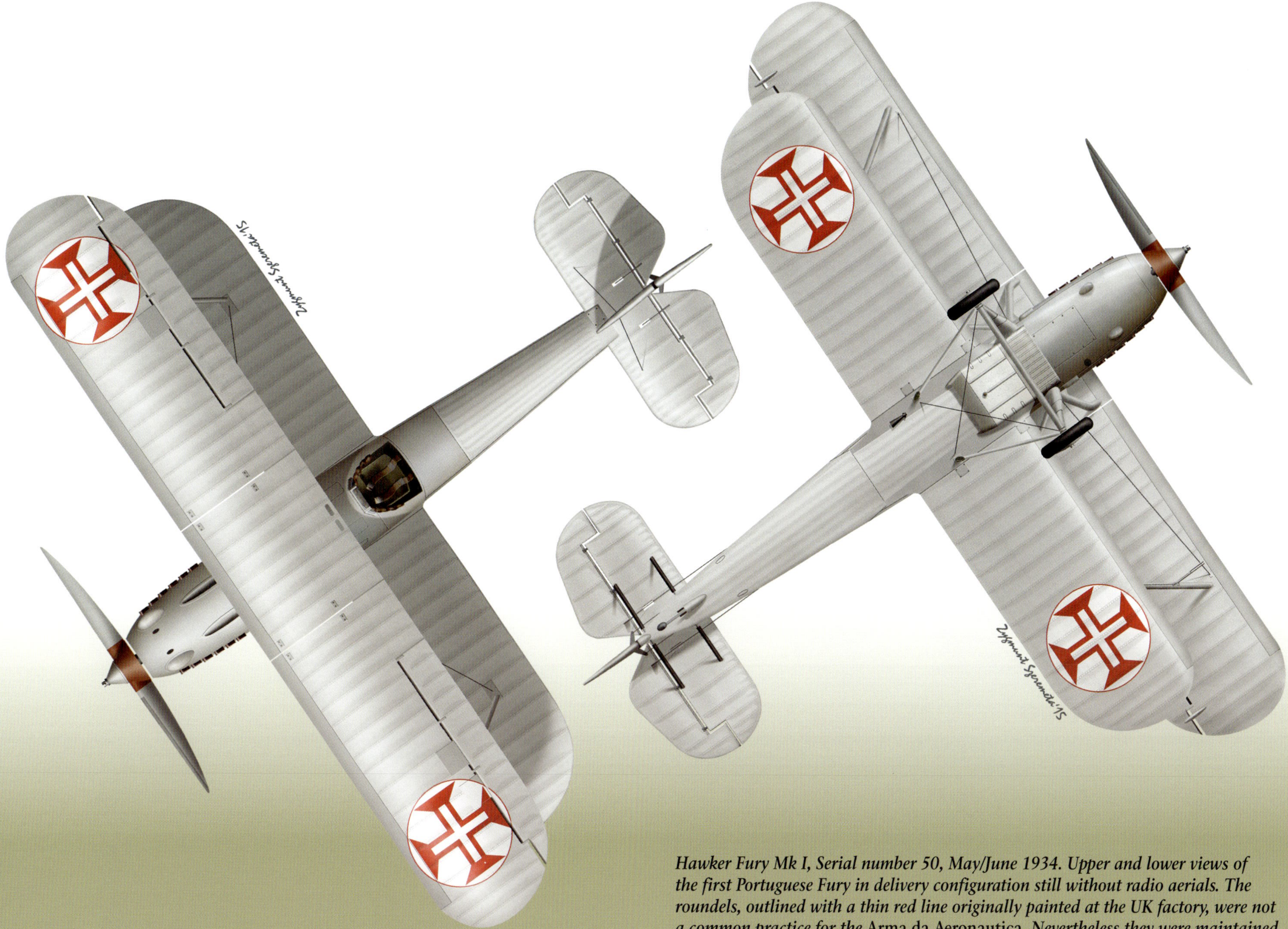

Hawker Fury Mk I, Serial number 50, May/June 1934. Upper and lower views of the first Portuguese Fury in delivery configuration still without radio aerials. The roundels, outlined with a thin red line originally painted at the UK factory, were not a common practice for the Arma da Aeronautica. *Nevertheless they were maintained for the duration of the service of the three aircraft.*

Hawker Fury Mk I, s/n 50 with National Coat of Arms, and radio antenna, late 1934. It was after its arrival in Portugal that the Furies were fitted with radio equipment, becoming the very first aircraft in the Peninsula to use this kind of communication system. Also the external appearance changed slightly with the addition of the Coat of Arms to the fin flag, maintaining the original silver dope painting.

The three Portuguese Furies serial numbers 50, 51 and 52 after their arrival at Tancos Air Base. (Força Aérea Portuguesa /AHFA)

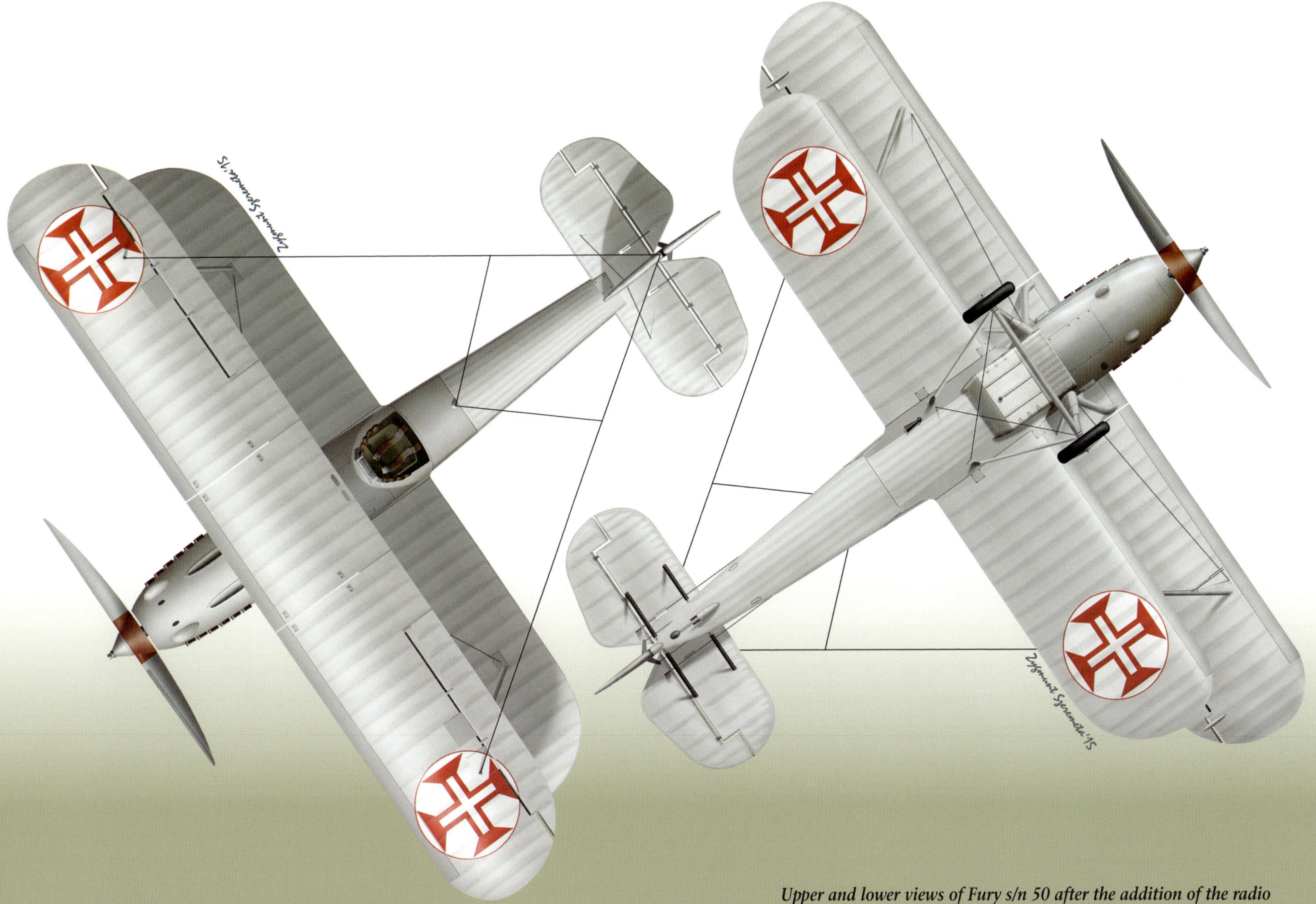

Upper and lower views of Fury s/n 50 after the addition of the radio equipment as denoted by the respective aerials. See text for detais.

Hawker Fury Mk I, serial number 402, mid/end of 1935. Aircraft in original factory livery of fabric surfaces doped silver with highly polished metal parts. From 1935 onwards the Arma de Aeronautica changed the identification system of their aircraft, the serial numbers in the "400 block" being applied to the Fury. This way, the aircraft with the previous serial number 52 became 402.

Complying with the new rules regarding the change of serial numbers, this Fury shows its new three digit identity (402). (Força AéreaPortuguesa /AHFA/ Coll.Gualter Meira)

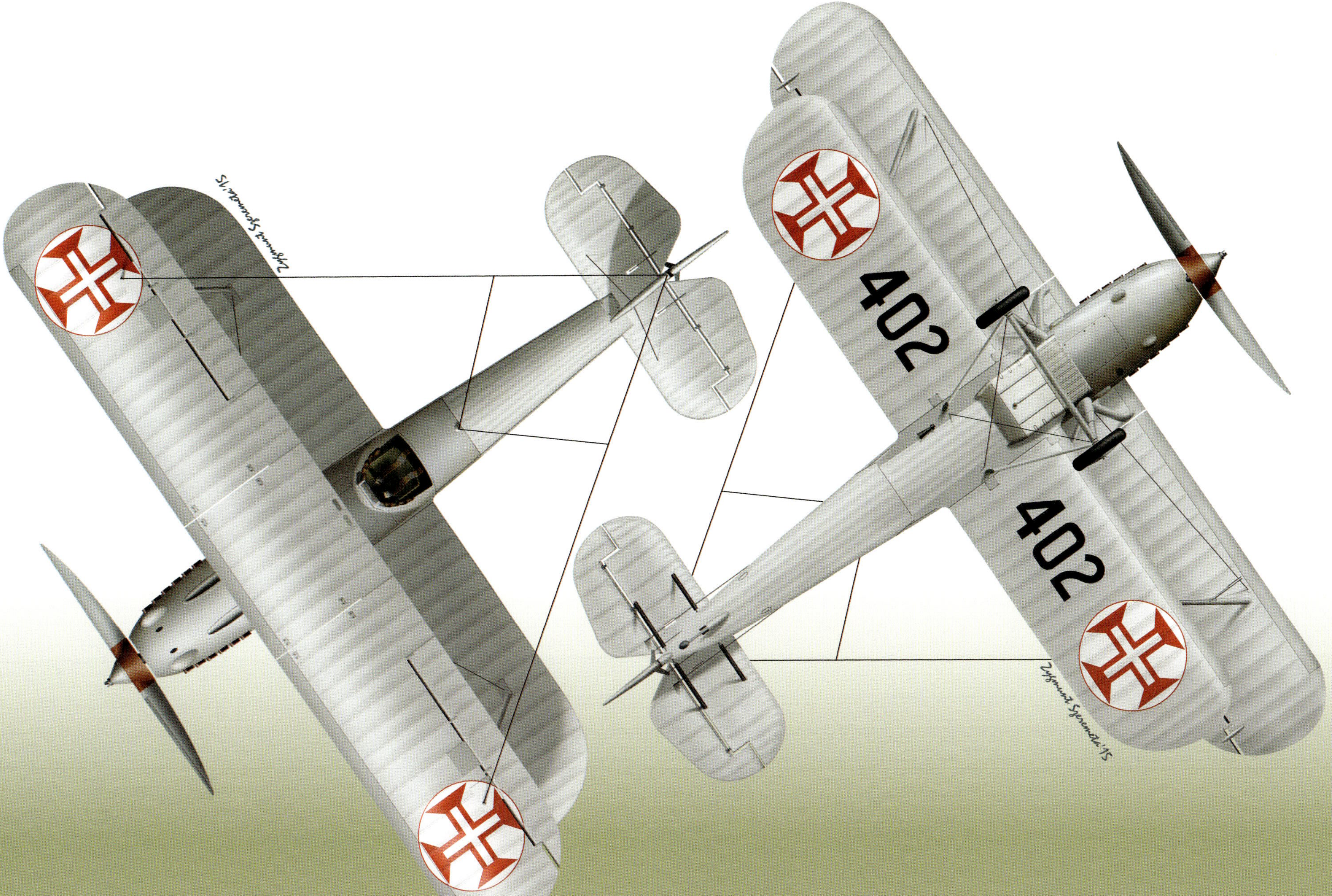

Hawker Fury Mk I, serial number 402, mid/end of 1935. Underside view of former aircraft s/n 52, after the change of the identification system enforced by the Arma da Aeronáutica *in 1935. See text for details.*

Gloster Gladiator Mk II

Background

The British Air Ministry issued Specification F.7/30 in 1930, with the intention of securing a fighter to serve in the Royal Air Force that was able to face any aircraft that might possibly attack the United Kingdom by air. The specification explicitly identified, among others, the following characteristics for the new aircraft:

- Single-seat fighter, with day and night fighter interception capabilities;
- Maximum speed of over 250 mph;
- Four Vickers machine-guns as armament;
- Preferred use of the Rolls-Royce Goshawk engine.

Gloster decided not to develop a completely new proposal in response to F.7/30, but instead took advantage of an existing type, already in service with RAF, the new biplane fighter Gloster Gauntlet, and elected to evolve the design.

A long period of time elapsed between the origin of the specification and the development of proposals from the industry. Only in February 1934 was Gloster finally able to present a fighter proposal issued from the Gauntlet design. The new aircraft would use the new version of the Bristol Mercury radial engine, the ME.30, which, in Gloster's opinion, would allow the aircraft to attain the required speed of 250 mph. The new engine, with its 700 bhp output, would also easily allow the extra weight of two more machine-guns to be carried as per the requested armament. Thus, the aircraft fully complied with Specification F.7/30 (with the caveat of not using the preferred Goshawk engine) but, surprisingly in view of its evolutionary design, it also becomes the last contender to be shown to the RAF. The other contenders for the new fighter included unconventional Blackburn and Westland biplanes, and the Supermarine Type 224 monoplane, the original 'Spitfire', with its inverted gull wing and fixed undercarriage.

The Gauntlet-based prototype was flown for the first time on 12 September 1934, equipped with a 645 hp Bristol Mercury VIS engine. With this fitted, the prototype, now identified as the

Gladiator 465. This photo of a brand new aircraft clearly shows the upper surface colours covering both wing leading edges. (FAP/AHFA)

SS.37, attained a speed of 242 mph at an altitude of 11,500 ft, while fitted with two fuselage and two wing machine-guns, as required by F.7/30. By 5 April 1935 the SS.37 was transferred to the A&A.E.E. (Aeroplane and Armament Experimental Establishment) for trials, bearing the RAF serial K5200.

By this time, five years after the issue of the original specification, the need to re-equip the British armed forces had become pressing in the extreme, and given that the new Gloster prototype fully satisfied expectations, a Production Specification (F.14/35) was quickly prepared, and the first 23 production aircraft ordered. On 1 July 1935 the new aircraft was named Gladiator.

A follow-up order for another 180 aircraft was placed in September 1935, when the prototype had already been subjected to several modifications. The initial flights of the first three production aircraft were completed in January 1937, and No.72 Squadron formed at Tangmere on 22 February, the first of the nine squadrons that would equip with the new fighter in 1937[1].

1 To illustrate the situation in which the Royal Air Force found itself by 1938, it is worth mention that while Gloster Gladiators in service were receiving their new 3-blade propellers, a new monoplane fighter with a vastly superior performance, the Hawker Hurricane, was already being delivered to front line squadrons.

Of very poor quality, this photo has the interest of showing the surroundings of the Lajes Airfield (Azores), where the Gladiators operated during W.W.II. (FAP/AHFA)

Gladiator 461. The size and format of the Cruz de Cristo *can be discerned on this view, as well as the positioning of the underwing serial numbers. (FAP/AHFA)*

Line-up of Gloster Gladiator aircraft on the Ota airfield. The aircraft serial number 452 and its two companions are in mint condition, denoting their recent arrival. (Coll. M.de Barros)

Four squadrons of Gladiators and one of Gauntlets were based in Palestine from 1938. The heavy use of the aeroplane in that region led the RAF to order several modifications from the original design, which were carried out in the RAF's Shawbury maintenance facilities during January-February 1939, to include the installation of the Bristol Mercury VIIAS of 830 bhp engine, new cockpit instrumentation, a Vokes air filter, electric starting equipment and a Fairey three-blade metal propeller of 10ft. 6in. diameter. This new aircraft was then called Gladiator Mk II.

With the onset of war in Europe in 1939, it should be stressed that even though the Gloster Gladiator was no longer a state-of-the-art fighter, its role was nevertheless important in the first part of the conflict. This was because it represented the only reasonably modern fighter aircraft instantly available in the North African, Middle East and Mediterranean campaigns, performing gallantly and facing machines very often with superior performance on paper.

Gladiator pilots that formed one of the "three aircraft patrols" in service in the Azores as mentioned on the text, being from left to right Alferes Oliveira Seixas, Furriel Gomes dos Santos and Furriel Melo. (Coll. M. de Barros)

The Gladiator was used by 16 different countries, (including Germany, which captured a number of aircraft). Several variants of the Gladiator were built, including the Sea Gladiator, involving extensive modifications relating to the many export orders, including those from Portugal.

The total numbers of 747 aircraft produced can be listed as follows:

- 1 prototype – (1934)
- 378 Gladiator Mk I – (1935–1938)
- 38 Sea Gladiator interim – (1937–1938)
- 60 Sea Gladiator – (1938–1939)
- 270 Gladiator Mk II – (1938–1939)

Gloster Gladiator in Portugal

In the 1930s, the world saw the development of the conditions that would lead to the beginning of the Second World War in September 1939 – the rise of aggressive and totalitarian regimes such as Germany, Italy and later Japan, and the general apathy of other major powers towards this development.

Politically speaking, Portugal entered this decade attempting to achieve stability after a long period of turmoil (1910–1926), in which the young *Republica Portuguesa* witnessed a succession of coups and counter-coups, civilian or military, that led to seven different Parliaments, eight Presidents, 39 Governments, 40 Prime-Ministers and numerous Boards and Interim Executives. This instability, born from internal disagreements within the political Parties that had toppled the Monarchy and established the Republic, descended into a climate of civil war, finally leading to yet another military coup on 28 May 1926. This established a Military Dictatorship, later to be known as the National Dictatorship, and later still, as the *Estado Novo* (New State).

Restructuring the armed forces and furnishing them with new equipment was not one of the main priorities of the Prime Minister of the new Government, Antonio Salazar. This had to be postponed in the first years of his consulate while he attempted to maintain an internal climate of peace, by force if needed, in order to balance the state finances and recover lost international prestige, maintaining a strict neutrality towards any conflicts near or far from the country's borders.

However the sudden emergence of the Spanish Civil War in 1936, with the risk of the conflict crossing into Portugal, led the Portuguese government to accelerate a policy concerning the strength of the armed forces, in order to show an acceptable capacity to react to any provocation.

Three Gladiators s/n 459, 460 and an unidentified one flying over Angra do Heroísmo (Azores). (Coll. M. de Barros)

Three Gladiators s/n 457, 458 and 461 at the temporary airfield of Achada on Terceira Island (Azores). (Coll. M. de Barros)

One of the requirements deriving from that strategy was the search for a new fighter to equip the *Arma de Aeronáutica*, as the only examples available in Portugal in the mid-1930s were the three Hawker Fury aircraft bought in 1934, described above.

Taking this into consideration and wishing to reinforce ties with Great Britain, on the basis of the 600 year-old alliance (the oldest in effect between two countries in the world), in October 1937 the Portuguese Government placed an order for 15 Gloster Gladiators. This would also help to balance likely German military influence resulting from orders that had been placed with that country for Junkers bombers. The re-arming plans included three fighter Flights of 15 aircraft each, which would be stationed with the bombers at a new air base to be constructed near Ota, a small village 49 km from Lisbon, and at Tancos, the old fighter base[2].

In the summer of 1938, a Portuguese military mission visited the UK during which they paid a visit to the Gloster factory, and were also able to test fly several aircraft, as had been the case in Germany. The Portuguese Gladiators, designated Model G.5 by Gloster, were similar to the RAF Gladiator Mk II except in the armament, which consisted of four Belgian FN (Fabrique Nationale) 7.92 mm machine guns instead of the British Vickers .303 in. weapons. The fifteen aircraft were taken from a British order, and had already allocated RAF serials N5835 to N5849. The prototype was test flown at the A.&A.E.E. between 19 and 27 July 1938.

By September that same year the first Portuguese Gladiator was assembled at the Alverca depot with the assistance of British technicians, being immediately test flown by a Gloster test pilot. When completed, the group of aircraft received the temporary serials P.1 to P.15, later to be changed to the definitive *Arma de Aeronáutica* serials 451-465, as soon as they joined their intended Flight[3].

During the final months of the year *Capitão* Moreira Cardoso from the Tancos base led the team of pilots receiving the new fighters after they were cleared by the British pilot. The aeroplanes were gradually put into service in the Alverca depot facilities, as the new Ota Air Base was yet to be

2 The British delegation, visiting Portugal during 1938 to help define the country's needs regarding additional military equipment, actually recommended the purchasing the Spitfire Mk I and not a biplane fighter such as the Gladiator. The Portuguese authorities followed this advice, but at the time RAF needs prevented the fulfilment of the order placed for Spitfires, at least immediately. As it is explained elsewhere, this acquisition was to have an effect later on.

3 The Flight in the *Arma da Aeronáutica* was organised in two sections of six aircraft each, with three aircraft in reserve or maintenance. The sections could also be divided into patrols of three aircraft each.

completed. In February 1939 *Capitão* Machado de Barros replaced Cardoso as C.O.

That same month, the Portuguese Government ordered a new batch of 15 Gladiator Mk IIs diverted from Air Ministry contract 773235/38. This new batch was intended to equip the Tancos air base, home of *Grupo Independente de Aviação de Protecção e Combate* (G.I.A.P.C.), equipped until now with the remaining Morane-Saulnier 233 and Hawker Fury aircraft. In the interim, the first Flight, still based at Alverca, undertook training sorties during the remaining of the year and the beginning of 1940.

Finally in April 1940, the new air base at Ota was inaugurated and the Gladiator Flight moved to its new home, although since November 1939 several aircraft had been flying to and from Ota for tests, as records of such flights by aircraft 452, 465, 458, 454 and 455 attest.

Tenente *Machado de Barros with his Gladiator. The mosquito insignia can be clearly seen.* General *Machado de Barros, then a Lieutenant (*Tenente*), in a letter addressed to the Air Force magazine* Mais Alto *in April 2004, confirmed that he and other pilots tentatively tried the interception of Fw 200 Condors from KG.40 that overflew the Azores, on board their Gladiators but without success. Please refer to the text. (Coll. M. de Barros)*

The customary missions flown from Ota included aerobatics, altitude tests to approximately 4,000 m (13,100 ft), photographic sorties, radio tests (with aircraft 462 in August 1940) and patrol flights. On 12 June 1940 aircraft 458, piloted by *Alferes* Mário Alvarenga Rua, performed an altitude test to reach 6,000 meters (19,700 feet), a height attained and controlled by radio, the duration of the flight being circa 1hrs 20 min. The highest altitude reached by a Gladiator over Portuguese territory was 6,500 m (21,325 ft) on 1 April 1941 by aircraft no. 460. Temporary assignments to the Northern coastal airfield of Espinho took place during August 1940 to perform a number of tests, including air to ground and air-towed target shooting, and photographic missions.

The first Gladiator batch was to be known for two interesting details. The pilots found it difficult to cock the machine guns while airborne, so an O.G.M.A. mechanic designed a simpler pneumatic device that greatly facilitated this task. On the other hand, the Gladiator was the first aircraft in the Portuguese military aviation to have a dual-channel radio communications system installed, one channel to communicate with in-flight aircraft with another to communicate with ground forces.

The second batch of 15 Gladiators arrived at Alverca by October 1939 and, once assembled, were test flown by Portuguese pilots, the first flights starting in 15 February 1940 by *Major* Cardoso in the aircraft P.11 and *Tenente* Costa in aircraft P.13. Oddly enough the aircraft, once assembled, were allocated the same O.G.M.A. test serials, P.1 to P.15, as the previous batch had received. Permanent serials 466-480 were subsequently applied, all aircraft being fully operational at Tancos by May 1940[4]. However, the operational records show that Tancos aircraft continued to use the O.G.M.A. serials, and only by February 1941 were they recorded sporting the new serials operationally, with a few exceptions, these being 468, 470, 471, 473 and 475.

The first accident recorded involving a Gladiator occurred in September 27, 1940 when *Tenente* Sousa had to make use of his parachute to abandon aircraft no. 475, after a collision with another aircraft damaged its tail. The same month, during exercises held with the Army that involved combat aircraft on a scale never before seen in Portuguese territory, the two Gladiator Flights, now fully operational at Ota and Tancos, were employed. Besides the aforementioned episode with aircraft 475, on 25 September aircraft P.8 performed an emergency landing leading to the aircraft being written off. Aircraft no. 463 completed another such manoeuvre but avoiding the loss of the

4 As a matter of curiosity, the available records show that in May 1940 Tancos aircraft performed 135 flights totaling 76 hrs, in July 120 flights with 60.5 hrs on the log-books and in October 110 flights with only 41 hrs 36 min. on the clock.

Gladiators 456, 462 and 465 flying in formation, performing aerobatics over the town of Angra do Heroismo, Azores. This photo clearly shows the position and format of the Cruzes de Cristo *and the serial numbers. (Coll. M. de Barros)*

aircraft, as it was recorded flying again in January 1941. These events accounted for the loss of two aircraft, 475 and P.8 which, had it survived, would have become 473. Aircraft no. 468 apparently disappeared from the records by September 1940 to reappear only in September 1943 at O.G.M.A. (Alverca) for unknown reasons.

The "Azores Connection"

The Second World War opened with sweeping advances by Nazi Germany and the spreading of the conflict area to the Atlantic. The conseqent interest of both sides in the Azores Islands, located between Europe and America, prompted the Portuguese Government to mobilise forces to reinforce the islands' garrison. At the same time, it was made known that an attempt to take the Azores by force by any of the belligerents would result in resistance by the available Portuguese forces, even though such resistance would effectively be token in nature.

The mobilisation that followed brought the total number of troops in the Azores to 30,000-32,000 men, sent to the islands with corresponding equipment, in several shipments from Lisbon. The strengthening operation started in the spring of 1941. As a consequence of that decision, the two Gladiator flights were simultaneously mobilised along with half of the existing ten Ju 52 bombers, anti-aircraft guns, materiel and men, all departing from Lisbon on 4 June 1941. In the first shipment, 18 Gladiators were to be loaded, with another seven aircraft to follow. Five aeroplanes from the available number, aircraft nos. 460, 464, 468, 475 and 473/'P.8', would never be used in the Azores. The aircraft were to find a new home at two recently prepared airfields, one in Rabo de Peixe, S. Miguel Island, the other at Lajes, Terceira Island[5].

5 From mid-1941 the air strength in Continental Portugal was practically non-existent, as available aircraft consisted of only two Hawker Furies, five Gladiators in reserve without pilots, five Ju 52s and 10 Ju 86 day-bombers. Effectively, the reinforcement of the Azores Archipelago left the Continental Territory defenceless.

The Azores aircraft would form two Flights. the *1ª Esquadrilha Expedicionária de Caça* (First Expeditionary Fighter Flight), abbreviated to E.E.C.1, stationed at Rabo de Peixe, and the *2ª Esquadrilha Expedicionária de Caça* (Second Expeditionary Fighter Flight, or E.E.C.2) based at Lajes. In the latter case, the airfield facilities were not completely ready so the aeroplanes were temporarily sent to a rudimentary airfield at Achada on Terceira Island. The two Flights' commanding officers were, respectively, *Capitão* António Rodrigues Costa and *Tenente* Manuel Machado de Barros.

Under a restructuring process coincidently taking place within the *Arma de Aeronautica*, the Azores airfields were soon to be given identification numbers. Rabo de Peixe Airfield would become *Base Aérea nº 4* (B.A.4) and Lajes, *Base Aérea nº 5* (B.A.5). At that time, the three existing air bases in Portugal itself became B.A.1 at Sintra, B.A.2 at Ota and B.A. 3 at Tancos.

By the end of July 1941. and as soon as the Gladiators were considered operational, a system of alert patrols was put in place with three aircraft always ready to scramble and two in reserve on each airfield, for daylight operations. According to pilot's logbooks and operation diaries, the typical missions consisted of:

- Reconnaissance flights at 2,000 metres;
- Aerobatics training at 500, 1,000 and 3,000 metres;
- Combat tactics training at 1,000, 1,500, 2,000 and 3,000 metres;
- Bomber interception at 1,000 metres;
- Combat air patrol at 1,000 metres;
- Ground attack practice with three aircraft;
- Meteorological flights at 3,000 metres;
- Climbing tests to 6,000 metres;
- Climbing to 5,000 metres with a three aircraft patrol;
- Converging attack to moving target.

By July 1942 there were 12 aircraft at Lajes, Terceira, although most of them were non-operational. By December there were another 12 aircraft at Rabo de Peixe, S.Miguel Island, but these were also reported to have many problems. By late 1942, flying activity was severely curtailed by

Gladiator 453 with the mosquito insignia. During their assignment to the Azores the Gladiator flight from Lajes Airfield had three different types of "mosquito" insignias, differing in the details only. (FAP/AHFA)

the poor state of the airframes, which were heavily affected by the typically inclement Azorean weather. The difficulties experienced grew during 1942 and 1943, with numerous problems related to the regular supply of aviation fuel and the increasingly bad condition of airframes and engines. The lack of aircraft fuel would ultimately be the the reason for the grounding of all the *Lajes Esquadrilha* aircraft from 26 March to 16 May 1943.

Meanwhile, not everything was bad news for the pilots stationed in Azores. An important event would take place in the summer of 1942 with the arrival at BA5 of two Miles Master training aircraft, serials 417 and 418, which allowed flight training on monoplanes, forecasting the future use of this type of fighter.

Several serious accidents occurred during the period of the Gladiators' service in the Azores: the first fatal accident happened in October 1941 with the crash of aircraft 480 on S.Miguel Island.

On 9 April 1943, Miles Master serial 417 crashed on high ground in Terceira Island, the bodies of the two crew being found a few days later. Four days later, Gladiator no. 467 crashed against Pico da Vara, the highest mountain in S.Miguel Island, killing the pilot *2°. Sargento* Manuel Cardoso.

A much repeated but never confirmed story originated in 1976. *General* Machado de Barros, *Tenente* and Commanding Officer of E.E.C.2, stated in an interview with one of the authors that in different occasions 'his' Gladiators had tentatively tried to intercept German Fw 200 Condor aircraft that overflew the airfield (Lajes), but were never able to accomplish the interception. Many years after this interview, Mr. Guenther Ott, the official historian of KG 40, the Fw 200 unit based in Bordeaux, France that was responsible for Atlantic convoy-hunting operations, confirmed that no such incidents were recorded in the operations books of KG.40. It is believed that the over-flight of the Azores would be a mission practically on the limits of the Fw 200's range, unless conditions were very favourable.

The return to Continental Portugal and the final years

In the first half of 1943 the decision was taken to send all the remaining Gladiators on the Azores back to the Continent. This was not immediately implemented due to logistical difficulties, mostly relating to the dismantling and crating of the aircraft and cargo transportation availability. Finally by September 1943, after many technical hitches, all the remaining aircraft arrived safely at Alverca, with Gladiator 451 bearing in its logbook the distinction of carrying out the last recorded Gladiator flight in the Azores, which took place in August 1943. Oddly this aircraft had been grounded for a long time and had not flown since June 1942.

From August 1943 to October 1944 the Azores air space was left without any Portuguese air presence. However, 269 Squadron RAF, under the recently signed agreement between Portugal and England for the use of the Lajes Air Base facilities, received a number of Spitfire Mk VB aircraft in February 1944. The RAF Spitfires would remain there until March 1946, sharing the Lajes base with Hudsons, Martinets and Walruses of the same Squadron. The chief mission was probably air-sea rescue and protection of ditched crews until they could be retrieved. However, it is arguable that these RAF aircraft, in some respects, provided the Azores, or at least Lajes, with a measure of air defence from February 1944 onwards, an odd situation for a technically neutral country.

Meanwhile, the Portuguese Government vainly tried to obtain additional fighter aircraft. The only available equipment from Great Britain, its traditional supplier, was a small quantity of Curtiss Mohawk fighters, which arrived in the Azores in July 1944, almost a year after the last Gladiators left the Archipelago!

Gladiators returning from Azores were completely refurbished at Alverca and from August 1945 they were sent to Tancos B.A.3, with Ota B.A.2 receiving its allocated fighters from February 1946. Despite no longer being a front line aircraft, they were nevertheless useful for aerobatic training, as many of the current Hurricane and Spitfire pilots were former Gladiator pilots. This was not, however, the only use they were put to, as a record exists of no. 455 making a test climb to 5,000 m (16,400 ft) with the use of oxygen on 19 June 1946 .

Gladiator no. 466 with greyhound insignia. The Gladiator Flight bearing the Galgo *insignia was based on Rabo de Peixe Airfield on São Miguel Island, Azores. (FAP/AHFA)*

The gradual retirement of the Portuguese Gladiators was initiated from 1947, with seven aircraft still operational in 1952 (Gladiators 456, 457, 459, 463, 465, 470 and 476). The last four aircraft (457, 459, 464 and 476) were delivered to the Alverca Depot in 1953 for storage and, ultimately, scrapping, thus ending the biplane fighter era in Portugal. By this time the first jets were already flying with the Portuguese Air Force!

Camouflage and Markings

During the aforementioned interview with *General* Machado de Barros in 1976, the Gladiators' camouflage and markings was discussed. This confirmed that the aircraft carried an unchanged colour scheme during its service in Portugal, i.e., green on the upper surfaces and light blue on the lower surfaces. The colour of the spinner was also confirmed to be the same gloss light blue, as were the landing gear legs and wheel covers. The three-blade Fairey propeller was painted black with three thin yellow stripes at the tip. There is no record of a two-tone upper surface camouflage as is sometimes suggested.

In the absence of known colour photographic evidence, it seems most likely that the precedent set for colours and markings during previous aircraft acquisitions by Portugal was followed. In other words, for at least the first part of their Portuguese service, the Gladiators retained the original colours in which they were painted in the UK, i.e. Dark Green upper-surfaces and Sky Blue under surfaces (including spinner and undercarriage) as established by British Air Ministry orders[6].

The aircraft also wore the green and red National Flag with Coat of Arms on the rudder in the usual fashion. Unusually, the cockade bearing the red *Cruz de Cristo* on a white disk was, at least

6 Colour chips for these and other colours used by British aircraft manufacturers for the period of W.W.II and before, as well as facsimiles of Air Ministry orders, can be found in Vol.3 of RAF Museum Series book 'British Aviation Colours of WWII – The Official Camouflage Colours and markings of RAF aircraft 1939–45' – Arms and Armour Press London 1976.

in some cases applied on the lower wing under surface only, as existing photos prove. There is no logical explanation for this, as at the time of the Gladiator service the usual procedure called for the national cockade to be painted in four positions on the wings. In the absence of an official written directive on the subject, it cannot be guaranteed that this practice was always followed. Serial numbers were painted black on the wing lower surfaces, reading from the front, and white on the fuselage, roughly at a quarter of the distance between the wing trailing edge and the tail plane leading edge. (Some sources state that the fuselage serial numbers were painted yellow. In the absence of official evidence on this issue, this is open to debate). The space in front of the serial was used for the application of an emblem identifying the Flight. In the case of the aircraft belonging to the Tancos fighter base, the *Galgo* was painted in yellow. During the period of time spent in the Azores, an insignia was created by General Machado de Barros representing, in his own words "...the state of mind at the Flight: on the defensive, but ready to bite!". This insignia, a fighting mosquito wearing boxing gloves, is known to have had three different designs.

Under the 1950 reorganisation of the Armed Forces and the creation of the *Força Aérea Portuguesa*, a block of serial numbers was reserved for the Gladiators in the range of 41** , but as far as is known, these were not applied before the aircraft were retired.

Gloster Gladiator – Individual Aircraft Histories

RAF Serial (1)	Arrival Date	A.M. Serial	Retired (S.O.C.)	Remarks
	9/1938	451	1950	LFR Azores : 8/43
	9/1938	452	1950	LFR Azores 2/42
	9/1938	453	1950	LFR Azores 1/43
	9/1938	454	1947	LFR Tancos 1/47
	9/1938	455	1950	LFR Tancos 3/48
	9/1938	456	1952	Operational Ota 3/52
	9/1938	457	1953	Operational Tancos 8/52
	9/1938	458	1950	LFR Tancos 10/46
	9/1938	459	1953	Operational Tancos 7/52
	9/1938	460	?	LFR Tancos 1/50
	9/1938	461	1950	LFR Ota 1/48
	9/1938	462	1950	LFR Azores 7/42
	9/1938	463	1952	Operational Tancos 5/52
	9/1938	464	?	Operational Tancos 12/51
	9/1938	465	1952	Operational Tancos 7/52
P.1 (2)	10/1939	466	1950	Operational Tancos 7/50
P.2	10/1939	467	-	Destroyed 13/5/43
P.3	10/1939	468	1952	Operational Ota 5/51
P.4	10/1939	469	1950	LFR Tancos 10/50
P.5	10/1939	470	?	Operational Tancos 6/52
P.6	10/1939	471	1952	LFR Ota 11/49
P.7	10/1939	472	1946	-
P.8	10/1939	473	-	Destroyed 25/9/1940 still as P.8
P.9	10/1939	474	1950	LFR Tancos 1/47
P.10	10/1939	475	-	Crashed and destroyed 25/9/1940
P.11	10/1939	476	?	Operational Tancos 1952
P.12	10/1939	477	1950	LFR Tancos 8/49
P.13	10/1939	478	1947	-
P.14	10/1939	479	?	LFR Ota 3/51
P.15	10/1939	480	-	Crashed and destroyed 10/1941

Notes: The RAF serial numbers of the first batch of aircraft received were N5835 to N5849, but the correlation between these and Portuguese A.M. serial numbers cannot be established.

Aircraft s/n 466 to 480 arrived without RAF serial, receiving a temporary serial when assembled in Alverca. This system of temporary serials was also used with the first batch, as mentioned in the text.

L.F.R. : last flight recorded.

S.O.C : Struck off Charge

Aircraft Characteristics Gloster Gladiator Mk II	
Quantity used:	30
Crew:	One
Years of Service:	1938–1953
Span:	32' 3" (9.83 m)
Length:	27' 5" (8.36 m)
Height:	10' 7" (3.22 m)
Wing Area:	323 sq ft (30 m²)
Empty weight:	3,444 lb (1,562 kg)
Normal loaded:	5,750 lb (2,608 kg)
Max. speed:	323 mph (520 km/h) at 15,100 feet (4,600 m)
Max.range:	1,003 mls (1,614 km)
Armament:	2 x Fuselage and 2 x wing – mounted .303" (7.7 mm) Browning machine guns
Engine:	One 830 hp *Mercury VIIIA/AS*

Gladiator serial no. 459 flying over the Azores landscape in the '40s. This aircraft exhibits a strip of a different colour on the tail area, being the only photo showing it with such "adornment". As in all photos of the Portuguese Gladiators the absence of a colour band around the fuselage is notorious, it is assumed that such dissimilarity of colour represents some kind of fuselage repair. Allegedly, the strip/repair would be silver doped. (FAP/AHFA)

Gloster Gladiator Mk II, circa November 1939. This was the general aspect of a Portuguese Gladiator, on reception and after receiving its final serial number. These aircraft were factory painted in a two colour scheme of Dark Green upper surfaces and Light Blue under surfaces, which was maintained for their operational service life with Arma da Aeronáutica. Note the National flag on the rudder complete with Coat of Arms.

This photo of what looks like an "inspection line" or parade of Gladiators while at the Ota Air Base clearly demonstrate the absence of the National Insignia, the Cruz de Cristo, on the upper surface of the top wings. (FAP/AHFA)

General upper surface view of the Gladiator, showing to advantage the absence of national markings on the upper wing surface. For an unknown reason and against the use at the time, these aircraft did not carried the Cruz de Cristo on their upper surfaces, maintaining them however on the lower wing.

View of a typical lower wing under surface of a Gloster Gladiator. Of note is the black painted serial number on both wings facing forward, placed between the Cruz de Cristo and the machine guns pods.

Gloster Gladiator Mk II s/n 472, Tancos Air Base, 1941. Aircraft in original factory painted colours. During its detachment to the Azores Archipelago in 1941, the Tancos Gladiators maintained their Galgo (Greyhound) emblem that became the identification symbol of the 1ª Esquadrilha Expedicionaria de Caca (First Expeditionary Fighter Flight). The Esquadrilha was based then at the Rabo de Peixe Airfield, S. Miguel Island.

Gladiator 472 after its crash. It is assumed from the photo that the damage incurred by the aircraft in this ground loop did not prevent its quick repair and return to service, as the records shows that its final fate occurred in April 1946 when it was struck off charge and used for spares. (FAP/AHFA)

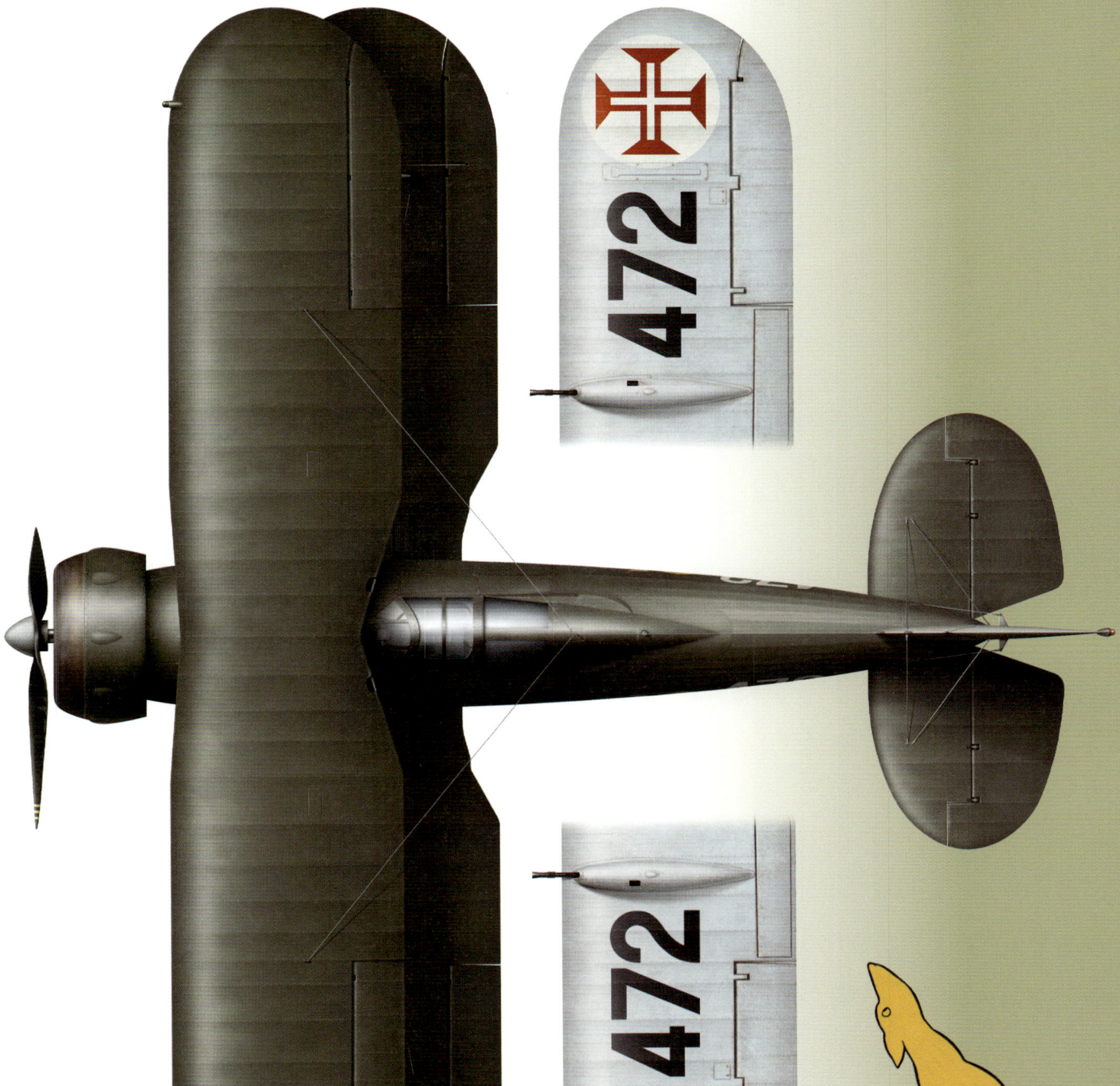
472
472

Gloster Gladiator Mk II s/n 459, Azores Archipelago, 1941. Aircraft in original factory painted colours. Seventy-five years have elapsed since the use of the Gloster Gladiator by the Portuguese Armed Forces (Arma da Aeronáutica) and yet the controversy on the colour of the fuselage painted serial numbers is not solved. With different sources claiming white figures and others suggesting that the yellow was more appropriated for the numerals, until now no credible official document surfaced from the archives to finally settle this matter. On other hand, and bearing in mind how hazardous is the exercise of establishing the authenticity of colours based on the examination of black and white photos only, certain documents compel the observer to lean to one of the proposals while others, of the same subject but under different lighting, have exactly the opposite effect. Thus we took the initiative to present the two variants, i.e., profiles with numerals in white (see profiles of aircraft serial number "455" and "472") and the present one, serial number "459", in yellow. The available photo showing it over flying the Azores landscape seems to demonstrate that the serial number is painted in a different colour than white. The other element of the decoration of this particular aircraft is the emblem of the "boxing mosquito", which had three different designs. General Machado de Barros, then a Tenente (Lieutenant), when he created the emblem, explained in an interview that his intention was not only to demonstrate the spirit of his fellow aviators (in his own words...on the defensive, but ready to bite...) but also identify the aircraft belonging to the Flight stationed on Terceira Island, Azores. The aircraft also shows signs of some kind of repair or maintenance, via a strip or band of a different colour, presumed to be aluminium. The landing gear is also in a darker colour alleged to be dark green, probably the result of the same repair or maintenance.

Curtiss Mohawk

Background

When in 1935 the US Army Air Corps (USAAC) issued a specification for a new fighter, the Curtiss-Wright Corporation answered with its new private venture, the Model 75. The other three companies that submitted designs also presented evolutions of already existing models – Seversky offered a fighter development of a two-seat amphibian from 1933, Chance-Vought, their V-141 development of the Northrop 3A, and Consolidated, a single-seat version of their PB-2A twin seat fighter.

The Model 75's design presented several novelties for the time, not only for the manufacturer but also for the USAAC The aircraft was of all-metal construction, structure and skinning (the control surfaces were the only fabric covered parts), and powered by a new 14-cylinder radial air-cooled Wright XR-1670-5 of 900 hp. Uniquely among the designs on offer, Curtiss employed an innovative landing gear system, designed and patented by Boeing, in which the wheels rotated 90° to rest flat inside the wing. To comply with the terms of the USAAC request, the Model 75 was armed with one 0.30 in. (7.62 mm) machine gun and one 0.50 in. (12.7 mm) machine gun, both firing through the propeller arc, in a typical arrangement for the day. The Model 75 was devoid of cockpit armour and self-sealing fuel tanks, though this was customary for US fighters at the time. The armament standards established in the USA were inferior to those set up and used in Europe during the same period. The armament of the initial production models would be replaced by a pair of Colt-Browning 0.50 in. guns, while the export version known as the Curtiss Hawk 75 received all kinds of different armament arrangements in conformity with the customers' specifications.

In May 1935, the proposed date for the presentation, the Model 75 was the only prototype ready for trials with the USAAC The Seversky Aircraft Company, was granted an extra three months to present its project, which made its debut in August 1935. Changes to submission dates, equipment and design occurring during the evaluation process led to disagreements between the contenders and ended with USAAC performing preliminary tests of the all of the competitors'

Curtiss Mohawk serial number 482 at Ota, its engine running, ready for take off. Of note are the position and style of the National Insignia and the absence of serial number under wings. (FAP/AHFA)

Capitão *Machado de Barros with other unidentified pilots standing in front of one of the Curtiss Mohawk from the Ota Air Base. (Coll. M.de Barros)*

proposals, requesting modifications from all of them, the main one being a change of engine. Curtiss responded, changing to the 9-cylinder Wright R-1820 Cyclone of 850 hp, this version of the prototype being designated Curtiss 75B. When the judgment was announced, the winner was the Seversky model, which would become the new P-35 pursuit (fighter). Nevertheless, the USAAC saw the value of the Curtiss proposal and ordered three aircraft for evaluation purposes bearing the designation Y1P-36, to be equipped with the R-1830 Twin Wasp engine.

Thus equipped, the aircraft performed so well that in 1937 it won a further competition and saw an order placed for 210 of the P-36A variant, the largest single US military order since WWI. Although the aircraft had a short career within the USAAC (ending in replacement by its stable-mate the P-40 shortly after the attack on Pearl Harbor) its employment by foreign air forces was widespread and diverse. Below is provided an explanation of the models used by the French *Armée de l'Air* and RAF only, as it was from these supplies that the Portuguese Mohawks came.

- Model 75 – Original prototype, civil registration X-17Y and c/n 11923
- Model 75A or H75-A – Main export version using variants the Wright Cyclone or Pratt & Whitney Twin Wasp. Firepower was lacking but the aircraft structure was strong, able to absorb a lot of punishment, as French pilots would later confirm after facing the German Messerschmitt Bf 109. The armament for this version was two synchronised machine-guns in the nose and two in the wings.
- H75-A1 (RAF Mohawk Mk I) – 100 aircraft built for France from December 1938, identified in French service as the H-75C-1 (C for *Chasse* – fighting). After the fall of this country in 1940 a small number of Hawks were flown to England where they were included in the RAF inventory as Mohawk Mk I aircraft: AX880-898, BJ876-878, BK876-879 and BL220/223. The armament was four FN Browning 7.5 mm calibre machine guns (two in the nose and two in the wings).
- H75-A2 (RAF Mohawk Mk II) – Another group of 100 aircraft delivered to France from May 1939. The armament of these aircraft was revised to include two additional 7.5 mm guns in the wings. Again, a small number was able to reach England in 1940, becoming Mohawk Mk II.

- H75-A3 and A6 (RAF Mohawk Mk III) – France ordered another 135 aeroplanes to include an improved 1,200 hp R-1830-S1C3G engine with armament as in the A2. Deliveries started in February 1940, with approximately 60 aircraft reaching France. Other aircraft went directly to French Morocco, while more than 20 aircraft were incorporated in the RAF as Mohawk Mk III. They were allocated the serials BK569-588 and AR630-694 (the latter serial block being shared with Mohawk Mk IV aircraft). After being fitted with British equipment they were supplied to India, South Africa and Portugal.
- H75-A4 (RAF Mohawk Mk IV) – A total of 284 H75-A4 aircraft were completed of the 795 aircraft originally ordered by France, being armed as the A3 variant but with the new 1,200 hp Wright R-1820-G205A engine. The armament was the same as that in models A2 and A3, six FN-Browning 7.5 mm machine guns, two in the nose and four in the wings. With only six delivered to the French *Armée de l'Air* before France's surrender, another four aeroplanes lost at sea and 23 that reached Martinique, the remaining aircraft were taken up by RAF as Mohawk Mk IVs. The exact number of aircraft cannot be determined, as they were merged in the serial blocks of the Mohawk Mk II and Mk III without distinction. Other aircraft from different foreign orders also became Mohawk Mk IVs, meaning the total figure should be close to 280. Upon arrival in England between July and September 1940 they were assembled, receiving new equipment according to RAF specifications, and were stored, held in reserve, in Maintenance Units in the event that they might be needed to help defend the UK. In the event, they saw no service in Western Europe under Allied colours, and the great majority were shipped to the Far East.

While as many as 20 different variants were operated by numerous countries, it is beyond the scope of this book to detail of all of them.

Curtiss Mohawk in Portuguese Service

As mentioned elsewhere in this book, the British Government refused to supply Portugal with the 15 Supermarine Spitfire Mk Is ordered in 1939, as the United Kingdom was then facing the possibility of an imminent German invasion.

The Portuguese Government insisted nevertheless on the supply of modern, monoplane fighters. With the transfer of the Gladiator Flights to the Azores, and the third fighter Flight, planned in the renewal of *Arma de Aeronáutica*, not having yet been formed, the Portuguese mainland was left without any credible air defence (see the Gloster Gladiator chapter).

The British Air Ministry, trying to answer the desperate Portuguese requests, allowed the release of a number of Curtiss Mohawks (Curtiss Hawk H75-A4) held in the RAF reserves in the

Curtiss Mohawks XY+B s/n 481 and XY+C s/n 482 at Ota Air Base summer 1943, ready for take off. (Coll. M.de Barros)

United Kingdom. As a result, 16 Mohawks were shipped to Portugal by the summer of 1941. Unfortunately, of the initial batch of 16 received by the Portuguese, five were heavily damaged during the transport to Lisbon, the airframes requiring lengthy repairs before they were usable[1]. By January 1942 eleven aircraft were ready for flight following assembly at Alverca and engine overhauls. The aircraft received the Portuguese serials 480[2] to 490, and were flying from Ota base by April.

However, accidents began immediately to affect the Mohawks. The first happened on 15 April 1942 when aircraft no. 489 crashed near Lisbon, killing the pilot, after participation in a commemorative flight over the Ota air base. On 13 May 1942 the pilot of aircraft no. 490 lost engine power and was forced to make a wheels-up landing in a field off the end of the Ota runway. Although the aircraft was damaged beyond repair, the pilot fortunately suffered only slight bruising.

In the meantime, *Capitão* Machado de Barros had left Lajes in the Azores and the Gladiator Flights, and was charged with the creation of *Esquadrilha Expedicionária de Caça nº 3* (E.E.C. 3) which was to include the Mohawks. This new flight would replace the Gladiators of E.E.C. 1, then based at Rabo de Peixe on S. Miguel Island, which soon would return to Continental Portugal (see the Gloster Gladiator chapter).

It was at this point, and for the first time, that Flight codes were applied to Portuguese fighter aircraft, the Mohawk flight receiving the code XY, with each aircraft being identified by a third letter, following the RAF practice.

A year later, the transfer to the Azores had not yet been accomplished and, by June 1943, Mohawks were still flying from Ota, with one more aircraft, no. 485, lost in July. (The pilot was able to bail out safely). In October that year, another serious accident occurred, when aircraft no. 487 was totally written off in a crash landing, fortunately without harm to the pilot, leaving the Mohawk fleet reduced to seven operational aircraft.

After a long wait, on 14 July 1944, almost three years after their arrival in Portugal, the first Mohawk Flight was officially commissioned at Rabo de Peixe airfield (Airbase no.4), S. Miguel

1 The ex-RAF serial numbers were as follows: AR 636, AR 642, AR 643, AR 652, AR 664, AR 666, AR 668, AR 671, AR 673, AR 679, AR 680, AR 690, AX 680, AX 886, BL 220, BS 789. From the above AR 636, AR 642, AX 680, AX 886 and BS 789 are confirmed in Portuguese official documents, the other serials being obtained by cross-checking several sources and we entirely believe that they are correct with 90 % of certainty. The correlation between RAF serials and Portuguese serials cannot be ascertained at this moment.

2 As Gladiator serial number 480 had already been struck off charge, its serial was re-used.

Curtiss Mohawks XY+B s/n 481, XY+C s/n 482 and XY+H s/n 487 flying over Ota Air Base. (Coll. M.de Barros)

Curtiss Mohawk XY+F s/n 485. Capitão *Machado de Barros is the third from the left standing in front of the aircraft. Of note is the style of the figures composing the serial number. (Coll. M.de Barros)*

Curtiss Mohawks XY+B s/n 481 and XY+C s/n 482 at Ota Air Base in the summer of 1943. (Coll. M.de Barros)

Capitão *Machado de Barros at the cockpit of a Mohawk, the photo clearly shows details on the cockpit area of the aircraft. (Coll. M. de Barros)*

Island (Azores), becoming a component of E.E.C.3. They replaced E.E.C.1, which had disbanded in the meantime.

The number of Mohawk aircraft actually used in the Azores is revealed by the *Ordem de Serviço nº4* (Service Order nr 4 to the Airbase) of 30 October 1944, which referred to aircraft nos. 480, 481, 482, 483, 484, 486 and 488 in E.E.C.3. The same document also specifically mentioned Mohawks bearing ex-RAF serials AX680, AX886, AR642 and BS789 to be included on the flight. It is assumed that these were four of the five aircraft that suffered damage during transportation, as mentioned before, and which had not yet flown since their arrival in Portugal. It also seems that these aircraft did not receive any *Arma da Aeronáutica* serials, as there are records of flights of Mohawk 'BS789' in September 1944. The reason for this discrepancy is open to conjecture.

Mohawks did not have a bright career in the Azores, with continual fuel shortages preventing normal use of the aircraft and sufficient training for their pilots. One of the pilots' logbooks registered a total of around 17 hours flying time in 6 months! It was consequently not surprising that another accident occurred in December 1944, completely destroying aircraft no. 483 and resulting in serious injuries to the pilot, *Tenente* Quintela. Yet another accident took place on 23 August 1945. *Alferes* Carlos Burnay was forced to carry out an emergency landing with aircraft no. 484, and was seriously burned, having to be helped out of the aircraft by onlookers and requiring medical evacuation to Lisbon. The aircraft was completely destroyed.

Soon after this accident E.E.C.3 was disbanded, as fighter aircraft on the Azores had became irrelevant with the end of the war in Europe. Mohawks ceased their service and were apparently struck off charge at S.Miguel, not a single one returning to Continental Portugal[3].

3 From January 1944, a number of Spitfire Mk VB aircraft belonging to 269 Squadron RAF were operational from Lajes airfield, probably to help on ASR operations. Nevertheless, they were also able to resist air attacks, even if by this stage of W.W. II it is hard to envisage where such an attack might have come from.

Of indifferent quality, this photo is quite interesting because it depicts Curtiss Mohawk serial number 488 without the usual Cruz de Cristo *(Cross of Christ), squadron and individual identification letters painted in the fuselage. For the colours of the aircraft please refer to the text in the "Camouflage and Markings" paragraph of this chapter. (Coll. M. de Barros)*

Curtiss Mohawk serial number 482 XY+C preparing for take off at Ota in the summer of 1943. (Coll. M. de Barros)

The Mohawk was not well-liked by Portuguese pilots. When interviewed, *General* Machado de Barros, first C.O. then *Capitão* of the Mohawk Flight, remarked that pilots with experience with Gladiators and other British aircraft disliked the Mohawk, with its fully electrical systems being prone to malfunctioning in an adverse environment. As the Azores Archipelago is known for its difficult weather conditions, with high humidity, salty atmosphere, high rainfall and winds, the likelihood of failure in the more delicate electrical apparatus was high. Other idiosyncrasies noted by General Barros and disliked by the pilots were, for instance, the location of some instrumentation on the cockpit floor. The unreliability of the engine, which triggered the majority of accidents, was another important factor in the general dislike of the aircraft.

Camouflage and Markings

From the available graphic documentation and photos, it can be confirmed that the Mohawk fleet in Portuguese service maintained the RAF camouflage of Dark Earth and Dark Green top surfaces and Sky under surfaces. Before their inclusion in the E.E.C.3 the aircraft probably flew with the red *Cruz de Cristo* on a white disc on the wings in four positions, only, and the Portuguese serial number in white on the rear fuselage. The green and red National Flag with Coat of Arms was painted on the rudder.

When in the Azores the aircraft also received the red *Cruz de Cristo* on a white disc on the rear fuselage with Flight letters (XY) forward of the Cross, with the aircraft letter to the rear, British style (XY-*). No Flight insignia is known to have been used by the Mohawk fleet.

Several sources maintain that, for a certain period of their operational life in the Portuguese *Arma da Aeronautica*, the Mohawks were painted in a single upper surface colour, i.e. green overall with the under surface either light blue or Sky. It is likely that this assessment is based on black and white photographs of a dubious quality, including one that shows the accident of aircraft no. 490 and another one depicting aircraft no. 488 in flight. Bearing in mind the career of the aircraft as described above, the 'single upper colour' interpretation is likely to be inaccurate.

- The Curtiss Mohawks arrived in Portugal in September 1941. They were part of a British reserve and probably wearing British colours (Dark Green/Dark Earth/Sky camouflage) or the approved US equivalents of these colours.
- The assembly and training process in the Portuguese territory was a long one, ending around the summer of 1943, period in which the accident of no. 490 occurred. Logically, the aircraft would continue to wear the painting scheme in which they were received, as there was

Curtiss Mohawk (*Curtiss Hawk H-75A4) s/n 490 – Several sources maintain that, during a certain period of their operational life in the* Portuguese Arma da Aeronautica, *the Mohawks were painted in a single upper surface colour, i.e., green overall with the under surface either light blue or duck egg blue. We believe that this assessment is based in two black and white photos of a rather dubious quality, one that shows the accident of aircraft 490 and another one presenting airplane 488 in flight, nothing else being presented or brought forward to confirm this opinion. To our knowledge, the Curtiss Mohawk fleet maintained their original British colours of* Dark Green *and* Dark Earth *upper surfaces and* Sky *under surfaces camouflage or perhaps the US equivalents of these colours. Please see text for complete explanation.*

Accident of Curtiss Mohawk serial number 490 at Ota, on 13 May 1942. This aircraft also does not have the Cruz de Cristo *and identification letters painted on the fuselage. For the colours of the aircraft please refer to the text in the "Camouflage and Markings" paragraph of this chapter. (Coll. M .de Barros)*

Curtiss Mohawk (Curtiss Hawk H-75A4) XY+H, s/n 487. With this aircraft began a new era in the Aeronautica Militar: It was the first monoplane fighter to serve under the Portuguese colours, the first of its kind to wear a specific "three-tone" camouflage (two upper and one under-surface colours) and also the first to use a three letters code system to identify the Flight and the plane within it. Until today doubt persists on the true colour of such codes and serials of aircraft of the WWII period, this being a subject of argument among enthusiasts. In reality, in some photos they appear as a spotless white, while in others they apparent to be darker then the white disc of the National insignia. We believe, however, that the correct colour for this particular aircraft would be white and, therefore, we opted to show them as such.

Curtiss Mohawk XY+H s/n 487 taking off from the runway of Ota Air Base. As mentioned elsewhere in this book, the squadron and individual identification on the aircraft were shown with the squadron letters in front of the National insignia and individual code letter to the rear. (Coll. M.de Barros)

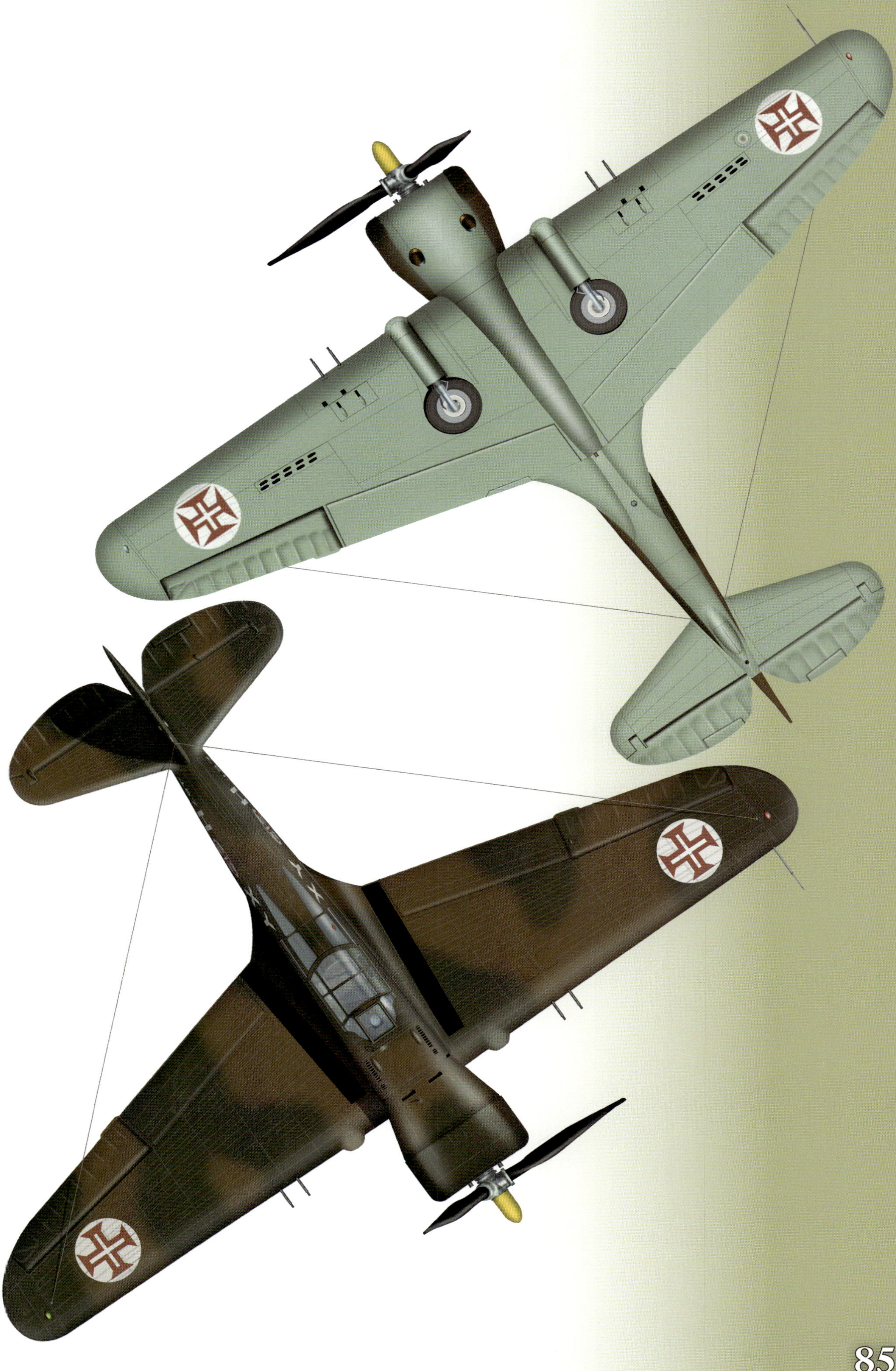

no immediate destination for them (Flight or base), meaning there is no reason to suppose a change of colour to markings associated with a unit or location.

- The idea of the three-letter code came during the formation and work-up of *Esquadrilha 3* before the move to the Azores. Another year passed before the Flight equipment and personnel were in fact transferred to the Azores in 1944. It is assumed that the aeroplanes' paint job, by then somewhat tired, had been retouched with local paints, similar in hue to the British originals, but maintaining the overall scheme. Photographs of the aircraft in a setting identified as the Azores, while black and white, clearly show the two-tone nature of the camouflage. Thus, the 'one-colour' Mohawk is most likely to be another urban myth, of which the History of Portuguese Military Aviation is littered.

Curtiss Mohawk IV – Individual Aircraft Histories				
RAF Serial (1)	Arrival Date	A.M. Serial	Retired	Remarks
Not known	Summer 1941	480	1945	-
Not known	Summer 1941	481	1945	-
Not known	Summer 1941	482	1945	-
Not known	Summer 1941	483	-	Destroyed in accident 12/1944
Not known	Summer 1941	484	-	Destroyed in accident 8/1945
Not known	Summer 1941	485	-	Destroyed in accident in 7/1943 (2)
Not known	Summer 1941	486	1945	-
Not known	Summer 1941	487	1945	Destroyed in accident 10/1943
Not known	Summer 1941	488	1945	-
Not known	Summer 1941	489	-	Destroyed in accident in 4/42
Not known	Summer 1941	490	1945	Destroyed in accident in 5/42

Notes:

(1) – Although the correlation between RAF and A.M. serial numbers is not known for any aircraft, a list of the original RAF serials is given under Note 1 in the main text. As mentioned above, the missing aircraft from the above list were not allocated with an A.M. serial.

(2) – Albeit marked as destroyed in an accident in July 1943, the Tancos tower movements logbook records this aircraft as still flying in September that same year.

Aircraft Characteristics (Hawk H-75A-4 or Mohawk IV)	
Quantity used:	16 received, but only 11 or 15, depending on the source effectively used (see text)
Crew:	One
Years of Service:	1941–1945
Span:	37' 4" (11.38 m)
Length:	28' 10" (8.79 m)
Height:	9' 6" (2.89 m)
Wing Area:	236 sq ft (21.92 m2)
Empty weight:	4,541 lb (2,060 kg)
Normal load:	5,750 lb (2,608 kg)
Maximum speed:	323 mph (520 km/h) at 15,100 feet (4,600 m)
Maximum range:	1,003 mls (1,614 km)
Armament:	Browning 0.303" in wings, 2 x 7.5 mm FN-Browning machine guns in the fuselage nose
Engine:	One *Pratt & Whitney* R-1830 – S1C3G "*Twin Wasp*", 1,200 hp

Lockheed P-38G Lightning

Background

The P-38 Lightning was the response of the Lockheed Aircraft Corporation to a specification issued by the USAAC in February 1937, 'Circular Proposal X-608', calling for a "high altitude fighter, able to operate at combat efficiency above 20,000 feet (6,100 m), with a... speed of 360 mph (580 km/h) at that same altitude, maintaining speed for at least one hour at full throttle". Added to this, the proposed fighter should be able to "take-off or land within a distance of 2,200 feet (670 metres) over an obstacle of circa 50 feet (15 metres)". The design emerged from the team leaded by Hall Hibbard and Clarence 'Kelly' Johnson.

These USAAC requirements were demanding and largely surpassed the potential of conventional fighter aeroplanes then being produced. There was little surprise that very few companies responded to the Circular Proposal, and Lockheed, competing with Bell and Curtiss, saw its unconventional conception, the Model 322, being accepted with an immediate contract issued for one prototype, later granted the USAAC designation XP-38. The first flight took place on 27 January 1939 from March Field, California.

At the time only the Dutch Fokker G.1 fighter[1] and the German Focke-Wulf Fw 189 had a layout similar to the configuration chosen for the P-38. The former was considered a powerful fighter-cruiser, attracting the attention of several countries when first shown in the Paris International Fair in 1936, but no more then 61 were built, with no further development pursued due to the

1 Another *Fokker* product, the D.XXIII single seat fighter, although presenting a similar design to the P-38 had its two engines mounted in a push-pull arrangement. Due to a variety of problems, the prototype had a brief existence not completing its tests programmes before the invasion of Netherlands.

The P-38G serial 300 at Ota Air Base. The weathering of the top surfaces mentioned in the text can be clearly seen. For a long time the overall aspect of this aircraft led to the assumption that the upper surface of the plane might have been painted in a two colour camouflage scheme. Today It is generally accepted that the only serviceable Lightning in the A.M. maintained its original US scheme of olive drab over neutral grey, the differences of shade shown on photos being due either to weathering and/or paint retouches with a local colour, close to the original. (FAP/AHFA)

Netherlands being overrun by German forces in 1940. The Fw 189 had quite a different role from the P-38, as tactical-reconnaissance and army cooperation aircraft, with a limited defensive firepower.

Lockheed was satisfied with the performance obtained by its prototype, and decided, after several adjustments to the airframe, to embark on a series of record-breaking flights and other 'publicity stunts' in an attempt to persuade the government to acquire a substantial quantity of the new fighter. With this in mind, a transcontinental flight was decided to prove the reliability and cross-country speed of the aircraft.

This attempt took place less then a fortnight after the first flight, and was staged between March Field in California and Mitchell Field in Hempstead, New York. On 11 February 1939 the prototype took off from the first airfield to arrive at its destination on the other side of the continent seven hours later, after a flight with two refuelling stops. Unfortunately, this challenge terminated in disaster for the P-38 prototype, when it struck trees on its final approach to the Mitchell Field runway, being completely destroyed. Nevertheless, the performance of the aircraft so impressed the authorities that an order for 13 prototype aircraft for further evaluation was issued, and the P-38 programme could be further pursued.

The untypical layout chosen by Lockheed would make this fighter aircraft unique. The central gondola in which weapons and pilot were contained allowed a concentration of firepower without the need for gun synchronising mechanisms, and a bubble-type canopy afforded 360° vision during flight. Furthermore, a tricycle undercarriage lent straightforward take-off and landing characteristics while careful streamlining and the power provided by two 12-cylinder Allison V-1710 turbo-supercharged engines contributed to a speed in excess of 400 mph.

With war breaking out across Europe, and as with other new US types, France and the United Kingdom were the first countries to demonstrate an interest in the new aircraft. Delegations from both countries toured the US looking for possible suppliers of modern aircraft in a variety of types, but mostly fighters. The purchasing commissions had already established contracts for the supply, among others, for a large number of Curtiss aircraft. Lockheed proposed also its new fighter type, of which the performance of the prototype very much impressed both delegations.

Considering the compatibility of spare parts with aircraft already ordered (i.e. export versions of the Curtiss P-40), the French in particular desired right-hand rotating engines instead of the

The same aircraft but now in company of five Airacobras from the same OK Flight. The nearest aircraft is Bell Airacobra P-400 A.M. serial 311, coded OK+L. The two other aircraft that can be clearly identified are P-400 serial 301 OK+A and P-400 serial 307 OK+H. Note the absence of the National Crest on the flag painted on the fin of the Airacobra closest to the camera, the only one of the four totally visible exhibiting this anomaly. (FAP/AHFA)

counter-rotating engines of the USAAC's P-38s. The aircraft ordered also lacked turbosuperchargers, which at the time were restricted for export. A total of 667 aeroplanes, 417 for the French *Armée de l'Air* and 250 for the RAF, were ordered. However, with the defeat of France in 1940, the United Kingdom took over the entirety of the order.

Lockheed proceeded with the development of the P-38 in parallel with the completion of the British order for the Lightning Mk I[2], experiencing a number of 'teething problems' with the airframe design to resolve. One of the more significant difficulties experienced related to compressibility[3], which was ultimately solved by the addition of dive flaps outboard the engine nacelles restricting speed in a dive. Meanwhile, the first 143 British would be produced following the initial specifications, but the RAF entered into negotiations to amend the contract, making the balance of 524 aircraft equivalent to the P-38E then in production. These aircraft would have handed engines and turbosuperchargers, and be supplied under the designation of Lightning Mk II. Lockheed's ongoing problems with high-speed handling and structural problems caused concerns in the UK, and the RAF began to reconsider its need for the aircraft. In the event, the United States' entry into the war meant the US Government took immediate measures to secure much of the military equipment then being produced for foreign countries, including the first 40 Lightning Mk I (Model 332F) aircraft. These were deployed to the West Coast in case of a possible Japanese attack. One month later, January 1942, all the remaining aeroplanes to be forwarded to the UK were held and taken over by the USAAF, becoming part of its order of P-38Fs. Consequently, all the aircraft ordered by the United Kingdom ended up serving in the USAA.F[4]. The first batch of 143 to serve mainly as trainers, with only 22 being built according to the original specifications with no turbosuperchargers and right-handed engines, the remaining being retrofitted to US preferred equipment and specifications.

With United States involvement in the conflict in Europe following Germany's declaration of war, a large volume of war supplies started to cross the Atlantic with the intention of building up a force stationed in the UK[5]. Among the first war materiel to reach England shores were the P-38 Lightnings belonging to the 1st Fighter Group that were intended to form part of the Eighth Air Force. In fact, the B-17, C-47 and P-38 aircraft comprising the first wave to cross the Atlantic under their own power were all to see limited service within the 8th A.F., being transferred to the 12th Air Force, under the command of General James H. Doolittle. They would go on to be deeply involved in Operation *Torch*, the invasion of the North African Territories occupied by Germany and French Vichy Forces on 8 November 1942.

Lockheed P-38 in Portugal

The reason for including this aircraft within this book is because more then seventy years after its 'acquisition' it continues to divide historians, researchers and modellers. Operation *Torch* brought to Portuguese skies and territory a huge number of aircraft en route to Northern Africa. The vast majority passed by, either directly over Portuguese territory, or more often, over the sea along the coastline. Some were forced to land in Portugal, due to mechanical or other problems

2 The proposed Lockheed Model 322 for France and the UK was designated Lightning Mk I by the British in April 1940, this name becoming popular and recognised by all belligerents during WWII.

3 Compressibility is an important factor in aerodymanics, experienced as airflow nears and sometimes locally exceeds the speed of sound. The associated aerodynamic effects were initially not well understood and made it very difficult for WWII-era aircraft to reech speeds much beyond 500 mph (800 km/h).

4 Meanwhile, in March 1943, the USAAF lent three of the twenty-two seized aircraft to RAF, to be test flown by the A&A.E.E. and RAE, with unfavourable results, the three aircraft being later that year returned to the Americans. NB the USAAC was superseded by the US Army Air Forces (USAAF) in June 1941

5 "Operation Bolero" was the code name used to designate the ferrying of US troops and other military hardware to the UK in order to build-up the necessary force to invade the Continental Europe. That would end-up two years later in the well-known "Operation Overlord".

and others, less lucky, were destroyed, some with the loss of life of their crews, while attempting emergency landings.

The first P-38 to land in Portugal was P-38F-1-LO 41-7587, from the 94th Fighter Squadron (F.S.), 1st Fighter Group (F.G.), flown by Captain Jack Illfrey, which arrived at Lisbon Airport on 15 November 1942. This Lightning was part of a group of aircraft of the 1st F.G. that left Chivenor in the UK destined for North Africa, 'shepherded' by four B-26Bs of 319th Bombardment Group (BG). Take-off took place in England between 0705 and 0748 hours, and Captain Illfrey's logbook records a six and a half-hour flight until his final destination was reached.

The well known and oft-recounted episode of Captain Illfrey escaping from his 'captors' is flamboyantly related in his book 'Happy Jack's Go Buggy – A Fighter Pilot's Story', in which the Portuguese authorities, pilots, and the horse-mounted G.N.R.[6], etc., take on the role of villains, outwitted by the heroic American pilot. The reality is less colourful. According to his book, Captain Illfrey's P-38F-1 was obliged to land owing to fuel shortage, due to the loss of one of its underwing tanks. After Ifrey was questioned, the Lightning had its tanks filled up with the intention of a Portuguese pilot flying it from the civilian airport of Lisbon to a nearby military base. Captain Illfrey was requested to instruct *Capitão* Costa Macedo in the bare minimum of how to fly the aircraft. With *Capitão* Macedo seated on the P-38's left wing, Ilfrey showed him the controls. While this was taking place, the noise of an approaching aircraft – in fact another P-38 (see below) – preparing to land created a momentary distraction. Seizing the opportunity, Captain Illfrey "threw a lot of power... with the idea to blow the pilot off the wing, which I did in just another second or two"[7]. Captain Illfrey "gave the plane full power, and without looking back went straight across the field, disregarding runways and everything else in my path...". Eventually he headed to Gibraltar, distant some 400 miles away, with an adventure under his belt to tell.

The second P-38 to land, and which unwittingly contributed to Ilfrey's 'escape', was P-38G-1-LO 42-12738, flown by Captain James A. Harmon. This aircraft was interned and its pilot placed under tight custody (especially in view of what had happened with Ifrey) to return a few months later, via the US Legation in Lisbon, to his home base and subsequently on to the front. *Capitão* Costa Macedo had, therefore, his opportunity to fly a P-38 when on 21 November he transferred this aircraft from Lisbon to the Sintra Air Base.

On the day Harmon landed at Lisbon, 15 November 1942, two more P-38s from the formation Illfrey's and Harmon's P-38s had been part of, experienced different fates. The first, a P-38F from the 1 F.G./27 F.S., hit Monte Mato, near Cabo Ortegal in the Galicia Province, Spain, resulting in the death of the pilot, Captain Robert N. Chenoweth, while the second, piloted by 1st Lieutenant Woolford, was able to reach Gibraltar safely.

The flurry of activity in Portuguese skies, in the direction of Northern Africa, continued during the following weeks. Three more P-38s reached the territory with different fortunes. On 23 December 1943, P-38 s/n 42-12825 belonging to the 96th F.S., 82nd F.G., was forced into an emergency landing in Quarteira, Algarve, with its pilot, Captain 'Buddy' Strozier, walking away uninjured from the aircraft. It is likely that the aircraft was not completely destroyed though its fate is unknown.

Among the unluckier Lightnings was P-38F, s/n 43-2146, which fell near Albufeira, Algarve, on 26 January 1943, probably due to fuel shortage. According to the report written by Captain Jara from the US Legation to Lisbon, its pilot, 2nd Lieutenant Richard L. Rope bailed out too late for his parachute to open properly. His body was found 400 metres from the wreck of his aircraft, and

6 G.N.R. – *Guarda Nacional Republicana* (National Republican Guard) similar to the French *Gendarmerie*, at the time in charge of policing outside urban areas. During wartime they were also in charge of Lisbon Airport's perimeter security. It is not conceivable that they were performing their duties in full ceremonial uniform, as described by Captain Illfrey in his book.

7 Years later, in the Azores Lajes Air Base, Illfrey and Macedo met again, but apparently – understandably the meeting was not very friendly... *General* Costa Macedo would become in 1952 the first Chief of Staff of the new *Força Aérea Portuguesa*.

returned to the United States with due honours. Another incident that led to the death of the pilot, 1st Lieutenant Donald Beals, was the crash of P-38F s/n 41-7576 from 83th F.S., 78th F.G., in an unknown location (probably also in the Algarve). The remains of the pilot were repatriated to his hometown of Twin Falls, Idaho. The available documents did not specify the cause of the accident or its location, but the likelihood that it happened in Portugal is suggested by the lack of evidence of such an occurrence on Spanish territory.

The saga of the P-38 in the Iberian Peninsula continues with other emergency landings or accidents in the neighbour Spain. However, there is more to say about the Portuguese experience with the type.

British and US documents consulted from 1943-44, signed by the respective Military Attachés from the UK and US Legations to Lisbon, reported the existence in Portugal of three P-38 Lightnings, with at least one serviceable. A US memorandum 'Force landed Aircraft in Neutral Countries' dated 5 March 1944, addressed to a Colonel Weckerling (?) in Washington, describes the number of aircraft interned in the Portuguese Territory and their acquisition by Portugal[8]. Among the aircraft listed three P-38s are mentioned as having been acquired, one being "unserviceable". This is, however, later contradicted by another memo from the US Military Attaché dated 1 July of the same year, referring to "two P-38s, one unserviceable".

In the light of the documentation, it is clear that the only operational aircraft integrated into the *Aeronautica Militar* was P-38G-1 42-12738, flown by Captain James Harmon, which landed in Lisbon, the other two being probably the aircraft of Captain Strozier, and what was left of 1st Lieutenant Beals' P-38.

Until the end of the war the number of aircraft today identified as having landed, in good or less good condition, crashed or destroyed in Portugal or its territorial waters, according to primary sources, amounts to 201 aircraft of all types, including bombers, gliders, fighters and long-range patrol seaplanes.

Lockheed P-38G-1-LO in Service with *Aeronautica Militar*

As stated above, and as recorded on *Capitão* Costa Macedo's logbook, on 21 November 1942, Lockheed P-38G-1-LO 42-12738 was ferried from the civilian Lisbon Airport to Sintra Air Base. On 17 June the aircraft was flown, by the same pilot, to Ota Air Base where it was included in the OK Flight then consisting of Bell P-39 Airacobras, and received the serial number 335. While at Sintra, a German agent attempted to photograph the aircraft, but was caught and arrested.

The service career of the P-38 was limited, and the aircraft flew only for short periods of time and distances. It was known by the nickname of "the general's plane", due to being taken from the hangar to be shown off during official ceremonies or visits by 'top brass'. The lack of spare parts, combined with the lack of pilots trained on twin engined fighters, seems to have been the main factor in its relative inactivity.

The most eventful flight occurred when *Capitão* Solano de Almeida, one of the more experimented pilot on the aircraft, who had in mind using the Lightning for a flight to the African colonies, took-off from Ota Air Base without the permission of the C.O. He took the P-38 to Lisbon, which he overflew several times, before returning to Ota. His reception on landing was, as could be predicted, less than warm.

While in Ota, Internal Service Order (*Ordem de Serviço*) nr. 279, dated 6 October 1943 amended the serial number of the Lightning from the previously attributed 335 to 300, with code letters OK+T. This change took place because Airacobra 301 had been written off in an accident and Airacobra no. 300 had taken its position within the Flight, leaving the serial number 300 open, so it was given to the P-38.

8 Further details of this acquisition are described in the Airacobra Chapter of this book.

Very rapidly, the general condition of the P-38 started to decline, the first signs being underwing fuel leakages. When in search of a solution, it was discovered that the fuel cells were deteriorating due to the quality of gasoline used. A similar phenomenon had already been experienced in Java, Indonesia with B-17s from the 19th BG after their arrival in January 1942. It was discovered that the rubber structure of the self-sealing fuel-system, the fuel pump and carburettor membranes were corroding when in contact with fuel with a high percentage of benzene, as supplied by the Dutch. Fabrication of new metal fuel cells was considered unfeasible, so all efforts to maintain the sole Portuguese P-38 in flying condition were abandoned and the airframe was scrapped in 1944.

Interned Crews

All nationalities crews of the interned aircraft that made emergency landings in the Portuguese Territory, after a mandatory questioning period by the Intelligence Services and/or Police, sometimes in the presence of their respective Military Attaché, were given civilian clothes and transported to hotels or guesthouses, after a brief stop in Lisbon, to locations outside the Capital, far from prying eyes. They were placed under the responsibility of the local civilian police or the infamous P.V.D.E. (*Policia de Vigilância e Defesa do Estado*). To the unfortunate crews that did not survive the emergency landings or crash of their aicaft, a funeral with military honours was given, or their remains repatriated to their home countries. In several Portuguese cemeteries it is still possible to see the final resting places of these airmen.

While interned, the airmen stayed first in the town of Caldas da Rainha, a small town 76 kilometres North of Lisbon, near the coast. Later on, this being considered too close to the capital, the border town of Elvas, 173 km East of Lisbon, was chosen to lodge the airmen. The airmen were not imprisoned, and remained free to do whatever they wanted as long as they remained in the town where they were interned. Lieutenant Littlejohn, pilot of an Airacobra that landed in Lisbon in 1942, interviewed some sixty years later by one of the authors, remarked that this period in Portugal was the best time of his life! Where he was lodged in the border town of Elvas, he was able talk to the residents, the students of the local High School being keen to take advantage of a native English speaker being on hand to practice their knowledge of the language with. He was also able to ride horses, walk in the fields, eat and drink in local restaurants, and mingle with the inhabitants.

Regrettably, a number of the airmen who landed safely in Portugal were not so fortunate after they were allowed to leave. Such was the destiny of the original pilot of the sole P-38 in Portuguese service, Captain James A. Harmon. He died on 17 April 1943 in North Africa, when his aircraft was hit after he had shot down a Junkers Ju 88. He was able to bail out, only to be strafed while descending by parachute.

Camouflage and Markings

For years the discussion of the colours and markings of the sole Portuguese P-38 had been a matter of debate for historians and modellers. Photographs of the P-38 in service with the *Aeronautica Militar* do not abound and, so far, no colour photogaphs of this aircraft have come to light. The very few black and white photos that are known are generally of poor quality, and, in some cases, of dubious origin, with some doubt existing as to whether they really portray the Portuguese P-38. The exception is one very good photograph that shows the P-38 amid the 'OK' Flight Airacobras.

Despite many years of arguments, it is almost certain that the Lockheed P-38G-1-LO of the *Aeronautica Militar* retained the original colours in which it arrived in Portugal, i.e., Olive Drab 41 upper surfaces and Neutral Grey 43 under surfaces, these colours corresponding on Federal Standard charts to FS 23070 and 36173 respectively. On its arrival in Lisbon the Lockheed P-38G 42-12738 was painted in the standard USAAF pattern for the period using the official two colours. National Markings, consisting of a white star on a blue background surrounded by a yellow ring, were painted on the booms together with the 94th F.S. Unit Code, 'UN', and the individual ID letter 'B', painted in white. Some sources suggested that the yellow serial number, 212738, was half concealed by a United States Flag on the fixed part of the fin. The name 'Jungle II' has also been suggested to have been painted in yellow on the external side of the left boom, close to the fin, although this has never been confirmed.

The two other identifying elements of the 94th F.S., 1st F.G. of a yellow band around the booms and the yellow wing tips were apparently absent on this aircraft. However, the existence of yellow rings around the base of the propeller spinners is reported.

As it is stated in 'Lockheed P-38, F-4 & F-5 Lightning – Camouflage and Markings nr 18', Ducimus Publications, transcribed here with the due credit, regarding the the upper surface camouflage, "...Dark Olive Drab was particularly prone to colour change with age and exposure to strong sunlight... some of the 1st and 14th original P-38Fs, which were active until the spring of 1944, had upper surface paintwork of a pale khaki shade in contrast to the dark olive of the new P-38Js" etc. Other authors, notably Dana Bell,[9] and Martin Waligorski from I.P.M.S. Stockholm, also relate this phenomenon of colour modification concerning Olive Drab. Considering that when the P-38 received its new identity, there would not have been identical specification paint in the *Aeronautica Militar* warehouses, the closest possible shade available would have had to suffice for the coverage of the original paint. This, together with the usual fading above referred, would be sufficient to explain the appearance of a two-tone camouflage visible in some photographs.

Knowing how hazardous trying to identify colours based only on period black and white photographs can be, it is the view of the authors that the general colour of the A.M. P-38 was Olive Drab and Neutral Grey, with the National Markings of the red *Cruz de Cristo* inside a white background disc placed in the usual six positions, the 'fuselage' circle being placed on the radiator intake housings, with the white 'OK' Flight codes ahead of the cockade and the individual identification letter 'T' behind, followed immediately by the serial number 300. Although is known that the aircraft had previously received the serial 335, no photographic evidence has appeared to confirm the painting of this serial on the aircraft.

The Red and Green National Flag with Coat of Arms was painted on the fixed portion of the fin. During its Portuguese career, the P-38 received the phrase '*Não faz mal*' ('It doesn't matter') painted white on the left side of the nose in a 'script' style. This is generally explained as a reference to the nonchalant attitude of the ground crew towards their duties.

9 "...Dark Olive Drab was prone to extreme fading, generally bleaching to a buff or brown colour, though some manufacturers produced paints that faded to a weak green or a greenish grey..." – Air Force Colours – Vol.2 – ETO & MTO 1942-45 – Dana Bell – Squadron-Signal Publications.

Lockheed P-38G-1-LO Lightning, s/n 300, former USAAF s/n 42-12738. The sole example of a serviceable aircraft of its kind to be used by the Portuguese Arma da Aeronáutica. *Due to the weathering and quick fading of the upper colour, leading to assume its "two colour camouflage", this aircraft has been for many years the subject of vibrant debate among enthusiasts. Today it is of general consensus that it maintained, for its brief career under Portuguese colours, its original scheme of Olive Drab over Neutral Grey. Wavy lines separated these colours and the sentence* Não faz mal *(It doesn't matter) was painted in white on the left side of the nose. As usual for the period, the aircraft had the nationality markings on the customary six positions, the Flight code and serial number being applied in white on the booms.*

Aircraft Characteristics Lockheed P-38G-1-LO	
Quantity used:	One
Crew:	One
Years of Service:	1943–1944
Span:	52 ft (15.85m)
Length:	37' 10" (11.53m)
Height:	9' 10" (3 m)
Wing Area:	327.5 sq ft (30.42 m^2)
Empty weight:	12,200 lb (5,534 kg)
Max. take-off weight:	19,800 lb (8,981 kg)
Maximum speed:	400 mph (644 kmh) at 25,000 ft (7,620 m)
Service ceiling:	39,000 ft (11,887 m)
Armament:	One 20 mm Hispano cannon, and four Colt-Browning 0.5 machine guns in the nose, besides two 325, 500 or 1,000 lb bombs in pylons.
Engine:	2 x 1,325 hp V-1710-51/55, with General Electric B-2 Superchargers

Bell P-39/P-400 Airacobra

Background

The idea of installing an engine behind the pilot, driving a tractor propeller via a long shaft, was not new in the late 1930s when the US Bell Aircraft Corporation began to study the layout. Recent experiments conducted in the Netherlands by Koolhoven and in the UK by Westland had not, however, led to aircraft of that configuration progressing beyond the prototype stage. This, however, was not helped by the lack of powerful engines and adequate transmission technology. Nevertheless, the layout allowed more space for heavy armament to be installed in the nose, the use of a tricycle undercarriage, and excellent forward visibility.

In the United States, the Bell Aircraft Corporation, a new company already known for its unconventional projects, decided to pursue this unorthodox design, when the Army Air Corps issued a specification for a new fighter aircraft in May 1937. The design team, headed by Robert Woods, initiated a project of an aircraft to be built around a weapon, instead of the more conventional practice of building the aircraft around an engine. The benefits of this design, besides those already set out, were to create an aerodynamic profile resembling the 'snout of a high velocity bullet' capable of boosting the speed in excess of the requested 360 mph (580 km/h) at altitude, and offering a climb time to 20,000 feet (6,100 m) in the order of six minutes.

The prototype XP-39 with the serial 38-326 took the air for the first time on 6 April 1939, powered by a turbosupercharged Allison V-1710 engine. It surpassed all performance figures stipulated in the USAAC specification and created considerable interest around the world. However, the prototype's initial configuration was 'light and clean', and did not include armament (intended to consist of the heavy 37mm Oldsmobile T9 cannon plus machine-guns), armour, nor self-sealing

Part of the Airacobra Flight (code OK) at Ota Air Base. Aircraft P-400 serial number 311 OK+L, P-400 301 OK+A plus two others can be identified. Note absence of the Coat of Arms on the Portuguese flag on the tail of aircraft 311. (FAP/AHFA)

fuel tanks. Consequently, thanks to its low weight and highly polished exterior, the performance of the aircraft was maximised.

When the XP-39 was handed over to the Wright Field experts for tests, in a closer configuration to production aircraft, the performance fell in such a way that the aircraft was described by the examiners as disappointing, with low ceiling, considered practically useless over 17,000 feet, a slow rate of climb, and a relative lack of manoeuvrability. However, while the P-39 was a poor pure interceptor, it would later prove outstanding in the low-level close support role, where it could absorb a great extent of battle damage, especially from small arms, and make a good use of its heavy weaponry, while gaining a reputation as a 'pilot's aeroplane'.

The story of the P-39 Airacobra, its development and use being extensively covered by many books and magazine articles, it falls beyond the scope of this book to tell the complete story. Readers interested in studying this unusual aircraft in more detail should consult the bibliography that accompanies this chapter. It is, however, appropriate to take some space to explore the British and French relationship with the P-39 here, in order to counter the widespread myth that the Portuguese Airacobras had their origin directly from the United Kingdom.

The Airacobras in the United Kingdom

With Europe embroiled in war and with considerable strain on their respective industries, French and British authorities wished to acquire large numbers of aircraft abroad in 1939-40. The first export contract was signed in 1939 between Bell Aircraft Corporation and France for an amount of $9,000,000 to cover 170 aircraft. None, however, were delivered in time to fight against the advancing German forces before France fell. As some $2,000,000 of the payment had already been made by France, this was used by Bell to enlarge its facilities and start the series production

Rear fuselage of Bell P-400 Airacobra serial 302 OK+C. Note the relative positioning of the Cruz de Cristo *to the serial number and the Flight code letters, as well as the limits of the camouflage colours. (FAP/AHFA)*

Bell P-400 Airacobra serial number 306, Flight code OK+G. (FAP/AHFA)

of the P-39. France would eventually receive the Airacobra some time later, after Operation *Torch*, in 1943.

The British RAF, already in possession of excellent fighters such as the Spitfire and Hurricane, nevertheless felt the need to secure aircraft in quantity to counter the threat of the *Luftwaffe* crossing its shores, especially when parts of the British aircraft industry were vulnerable to bombing. The British Direct Purchase Commission in the United States, ordered 205+300 aircraft, identified as P-39 Model 15, similar to the US P-39D, plus the 170 undelivered Model 14s originally destined for France, making a total of 675 aircraft. For a very short time the aeroplanes were named Caribou by the British authorities, but Bell suggested the name Airacobra, which was accepted in July 1941. The RAF therefore named them Airacobra Mk I and Airacobra Mk IA, the letter 'A' denoting the aircraft directly purchased, the others being forwarded under the Lend-Lease agreement.

The first machines arrived in the UK in July 1941, and were immediately transferred to the Aeroplane and Armament Experimental Establishment (A&A.E.E.) at Boscombe Down, and to the Air Fighting Development Unit (A.F.D.U.), Duxford, where it became apparent that the data forwarded by Bell did not match the performance of the aircraft supplied. The shortcomings discovered at the testing establishments did not concern only speed, but also equipment failure, ingress of mud damaging the controls and landing gear, excessive accumulation of fumes from the guns inside the cockpit, and a series of other problems.

Despite all those shortcomings, four aircraft were considered operational and joined 601 Squadron at Duxford in October 1941, carrying out nine strafing missions across the Channel to ports and ships in occupied France, with no further operations being attempted. By December that year, the approximately 160 Airacobras meanwhile received by the UK (mostly still in their original crates) were transferred either to the USSR or back to the United States, which was by now also involved in the conflict. Sources vary as to the number passed to the USSR, the figures generally quoted being 65 or 90 aircraft. The impressed British Airacobra Mk I and Mk IA aircraft were designated P-400 in the United States, in the same way that the Lightnings were designated P-322.

First arrivals to the Portuguese shores

By November 1942, with the Allied Operation *Torch* in full progress, the West coast of Portugal was to become the backdrop to a major air operation: the transfer of the 81st Fighter Group from the United Kingdom to the French North Africa Theatre of operations. This Fighter Group, equipped with P-39L/M Airacobras and the former British export version, the P-400, started the move to its new operational theatre during late 1942/early 1943. The transfer was made by dispatching several groups of aircraft per day, led by twin-engined bombers (North American B-25 Mitchell or Martin B-26 Marauder).

The pattern of the transfer operation was for the formation to take-off at dawn from a base in the South West of England, in order to reach North Africa or Gibraltar after a 6-7 hour flight. Meanwhile, in the course of the journey, they had to avoid interception by German Junkers Ju 88s of KG40 based at Bordeaux, which was not always successfully achieved.

One piece of advice that the pilots received before leaving England was that, in case of extreme difficulty (engine failure, loss of communications, shortage of fuel, etc.), they should try to land in Portugal. Although being a country living under an authoritarian regime and known to have German sympathizers, Portugal carefully maintained its neutrality and was more sympathetic towards Allied belligerents than its neighbour on the Iberian Peninsula. Furthermore, the interest demonstrated by the Allies in the Azores and negotiations on their use by the British and US Governments, led the Allies to believe that Portugal was a safer place for aircrew in distress.

Following this advice, on 27 December 1942 five Airacobras, from a group of around 50 aircraft of the 91st and 92nd Fighter Squadrons (81st F.G.), landed in Portugal due to fuel shortage or equipment malfunction. Two of them landed at Lisbon (Portela Airport), one at the *Granja do Marquês* Air Base (Sintra), another at Santa Cruz beach, north of Lisbon, and the last on a beach at Vila do Conde, on the Northern Portuguese coast, near Porto.

The first pilot arriving at Lisbon, Lieutenant Littlejohn, reported a total electrical failure that obliged him to manually lower the landing gear and land without flaps, with the result that his aircraft stopped a mere 15 metres from the end of the runway. The second pilot that landed in Lisbon was Lieutenant Colonel Wade, the Commanding Officer of the 81st Fighter Group!

During the war years, Lisbon was renowned for being a hotbed of spies of all nationalities. Therefore, the Portuguese authorities were keen to move the Airacobras from Lisbon, where they were in full view. Two days after their arrival, *Capt.* Costa Macedo, one of the leading Portuguese

Bell P-400 Airacobras at Ota Air Base air display line-up in May 1944. Identifiable on the photo are Tenente *Rogério Seixas (front) and just behind* Alferes *Rosa Rodrigues (right) and* Alferes *Braz de Oliveira (left). (FAP/AHFA)*

military pilots, took both P-39s from Lisbon to the Ota Air Base, doing the same for the aircraft at Sintra the following day. Although this was a short flight, it is notable given that the Portuguese Air Arm's most modern fighter was the Curtiss Mohawk, a 'taildragger'. Most pilots were still flying biplane fighters and none had any experience whatsoever with Airacobras.

Another Airacobra (RAF serial AP310) landed in Lisbon before the end of the year, the exact date not being known. It was also transferred by air to Ota.

On 15 January 1943 the tower logs of Portela Airport registered the largest arrival of aircraft to Portugal in a single day: ten landed at Lisbon, nine from the 350th F.G. and one from the 81st F.G., between 14:06 and 15:12 local time, and another landed at the Naval Air Station of S. Jacinto, on the Northern coast. All the Lisbon aircraft have been identified by type and serial, these consisting of eight P-400s and two P-39Ls, while the type and identity of the aeroplane landed at S. Jacinto is unknown.

The procedure to ferry the aircraft to Ota was repeated by *Capitão* Macedo, now assisted by another pilot, *Tenente* Seixas.

During 1943 the arrivals continued, following the evolution of the combat in North Africa. On 8 February, the Portela Airport saw the arrival of a P-39L from the 350th F.G.; on 27 April, three Airacobras, two P-400 and one P-39M-1 model, arrived at Lisbon; on 3 June one P-400 made an emergency landing at Aljezur, on the Southern coast of Portugal, close to Algarve.

By now Portugal was the recipient of 22 aircraft, plus one of unknown origin but mentioned in official documents and identified by its s/n as "BX128 delivered to Portugal in 16 August 1943". (There must be an error here, as the serial BX128 corresponds to a Hurricane. The author of the mentioned document probably transcribed the wrong serial. The RAF serial block BX135-434 was allocated for Airacobras).

Negotiations with the previous owners of the Airacobras to transfer full ownership of the aircraft to Portugal started almost immediately, in March 1943. The country was, at the time, involved in discussions with the Allies to grant permission for the use of the Azores Islands facilities, and the prospect of having an up-to-date equipment for its Air Arm was appealing. In accordance with official documents in the Air Historical Branch (UK) archives, in April 1943 permission was granted to sell "...16 Airacobras and one Lightning[1] for the sum of USD 20,000.00 each, and offer four crated airplanes, two of which are not seriously damaged... (also) the Americans declined to supply spare parts for the aircraft and the (above) offer depends on the liberation of the interned crews..." At the date of the documents, Portugal already had 18 Airacobras on its territory, the discrepancy in numbers possibly arising through bureaucracy and slowness in the talks.

Another internal USAAF document sent from the US Legation in Lisbon and dated 5 March 1944, lists all the American aircraft already interned in Portugal by that date. This includes 22 Airacobras, as well as setting out the costs, and confirms that "The Portuguese have paid to date the amount of USD 700,000.00 cash, having bought 20 Airacobras at USD 20,000.00 apiece (the original bulk sale was for 24 planes, 1 P-38 and 3 P-39 considered without value..."[2]. Incidentally, the price of USD 20,000.00 for a Bell P-39 Airacobra could be considered a bargain, as its initial cost was USD 48,673.00.

Airacobra service in Portugal

With negotiations successfully completed, it was now possible for the *Aeronaútica Militar* (A.M.) to form one Flight of 19 aircraft by 23 June 1943 at Ota Air Base. The Flight was assigned the identification code letters 'OK'.

Of the 19 aircraft, there were 15 of the P-400 model, three of the P-39L model, and one P-39M. The A.M. intended to operate the Flight as two sub-Flights of seven aircraft, with different coloured

---

1 See the Lockheed P-38 Lightning chapter.

2 Considering the total sum paid, it is apparent that more than just the aircraft mentioned must have been included in the purchase, the excess probably consisting of a quantity of spare parts.

spinners colours, red and yellow, identifying aircraft from each (as described in the Camouflage & Markings section). Individual aircraft received the serials 300 to 318, and the code letters A to S (see table). Aircraft no. 300 to no. 314 were of the P-400 model, and from no. 315 to no. 318, P-39L/M models. Before long, Airacobra no. 301 was lost in an accident, and no. 300 was renumbered to 301 (leaving the empty number 300 to be applied to the P-38G Lightning attached to the Airacobra Flight (see P-38 chapter above).

Incorporating the Airacobras in the A.M. was not easy due to a lack of technical publications and an initial shortage of spare parts. Moreover, the Portuguese pilots had no experience of truly modern fighters, especially those with tricycle landing gear. To alleviate this situation, the Portuguese Government was allowed by the US authorities, to send three pilots to the USA to study the aircraft, its construction, maintenance and operation, while at the beginning of 1944, two USAAF instructors went to Ota Air Base to help the Portuguese pilots adapt to their new fighter

The Portuguese pilots' opinion of the new aircraft can be summarised from an interview conducted in the early 1970s of two of the former members of the Flight. *Sargento* Augusto Krug (a veteran pilot of the Spanish Civil War) said: "...For me it was not the ideal fighter, as besides having the propeller shaft revolving between my legs, I felt the intense heat of the engine on my back, due to not-so-good insulation. Besides, their maintenance and operation was not easy, as we had no manuals to start off, and had not received formal training on the aircraft. Once, one of our pilots taxied too fast as he did not know to fine tune the engine power, and slammed two other aircraft in front of him. Another one took off without controlling properly the power of the engine, which seized after a terrible noise, requiring an emergency landing at once..."

Tenente Solano de Almeida said: "... The comments of *Sgt.* Augusto Krug correspond to the reality, but on the other hand it was an aircraft with a very good performance at sea level, allowing us to leave behind our comrades flying the Spitfire Mk I. Of course in altitude the performance was degraded, and we had to be very careful with the control of the engine r.p.m., due to a problem with propeller shaft vibration at low r.p.m.. When performing the taxi rolls, brakes had to be applied to allow the use of higher r.p.m. This was the origin of excessive wear of brakes and of accidents with other aircraft rolling in front".

Nevertheless the operational career of the Airacobras progressed, and the full Flight participated in the annual aircraft review at Ota Air Base in May 1944, where almost 200 military aircraft were present. By the end of October 1943, the Air Arm participated with the Airacobra Flight, two Hurricane Flights and one Spitfire Flight in 'War Games' held at Pegões, a region south of Lisbon, involving some 40,000 men in three Divisions.

Unfortunately the operational career of the Airacobras suffered from several accidents resulting in the destruction or damage beyond repair of the aircraft, one pilot being killed:

- 1 August 1943 – Airacobra 309: Emergency landing. Aircraft damaged beyond repair;
- 16 August 1943 – Airacobra 304: Crash landing killing the pilot, *Sgt.* Augusto Alves Ferreira;
- September 1943 – Airacobra 301: Lands on a beach near Lisbon, damaged beyond repair;
- 9 February 1944 – Airacobra 312: Emergency landing near Ota. Aircraft damaged beyond repair;
- 25 April 1946 – Airacobra 317: Emergency landing. Aircraft damaged beyond repair.
- On 1 January 1945 the Airacobra Flight was renamed Flight No.4.

The Airacobras were operational until 1946, being retired from the inventory by 1949-50, starting with aircraft 301, 302, 303, 305, 306 and 307 in June 1949, and concluding with aircraft 310, 311, 312, 313, 314, 315, 316, 318 in April 1950, thus ending the Airacobra's career in the *Aeronáutica Militar*. No example was preserved, all being reduced to scrap.

Camouflage and Markings

No colour photographs exist with which the camouflage type and colours of the interned Airacobras can be confirmed, while official reports are unclear on the subject. The general view until recently was that the Portuguese aircraft wore the British Day Fighter Scheme of Dark Green/ Ocean Grey over Medium Sea Grey. However, contemporary sources including the pilots mentioned

Head-on view of a Bell Airacobra of the Aeronáutica Militar *at Sintra Air Base. (FAP/AHFA)*

above when interviewed, referred the aircraft as "green overall" or "brown and green", with "yellow or red spinners". Recent research suggests that the latter description is the correct one where the P-400 aircraft are concerned. In fact, some of the P-39s and P-400s delivered to the 81st F.G. were part of a shipment originally destined for the Soviet Union on a convoy to Murmansk that was so decimated that it was forced to return to its original departure point.

The aircraft were then assembled in the UK to constitute the core of the US Fighter Group in development. The Airacobras were, for the most part, finished in the older British delivery scheme, applied in the US by the Bell factory, of Dark Earth and Dark Green over Sky undersurfaces. Elements of the equipment also followed British standards, such as the pilot's harnesses and armament, including a 20 mm cannon firing through the spinner. Considering that these aeroplanes were not anticipated to enter RAF service or stay in the E.T.O. area, no attempt to change the camouflage for the new British Day Fighter Scheme referred above was made, as it was the case for other US-built aircraft intended for British service arriving in the old scheme from August 1941.

The colours, although very similar to the British produced paints, were of a different manufacture, by the DuPont Paint Company, and therefore differed slightly. Equivalent references are:

- Dark Earth 71-009 FS 30219[3]
- Dark Green 71-013 FS 34079+FS 34092 (1+2 parts)
- Sky (Type S) 71-021 FS 36622

As noted by several authors, the American colours were generally similar to their British counterparts, although when brand new some differences could be detected. The erroneous reference by DuPont to the colour known in the UK as 'Sky' by the name 'Sky (Type S) *Grey*' has generated some confusion (and to further complicate the matters, DuPont also referred to 71-021 as 'Duck Egg Blue'!). The above camouflage description applies to the interned P-400s, while P-39Ls and the sole P-39M probably wore the original USAAF scheme of Olive Drab over Neutral Grey. For these aircraft there is no photographic substantiation of its colours, verbal descriptions describing the P-39s as "green overall and grey ".

When the aircraft entered *Aeronáutica Militar* service, national markings were applied following the procedure of the day, with a red *Cruz de Cristo* in six positions, four on the wings and two on the fuselage, each on a white background disc. The national flag, red and green, was applied on the

3 Today, these colour references and wartime or modern equivalents continue to be a subject of heated discussion between researchers and no final consensus has yet been reached. The debate of this theme falls beyond the remit of this book, so readers should be aware that the correspondence to FS (Federal Standards) given above is just one of several possibilities, the one used by one of the authors on its modelling subjects.

Spanish Air Force officers walking in front of a line-up of Bell Airacobras in April 1945 at the Ota Air base during a "goodwill visit". (FAP/AHFA)

fin, green leading. Contemporary practice called for the Portuguese Coat of Arms to be superimposed on the National Flag, but photographic evidence indicates that this was not always applied[4]. The white letters identifying the Flight and the airplane were placed on either side of the fuselage Cross. Coloured spinners, yellow or red, identified the two sub-Flights formed with the Airacobras.

Bell P-39/P-400 Airacobra – List of interned aircraft				
Type	USAAF or RAF s/n	Date interned	Unit	Remarks
?	?	27-12-42	81st FG	Landed Lisbon Airport
?	?	27-12-42	81st FG	Landed Lisbon Airport
?	?	27-12-42	81st FG	Landed Sintra Air Base
?	?	27-12-42	81st FG	Landed S.Cruz beach
P-400	BX 256	27-12-42	81st FG	Landed V.Conde beach
P-400	AP 310	12-42	?	Landed Lisbon Airport
P-39L	24495	15-1-43	350th FG	Landed Lisbon Airport
P-400	BX 306	15-1-43	350th FG	Landed Lisbon Airport
P-400	BX 292	15-1-43	350th FG	Landed Lisbon Airport
P-400	BX 412	15-1-43	350th FG	Landed Lisbon Airport
P-400	BX 434	15-1-43	350th FG	Landed Lisbon Airport
P-400	BX 297	15-1-43	350th FG	Landed Lisbon Airport
P-400	AP 273	15-1-43	350th FG	Landed Lisbon Airport
P-400	BX 369	15-1-43	350th FG	Landed Lisbon Airport
P-400	BX 432	15-1-43	81st FG	Landed Lisbon Airport
P-39L	24517	15-1-43	350th FG	Landed Lisbon Airport
?	?	15-1-43	350th FG	Landed S.Jacinto Naval Air Base
P-39L	24527	8-2-1943	350th FG	Landed Lisbon Airport
P-400	BX 175	27-4-1943	350th FG	Landed Lisbon Airport
P-400	AP 292	27-4-1943	350th FG	Landed Lisbon Airport
P-39M	24854	27-4-1943	350th FG	Landed Lisbon Airport
P-400	BX 187	3-6-1943	?	Landed in a field near Aljezur
???	BX 128 (??)	16-8-1943	?	?

4 See chapter on Markings and Insignia.

Bell P-39/P-400 Airacobra – Operational aircraft – Individual aircraft histories						
USAAF/ RAF serial number	Type	Date of entry service	A.M. serial	Struck of charge	Flight code letters	Remarks
?	P-400	23-6-43	300/301	June 1949	OK-A	See note below
?	P-400	23-6-43	301	---	OK-B	Damaged beyond repair Sept.43
?	P-400	23-6-43	302	June 1949	OK-C	
?	P-400	23-6-43	303	June 1949	OK-D	
?	P-400	23-6-43	304	---	OK-E	Damaged beyond repair 16-8-1943
?	P-400	23-6-43	305	June 1949	OK-F	
?	P-400	23-6-43	306	June 1949	OK-G	
?	P-400	23-6-43	307	June 1949	OK-H	
?	P-400	23-6-43	308	April 1950	OK-I	
?	P-400	23-6-43	309	---	OK-J	Damaged beyond repair 1-8-1943
?	P-400	23-6-43	310	April 1950	OK-K	
?	P-400	23-6-43	311	April 1950	OK-L	
?	P-400	23-6-43	312	---	OK-M	Damaged beyond repair 9-2-1944
?	P-400	23-6-43	313	April 1950	OK-N	
?	P-400	23-6-43	314	April 1950	OK-O	
24854	P-39M	23-6-43	315	April 1950	OK-P	
?	P-39L	23-6-43	316	April 1950	OK-Q	
?	P-39L	23-6-43	317	---	OK-R	Damaged beyond repair 25-4-1946
?	P-39L	23-6-43	318	April 1950	OK-S	

Notes:

1 – The correlation of RAF/USAAF serial numbers to the A.M. ones is not known except for aircraft 'OK-P'. Known serials are presented in the first table above.

2 – Aircraft 300 was re-serialled 301 when the original 301 crashed.

Aircraft characteristics Bell P-39L Airacobra	
Quantity used:	18 (14 P-400,1 P-39M, 3 P-39L)
Crew:	One
Years of Service:	1943–1950
Span:	34' 0" (10.36 m)
Length:	30' 2" (9.19 m)
Height:	11' 10" (3.70 m)
Wing Area:	213 sq ft (19.78 m^2)
Empty weight:	6,500 lb (2,948.4 kg)
Maximum take-off weight:	7,900 lb (3,583.4 kg)
Maximum speed:	At 20,000 ft 347 mph (558.4 km/h)
Service ceiling:	31,496.06 ft (9,600 m)
Armament:	4 x machine guns 0.30, 2 x machine guns 0.50, 1 x cannon 37 mm
Engine:	GM Allison V-1710-63 with 1,325 hp

Bell P-400 Airacobra, *serial number 311, from OK Flight in June 1943. Part of the batch that was interned, and later purchased, by the Portuguese Government to equip the* Arma da Aeronautica *then in badly need of a modern fighter plane, this aircraft carried for the entirety of its service the two tone camouflaged scheme of Dark Earth, Dark Green over Sky under surfaces with which it arrived to the Portuguese shores. As explained elsewhere, these colours were of US manufacture and although with a different nomenclature very similar in shades to the ones of British origin.*

Bell P-39M Airacobra, *serial number 315, from OK Flight in June 1943. This aircraft is the only one of which the correlation between the USAAF original serial number (42-4854) and the Portuguese one (315) is known. Although all original serial numbers of the received aircraft are known, its relationship with the Portuguese counterpart remained unidentified until today. This aircraft maintained also its original paint scheme of Olive Drab over Neutral Grey for all the time in service with the* Arma da Aeronautica.

Bell P-400 Airacobra, serial number 311, from OK Flight in June 1943 showing to advantage its original upper-surfaces camouflage scheme.

Bell P-39M Airacobra, serial number 315, from OK Flight in June 1943.

Supermarine Spitfire Mk I (F. IA)

Background

Without doubt one of the best known of all fighter aeroplanes, the Supermarine Spitfire served continuously through the Second World War. So much has been written about the aircraft that only a brief summary is included here.

One of the aircraft presented to the RAF in response to Specification F.7/30, the Type 224 offered by Supermarine Aviation Limited lost out to a more conventional but effective design, the Gloster Gladiator (see chapter on the Gladiator, above). The Supermarine Type 224 was of all-metal, partially stressed-skin construction, with an open cockpit and a large inverted gull wing, fixed undercarriage covered by 'trousers', each concealing a 7.7 mm machine-gun (with two more guns in the fuselage). The prototype of Type 224, later RAF serial number K2890, had a distinctly modest performance, but after receiving several minor modifications was submitted to tests by the Royal Aircraft Establishment (RAE) at Farnborough, mostly concerning engine development.

Supermarine's chief designer, Reginald Mitchell, was not happy with the performance of the prototype, and he and his team went back to the drawing board. The new design, which would emerge as the Type 300, drastically reduced frontal area and volume, and incorporated a wing with a very slim profile which would later prove to be a major contributor to the success of the

Supermarine Spitfire Mk Ia. The National Markings are yet to be applied to this aircraft. (FAP/AHFA/Museu do Ar)

aircraft. In addition, the cockpit was enclosed by a glazed canopy, retractable undercarriage was included and the Goshawk engine was changed to the new Rolls-Royce PV12. The Air Ministry had developed a standard for armament consisting of a battery of eight machine-guns, formalised in Specification F.5/34, and this armament was added to the developing Type 300 design, now all enclosed in the wings. In January 1935 the British Air Ministry accepted Type 300 and issued an order for the prototype of what would become known as Spitfire with the serial K5054. The first service example of the Spitfire Mk I was delivered to No. 19 Squadron, at Duxford, in May 1938.

The Supermarine Spitfire Mk I in Portuguese Service

By the end of 1937 the Portuguese *Ministério da Guerra* (War Ministry, today *Ministério da Defesa*, or Defence Ministry) had, as a result of the Spanish Civil War, realised that the air component of the Armed Forces would be crucial in the event of war. The decision to reorganise the Armed Forces was formalised in several Decrees, one of which referred specifically to the *Arma de Aeronautica*, creating Headquarters, Commands, Bases[1], Fighter and Bomber Flights, personnel organisation, etc., and replacing the existing structure dating back to the first days of the *Arma*.

The acquisition plan initiated required a number of bombers, to be supplied by Germany (Junkers Ju 52 and Junkers Ju 86), and ground attack aircraft, to be supplied by Italy (Breda Ba-65). The purchase of a new fighter was left open to be selected between German, Italian and British products, thus diversifying the origin of the equipment to be bought.

The first request for the acquisition of a number of Spitfire Mk I (between 10 and 15 aircraft) was addressed to the British authorities on the beginning of 1938, being received with "sympathy" by the Foreign Office. However, as more and more countries demonstrated an interest in this fighter, the Air Chief Marshal of the day, Sir Cyril Newall demanded in a letter signed November that year, that a priority list of deliveries should be established. The resulting list placed Portugal sixth.

In the intervening time, the Portuguese government became increasingly concerned that the Spanish conflict would spill into Portugal, or that Nazi Germany would make aggressive moves aimed at Portugal or its overseas territories. The British Foreign Minister, Lord Halifax, had meanwhile personally assured President Salazar of the United Kingdom's complete support in such an event, offering at the same time a credit line for the purchase of weapons, among then the much-desired Spitfire.

As stated elsewhere in this book, small groups of the *Arma de Aeronautica* officers were, in the meantime, travelling through those European countries with the most developed aircraft industries.

1 Only in 1940 were numerals to be introduced to identify Air Bases. Thus Sintra would become Air Base 1, Ota Air Base 2, Tancos Air Base 3, Lajes Air Base 4, etc.

Supermarine Spitfire Mk Ia s/n 375 (ex-RAF X4617), after a mid-air collision with its Flight "companion" s/n 372 in January 1944 (see text). Of note is the absence of the aircraft identification letter. (Coll.A.Cardoso)

Supermarine Spitfire Mk Ia, apparently the aircraft s/n 370, Flight code XZ+A as shown on the profile photo. Of notice are the placement and size of the Cruz de Cristo *under the wings. (FAP/AHFA)*

Their aim was to visit factories, and examine and test the new aircraft then in production, to inform the eventual purchase of a fighter for territorial air defence. By mid 1938, in the absence of a clear response on the requested Spitfires, the Portuguese Government put forward a request to the British Foreign Office for the purchase of a number of fighter aircraft[2], specifying both the urgency of the acquisition and a guarantee that, even in case of Britain becoming involved in a conflict, the order would be fulfilled. The intended destination for this equipment was to be the Azores, where they would act as a deterrent to the threat of a possible invasion.

With a decision yet to be taken on the final delivery of such a fighter, British advisers to Portugal, supported by the Ambassador, and alarmed by the pressure of the Italians and Germans on the Lisbon authorities for the acquisition of their own aircraft, pressed British authorities for the supply of the requested fighter, the Supermarine Spitfire Mk I. However, the slow delivery of Spitfires to the RAF led to a recommendation to Vickers-Supermarine that "no aircraft could be released [to foreign costumers] before the delivery of the ordered 150 units to the RAF," thus rendering the Portuguese demand impossible to fulfil. Nevertheless, as "a special concession to Portugal and to the *Arma de Aeronautica*" the Spitfire Type 336 (Supermarine's designation for the Spitfire Mk I for export to Portugal) was offered and accepted in March 1939, with fifteen aircraft of the type to be supplied within a period of three months. A letter of intent approved by the British Air Ministry, was signed on 10 August 1939 establishing the delivery of at least ten aircraft by March the following year. These ten aircraft were considered to be sufficient to constitute a Flight of Spitfires, as an interim solution before the purchase of more aircraft.

Due to the outbreak of war soon after the letter of intent, though, Portugal had to wait two more years to share with the United Kingdom the privilege of being the only other country to make extensive operational use of the Supermarine Spitfire Mk IA (though Turkey briefly operated three Spitfires of that mark). The first two airframes to reach Lisbon harbour arrived in November 1942 followed by an additional four the following month. The balance of four aircraft, to complete the agreed minimum of ten, finally arrived by the end of January 1943. Portugal received eight more Spitfire Mk IAs by the end of October, bringing the grand total of this mark to eighteen[3]. The Spitfires received by Portugal, although completed overhauled by the factory before their export, were not brand new, having logged a considerable number of flying hours according to their documentation.

The airframes of the received aircraft, all Supermarine-built between September 1939 and December 1940, were re-assembled at the O.G.M.A. facilities in Alverca in order to be transferred

2 See the Gloster Gladiator and the Curtiss Mohawk Chapters.

3 The British Authorities could now afford to pass a certain number of Spitfire Mk IA aircraft to friendly foreign countries because the RAF was by then being equipped with more advanced types.

to the base for fighter aircraft, *Base Aérea nº 3* at Tancos, where they would constitute 'XZ' Flight. A number of pilots led by *Capitão* António Sarmento were detached to the *Oficinas Gerais* to be present during the assembly process and proceed with the preliminary flights. The first Spitfire Mk IA took off on the morning of 30 December 1942 for a low-level test flight with *Tenente* José Ribeiro Ferreira at the controls, being the first aircraft of this type to fly in Portuguese skies. While the flight was unproblematic, the same could not be said about the landing, the Spitfire nosing over and causing damage to the airframe, though fortunately no harm to the pilot.

Until the summer of 1943, the Spitfires were still flying with their original British serial numbers but Portuguese identification chalked on the fuselage. At this time, the aeroplanes received their *Arma de Aeronautica* serial numbers, registered in the '400' block (420 to 430). This serial block had been allocated to the Miles Masters in use at *Base Aérea nº 1* (Sintra) for conversion-training Tancos pilots onto monoplanes. In fact, from June to August 1943 there are records of simultaneous flying with Masters and Spitfires bearing the same serial numbers, including 426, 427, 428 and 429. The existence of the 400-series serials on Spitfires would not last long though, as from August 1943 they received their definitive serial numbers within the 300-block, between 370 and 387. According to official sources, the numbering sequence followed the order of arrival of the aircraft to Portugal. Although the British serial numbers of the aircraft received are known, the correlation between them and the Portuguese serials is not easy, due to the lack of reliable documentation, though contemporary photographs reveal some aircraft's identities.

In August 1943 several flights were recorded in the Tancos Air Base Movements Log Book for aircraft 370, 373, 374, 376, 381, 382, 383, 384 and 385. While there are no known photographs in evidence in the official Portuguese archives showing airframes bearing 400-series serial numbers, an entry in the Air Movements Log Book of the Lisbon Airport, dated 1 August 1943, indicates the arrival and departure of Spitfires 426, 427, 428 and 429, confirming the use of such serials. A further Mk IA serial number 425 appears on 26 September 1944, on a 35 minutes flight between Alverca and Tancos, at an altitude of 1,000 meters, as late as a year after the change of serial numbers. Conversely, in January 1944 not all aircraft had their Flight code letter painted in their fuselages, as proved by several photographs.

Supermarine Spitfire Mk Ia s/n 372 XZ+C, the other victim of the mid-air collision in 27 January 1944 with 375 (see text). (Coll.A.Cardoso)

Supermarine Spitfires Mk Ia s/n 373 and s/n 374 at the Tancos Air Base, in September 1943. (Coll. M. Palma)

Another mystery surrounding Portuguese Spitfire Mk IAs concerns the 'phantom' Spitfire Mk IA numbered 388, marked in the Movements Log Book of Tancos Air Base on several flights between February and November 1944. The highest number allocated to a Spitfire Mk IA should have been 387 so the appearance of a Spitfire marked 338 is perplexing.

Though the new fighter and its flying characteristics were well appreciated by its new owners, a major problem was soon detected – a tendency for the Spitfire's engines to overheat, exacerbated by the hot climate. The Spitfires were, however, deemed fit for deployment to the Azores, where the aircraft would equip *Esquadrilha Expedicionária de Caça nº 4*, or E.E.C.4 (Expeditionary Fighter Flight number 4), to be stationed at Lajes Airfield (*Base Aérea nº 4*). The Curtiss Mohawk flight, which, meanwhile was also at O.G.M.A. for engine overhaul, would depart at the same time to form *Esquadrilha Expedicionária de Caça nº 3* (E.E.C.3) at Rabo de Peixe Airfield, replacing the old Gloster Gladiators.

In the event, only the Mohawks were deployed to the Azores, as the 'Azores Agreement'[4] was signed in August 1943. The agreement set out that Portugal conceded use of naval and air bases for the deployment of Allied forces, and in return the RAF took responsibility for the defence of Lajes Airfield and, in consequence, of a large area of the Islands. The RAF deployed 269 Squadron, equipped with Spitfires.

By that time, the Continental territory of Portugal had 37 air defence fighter aircraft as follows: ten Spitfire Mk IA earmarked for E.E.C.4, nine Curtiss Mohawks from 'XY' Flight and 18 Bell P-39 /P-400 Airacobras from 'OK' Flight.

Meanwhile, the backbone of Portuguese air defence was provided by interned aircraft forced to land in Portugal due to problems en route to North Africa, mostly Bell Airacobras. The received Spitfire Mk IA aircraft were not new, and though they had been refurbished and updated, failures and accidents happened. The most spectacular example of this arose at the beginning of 1944 during the final leg of a patrol flight from Tancos Base. Spitfire 372 (XZ-C), with *Tenente* Ismael

4 The discussions and correspondence exchanged at the highest level between the Portuguese and British Governments largely exceeds the parameters of this book. Much has been published on the subject of the Azores Agreement, but on the question of the aircraft negotiations, readers are referred to *Spitfires e Hurricanes em Portugal* by *Engº* Mário Canongia Lopes, not only for its bilingual characteristics but also for its in depth focus on the political aspects.

Supermarine Spitfires Mk Ia lined-up at the Ota Air Base for the air display of May 1944. In the background part of the Airacobras OK Flight is discernible. (FAP/AHFA/Museu do Ar)

Canavilhas at the controls, could not lower its landing gear. His wingman in Spitfire 375 (XZ-F) attempted to fly beneath 372 to carry out an inspection, but, miscalculated and the two Spitfires collided. Canavilhas' aircraft lost its tail, while Spitfire 375 suffered damage to its propeller. Both pilots were able to belly-land at Tancos without sustaining physical injuries.

The Portuguese Government maintained contact with Britain, insisting on the supply of more Spitfires, of a more recent type, the Mk V. The British Ambassador to Lisbon was supportive, demonstrated by a note to the Foreign Office dated 19 August 1943, emphasising the obsolescence of the existing equipment. The request was not turned down, but it was put off to an unspecified later date. As the military situation in Europe was changing rapidly in favour of the Allies, the former position was quickly amended. A month after the Ambassador's memo, the Portuguese Authorities were offered a larger number of aircraft even than they had requested (see following chapter).

In addition to their role of defending Portuguese air space, the Spitfire Mk IA Flight was involved in a number of exercises involving other elements of the Armed Forces. Six aircraft of 'XZ' Flight were engaged on Army support exercises held on 24 August 1944, while five days later six more aeroplanes practised air-to-air gunnery.

On 5 December 1944, all the operational Spitfire Mk IAs were transferred from *Base Aérea nº 3* (Tancos) to *Base Aérea nº 2* (Ota). The serials of these aircraft were 370, 373, 374, 375, 376, 381, 382, 383, 384, 385, 386 and 387. Later, aircraft 379 would join. There they were incorporated into a Flight comprising the remaining Airacobras and some Spitfire Mk V aircraft, wherein the Mk Is were generally allocated to the younger pilots. By January 1946 only five of these aircraft were in flyable condition.

When by May 1947 nearly 60 Spitfire Mk Vs were received from RAF stocks, a new flight with the code letters 'ZE' was formed, including the three remaining flyable Spitfire Mk IAs, 379, 380 and 387. Two of the last three aircraft, 387 and 380, were subsequently lost in accidents, in September 1947 and April 1949 respectively.

Finally in December 1950, the last ten Spitfire Mk IAs, then in storage, (serial numbers 370, 373, 374, 375, 376, 381, 382, 384, 385 and 386), were struck off from the inventory of the *Arma da Aeronautica* (379 had already suffered that fate in 1948). Thus ended the career of the Supermarine Spitfire Mk IA in the *Arma de Aeronáutica*, without a single example set aside for preservation in a museum.

Camouflage and Markings

The British camouflage scheme for day fighters operating over Northern Europe changed in August 1941, replacing the original 'Temperate Land Scheme'. The two 'A' and 'B' variants of the disruptuve camouflage pattern were also abandoned from January that year, with only the 'A' pattern to be used on future aeroplanes. The new 'Day Fighter Scheme' comprised Dark Green and

Ocean Grey in a disruptive pattern covering all upper surfaces, with Medium Sea Grey under surfaces. The propeller spinner and an 18 in. band around the rear fuselage were to be painted Sky. Another innovation in this scheme was the inclusion of a 4 in. wide yellow strip painted along the outer portion of the wing leading edge, as a point of identification in the head-on aspect.

During their service with the *Arma de Aeronautica* Spitfire Mk IA aircraft mostly retained the above-described camouflage, apart from the rear fuselage band, which was omitted. It is not known if any paints in the aforementioned colours were included in the additional material received with the 18 Spitfires (including spare engines, propellers, etc.), but there is no evidence that any British paints were supplied. For refreshing the paintwork or repainting after repairs, it was probably necessary to resort to locally available paints.

As far as is known, the Spitfire Mk IA aircraft were the first in the *Arma de Aeronautica* where the red *Cruz de Cristo* national markings was applied on the fuselage without a white disc background. Following the British procedure, three letters marked the identification of each aeroplane, two Flight code letters placed in front of the Cross, 'XZ' in the case of the Spitfire Mk IA, and a third letter indicating the individual aircraft, placed after the national symbol. The serial number (3**...) was painted just ahead of the tail plane, also in the British style. Both code and serial were painted in white. It is assumed that the spinners maintained their original colour, Sky, but the band around the fuselage and the yellow identification strip on the wings were deleted. The national markings, including the white background disc, maintained their usual four positions above and below the wings, covering the existing British roundels. The green and red national flag, without Coat of Arms, was applied to the tail fin.

No other particular markings (names, drawings, mascots, etc...) are known to have been painted on the airframes, which maintained the same colours during the entire service period.

Supermarine Spitfire Mk I a – Individual Aircraft Histories			
RAF Serial (1)	**Date Arrival**	**A.M. Serial (2)**	**Remarks**
X4339 ?	21/11/42	370 XZ-A	---
X4589 ?	21/11/42	371 XZ-B	Accident 11/8/44(?)
R6920 ?	12/12/42	372 XZ-C	Accident 27/1/44 (See text)
R7159 ?	12/12/42	373 XZ-D	Accident 11/08/44(?)
X4855 ?	12/12/42	374 XZ-E	---
X 4617	12/12/42	375 XZ-F	Accident 27/01/44 (See text)
R6987 ?	20/01/43	376 XZ-G	---
R7027 ?	20/01/43	377 XZ-H	1st Accident 24/10/43 2nd Accident 06/05/44
R7123 ?	20/01/43	378 XZ-I	Accident 11/08/44(?)
X4920 ?	20/01/43	379 XZ-J	Accident (Date ?)
(*)	29/08/43	380 XZ-L	Accident 12/04/49

A very interesting and well-known photo of nearly half of the XZ Flight of Supermarine Spitfires Mk Ia at Ota Air Base. Distinctly the following serial numbers can be identified: 370/A, 373/D, 375/F, 376/G, 380/L, 383/O, 385/Q, 386/R and 387/S. Of note, again, is the proportion of the fin flag colours. Unlike other Flights, and for no apparent reason, the XZ Flight did not use the letter "K" to identify its aircraft. In the background two Supermarine Spitfires Mk V serial numbers 4, RL+D and 7, RL+G are discernible. (FAP/AHFA/ Museu do Ar)

"Family Photo" of the personnel of flight XZ, date unknown. (Coll. A.Cardoso)

(*)	29/08/43	381 XZ-M	Accident 30/11/43
X4857 ?	29/08/43	382 XZ-N	---
(*)	29/08/43	383 XZ-O	W/o Accident 28/01/46
K9991 ?	18/09/43	384 XZ-P	---
R7071	26/09/43	385 XZ-Q	---
X4716 ?	28/09/43	386 XZ-R	---
P9544 ?	07/10/43	387 XZ-S	Accident 12/09/47
?	?	388 ?	See text

The above listing was elaborated based on data published in *MAIS ALTO FAP* magazine. Nov./Dec. 2006.

Notes

(1) – The equivalent RAF/A.M. serial numbers could only be established in two cases, aircraft X4617 and R7071. The equivalence of the aircraft marked '?' follows their order of arrival, but could not be definitely confirmed. Aircraft marked (*) were identified as K9828, R6626 and R7146 and are believed to equate with A.M. serials 380, 381 and 383, but no confirmation was possible. According to one source, aircraft R7146 was a PR Type C version.

(2) – These aircraft were first included in the '400' serial block, 420-430. See main text for explanation. Strangely the 'XZ' Flight did not use the letter K as an individual aircraft identifier.

Aircraft Characteristics Supermarine Spitfire Mk I	
Quantity used:	18 (19?)
Crew:	One
Years of Service:	1942–1950
Span:	36' 10" (11.23 m)
Length:	29' 11" (9.12 m)
Height:	11' 5" (3.48 m)
Wing Area:	242 sq ft (22.48 m^2)
Empty weight:	4,409 lb (2,000 kg)
Fully loaded weight:	6,058 lb (2,760 kg)
Maximum speed:	362 mph (583 km/h) at 18,500 feet
Service ceiling:	30,500 feet (9,295 m)
Armament:	(Ia) 8 x Browning .303" with 300 r.p.g.
Engine:	One *Rolls-Royce Merlin II* 990HP at 2600 rpm liquid cooled twelve cylinder "V" engine

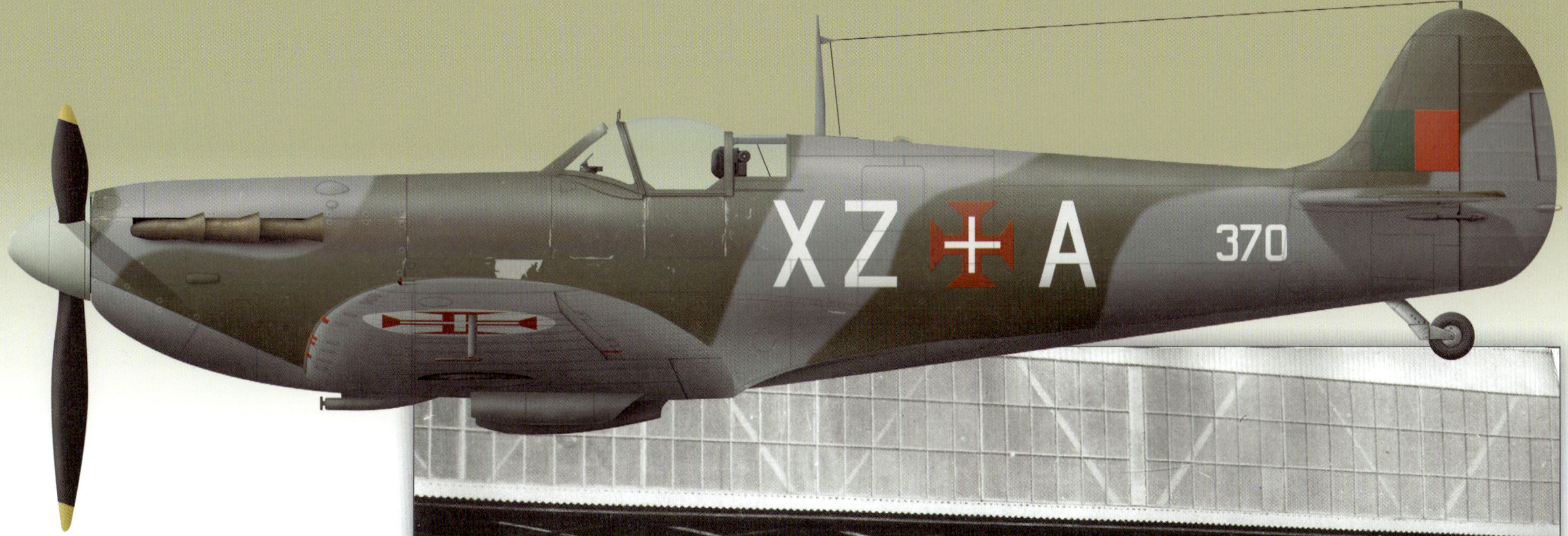

Supermarine Spitfire Mk Ia, serial number 370, 1943. Most probably the ex-RAF serial number X4339 (but without confirmation), this aircraft was the very first Spitfire to fly under Portuguese colours, its career ending in December 1950, when it was "struck off charge". As with all other aircraft purchased by the Portuguese, it maintained its original two-colour camouflage of Dark Green/Ocean Grey over Medium Sea Grey, following the British "A pattern" scheme. For the first time the *Cruz de Cristo on the fuselage was painted directly over the camouflage, without its white background.*

Nice profile photo of the first Supermarine Spitfire Mk Ia s/n 370, Flight code XZ+A of the Aeronáutica Militar. *Of note is the almost equal size of the green and red parts of the National Flag, contradicting the established norms of the day. (FAP/AHFA)*

Supermarine Spitfire Mk V

Background

The emergence of the Messerschmitt Bf 109F by late 1940 showed the pressing need for improvements to the Spitfire Mk I. The airframe basis for this new version was to be the combination of the earlier structure with reinforcement to the engine mounts for the more powerful Rolls Royce Merlin 45. The performance of this new version improved markedly and the first examples of the Mk V were delivered to 92 Squadron in February 1941.

There were also changes to the armament, which led, as an outcome, to different types of wings being attributed letter designations. Accordingly, the first aircraft of the mark, produced with eight 0.303 Browning machine-guns, were designated Mk VA, and with two Hispano 20 mm cannon and four machine-guns, the designation became Mk VB. Both these variants maintained the Supermarine Type number 331.

Another wing was later introduced, known as the 'universal wing', which was able to receive the armament of both Mk VA or Mk VB versions, or even four 20 mm cannon. Another modification applied to many Mk V Spitfires was the clipping of the wingtips in order to improve the performance, particularly roll-rate, at low altitude.

The engine was also subject to modifications during the production of the Mk V, with the addition of the Merlin 46, optimised for high altitude performance, and, with a new carburettor, the Merlin 50 series – 50A, 55, 56 or 45M, 50M and 55M depending on the specification of the supercharger. With the Mk V, letters to specify the role of the aircraft also made their appearance. As a result, when a Mk V was equipped with a Merlin engine optimised for low altitudes, it gained the prefix 'LF', while the standard fighter gained the prefix 'F'.

The Supermarine Spitfire V in Portugal

After the acceptance of the Spitfire Mk I aircraft, the Portuguese Government continued to push for enough modern fighters to form six day fighter Flights of 15 aircraft each, i.e., 90 aircraft in Continental Portugal and one second-line Flight on the Azores. By the time of the Azores Agreement in August 1943, there were 18 Airacobras, 9 Mohawks and 10 Spitfire Mk Is with the

Sequence of photos showing the recovery process of Supermarine Spitfire serial number 31, code MR+N after crash. The place and date of the accident are not identified in the photos, but it is assumed that it took place during a landing or take off operation, as the background shows what appears to be an airfield. (FAP/AHFA)

Again Spitfire s/n 31 during its recovery operation. As it appears by the photos, the condition of the airframe does not look too bad, assuming a possible repair of the aircraft. (FAP/AHFA)

The same aircraft and situation as described before. The photos show the recovery process, elementary to say the least and using a lot of "elbow grease" and all the available local help! (FAP/AHFA)

The Supermarine Spitfire serial number 31 coded MR+N being finally retrieved from its crash site. Although the date and place of this accident are unknown, the official records shown that aircraft s/n 31 was on active duty in March 1947 at Ota Air Base. (FAP/AHFA)

The interest of this photo is showing the aircraft in a line up that includes one Grumman SA-16A Albatross, thus establishing with certainty a given time frame, dating the photo from the early fifties. Of note also are the two aircraft close to the camera, both Spitfires LF Mk V. The airplane in the foreground depicts the use of a double code letter, DD serial number 46, as explained in the text, and oddly also the absence of the under-wing national insignia. Another oddity is the non-conformity between the spinner and the rear fuselage colour band. (FAP/AHFA)

Aeronautica Militar. The Portuguese Government established that, with the expected reception of an additional 12 Airacobras and five Spitfires, only 45 additional aircraft would be needed. Finally, agreement on the quantities and type of aircraft to be supplied was reached. These consisted of Spitfire Mk Vs, Hawker Hurricane Mk IIB/IICs and additional Spitfire Mk Is to bring the existing Flight up to full strength. The new fighters began to arrive at Lisbon by ship from the end of August 1943, and by the end of that year 26 Spitfire Mk Vs had been received. Some of the aircraft received were of the Mk VC type (universal wing) and others of the LF Mk VB (low altitude fighter).

For reasons unknown, the new aircraft received serial numbers running from 1 to 93, which did not fit into the current regulations for the issue of serial numbers. Furthermore, for a lengthy period, the new fleet of Spitfires retained part of their previous RAF serials. Records show flights by Spitfire '624' and Spitfire '311' on 2 December 1943, Spitfire '191' on 16 February 1944, and Spitfire '978' on 10 March 1944. It is likely that these were the Spitfires with the British serials BM624, BM311, AB191 and BL978.

An important detail concerning the allocation of serials to the Spitfire fleet (and unlike with the Hurricane fleet), no serials of retired or crashed aircraft were re-used in new aircraft as far as it is known. This means that 93 aircraft were received and the same number of serials were issued.

The new Spitfire Mk V Flights enter service

The first Spitfire Mk Vs received in October 1943 made possible the creation of 'RL' Flight, with 15 aircraft receiving, at least on paper, the serial numbers 1 to 15 and letters A to O, under the leadership of *Tenente* Rogério Seixas.

In January and February 1944 an additional eight aircraft were delivered, allowing the formation of 'MR' Flight, with six aircraft, and two more aircraft going to 'RL' Flight. During a demonstration of Portuguese air power at Ota Air Base on 6 May 1944, more than 200 aircraft were present, including a number of Spitfire Mk Vs from 'MR' Flight.

In July 1944, Ota Air Base (*Base Aérea nº 2*), was equipped with two Flights of Spitfire Mk Vs, 'MR' and 'RL', representing half of the *Grupo Supranumerário de Aviação de Caça* (Supernumerary Group of Fighter Aircraft). The Spitfire Mk I and Airacobra Flights made up the other half of the *Grupo*, identified respectively by the code letters 'XZ' and 'OK'. Also in 1944, additional Spitfire Mk Vs were received, raising the total number of aircraft to 34. The Spitfires, together with the

Hurricanes, assumed the role of day fighters. In addition, the list below, taken from several pilots' logbooks, demonstrates the diversity of missions performed by the aircraft:

1944:
Formation flights
Navigation (Ota-Coimbra-Ota, Ota-Fátima-Ota, etc.)
IFR flights

1945: (Information as recorded on a particular pilot's logbook)
Aircraft s/n 1 – June – combined exercises with A.A. artillery
Aircraft s/n 14 – Navigation – Ota-Elvas-Beja-Ota
Aircraft s/n 31 – September – Air display over Lisbon
Aircraft s/n 15 – September – Air target shooting practice
Aircraft s/n 7 – Navigation – Ota-Pampilhosa-Bussaco-Ota – 1h25m

1946:
Aircraft s/n 31 – February – Low-level flying (300 ft) Ota –Coruche –Ota (45 min)
Aircraft s/n 14 – February – Stalls, tight turns, "vrilles" (spins).
Aircraft s/n 10 – February – Training with A.A. artillery
Aircraft s/n 9 – March – Formation flight
Aircraft s/n 9 – June – Diving, low-level flying, aerobatics, low-level flying
Aircraft s/n 11 – August – Combat tactics
Aircraft s/n 10,12 and 14 – October – In support of Army manoeuvres

The final post-war deliveries

It was not until 1947 that another shipment of Spitfire Mk Vs was received by Portugal, when 60 more aircraft were bought. These aircraft had been refurbished at the Reid & Sigrist facilities where they were brought to the LF Mk V standards (low altitude day fighter) with Merlin 45M, 50M, and 55M engines, (the Merlin 50 engine being easily identified by its six exhaust stubs per side), and clipped wings.

Recently delivered Spitfires Mk V at Ota Air Base, in 1947. The Cruz de Cristo *(Cross of Christ), the A.M. serials and aircraft individual code letters in the fuselage are yet to be applied. As it is confirmed by the different exhaust pipes, these aircraft were received with different types of engine. The aircraft in the middle of the front column is ex-RAF serial EP785. (FAP/AHFA)*

Supermarine Spitfire LF Mk V Serial number 71 Code ZE+A. Although a black and white photo, one can distinctively discern the Flight colours, i.e., red spinner and rear fuselage band. (FAP/AHFA)

The delivery of this last group of aircraft was carried out by air between April 1947 and January 1948. The aircraft received the A.M. serial numbers 35 to 93. Of the total aeroplanes received, three were equipped with wing fittings to allow bombs to be carried.

During the delivery flight one aircraft, RAF serial AA753, was forced to perform an emergency landing in Spain, being offered to the Spanish authorities, who demonstrated the intention to repair it to flying conditions. However, this never happened and the airframe was eventually scrapped in 1951. Another aircraft was lost during the test flying period, bringing the number of aircraft effectively received by the A.M. during 1947-48 to 58.

With the deliveries of the Spitfires Mk V ending on 30 January 1948, a total of 92 aircraft were accounted as received. On the other hand, as the Air Base movement's logbook records confirm the use of the serial '93', which represents another unsolved mystery…

Although the number of Spitfires available suddenly increased with the 1947 deliveries, it was not possible immediately to form new Flights, mainly due to a shortage of pilots. Nevertheless, the

Sequence of photos taken at Tancos Air Base. Due to the absence of caption and date on the original photos, it is assumed that they were taken either as private souvenir or for instruction purposes. The flying suit in use by the Aeronaútica Militar until the advent of the US material in mid-fifties was of British origin and the same as used by the RAF. (FAP/AHFA)

Detail of flight suit. (FAP/AHFA)

Spitfire of Flight ZE at Tancos. (FAP/AHFA)

Blenheim Flight based at Ota, code letters 'ZE', was the recipient of a number of the new fighters, which operated alongside other types of aircraft.

In December 1947, a new Day Fighter Group was formed at Ota, made up of three Spitfire Flights, 'MR', 'RL' and 'ZE'. The latter also had in its ranks several Gloster Gladiators, North American T-6 Texans and Miles Magisters. During this period, individual aircraft within the flight were identified by two letters rather than the customary single letter, apparently because the quantity of aircraft in each Flight exceeded the letters of the alphabet, as demonstrated by photographs of aircraft wearing the codes MR-GG and (RL?)-DD.

In February 1952, the year of the creation of *Força Aérea Portuguesa* (Portuguese Air Force), of the 92 Spitfires initially received, 19 had already been lost to accidents. In April that year the 73 or 74 remaining Spitfires were reduced to 50, by the withdrawal of the aircraft in non-flyable condition. The survivors were then transferred to Tancos Air Base (*Base Aérea nº 3*), maintaining the three-Flight structure, but now with differing numbers of aircraft – the 1st Flight saw its

Supermarine Spitfires Mk V at the Ota Air Base parade in May 1944, with the Airacrobras of "OK Flight" in the background. Discernible in the distance at the end of the front row are six Bleinhems, one Mk V and five Mk IVs. (FAP/AHFA)

complement reduced to 16 aircraft, while the 2nd and 3rd Flights maintained 17 aircraft each. It is interesting to note that by then, the new American F-47 Thunderbolt fighters were already flying at Tancos.

In 1954 the Tancos Air Base movement logbook records flights of 23 aircraft[1], with the last Spitfire Mk V movement recorded on 1 March 1955 by aircraft no. 49.

Aircraft delivered, flight assignments and codes used:

As all the ex-RAF serial numbers of the Supermarine Spitfire Mk Vs supplied to Portugal are known and with the help of official documents that came to light several years ago, it is now possible to ascertain, in many circumstances, their correlation with Portuguese serials. On the other hand, where the codes correspond to a known serial, the reader may be interested these details in the list below.

Where possible, the aircraft subtype is also included.

Individual Aircraft Histories				
RAF Serial	Type	Date Arrival	A.M. Serial	Remarks
W3430	F. Vb	10/43	1	RL+A
?		10/43	2	RL+B
?		10/43	3	RL+C
?		10/43	4	RL+D
?		10/43	5	RL+E
?		10/43	6	RL+F, W/o in accident
?		10/43	7	RL+G
?		10/43	8	RL+H
?		10/43	9	RL+I
?		10/43	10	RL+J
?		10/43	11	RL+K
?		10/43	12	RL+L, W/o in accident.
?		10/43	13	RL+M, W/o in accident
?		10/43	14	RL+N, W/o in accident
?		10/43	15	RL+O, W/o in accident
AA 946	F. Vb	11/43	16	RL+P, later MR+A?

1 The following aircraft were recorded as fully operational and flying in 1954: serial numbers 1, 3, 5, 7, 18, 20, 21, 23, 34, 46, 49, 50, 52, 58, 61, 63, 64, 73, 79, 81, 87, 92 and 93, i.e., 23 aircraft.

BL 684	F. Vb	11/43	17	RL+Q, Later MR+B? W/o in accident
?		?	18	RL+R, later MR+C
BL 690	F. Vb	12/43	19	MR+D, W/o in accident
W 3803	LF.Vb	1/44	20	MR+E?
?		1 or 2/44	21	MR+F?
?		1 or 2/44	22	MR+G?
?		1 or 2/44	23	MR+H?
?		1 or 2/44	24	MR+I?
?		1 or 2/44	25	MR+J?, also RL+AA, W/o in accident
?		1 or 2/44	26	MR+K
W 3648	LF.Vb	1 or 2/44	27	MR+L?
?		1 or 2/44	28	MR+M?, W/ o accident
?		1 or 2/44	29	MR+N?, W/o accident
BL 978	F. Vb	1 or 2/44	30	MR+O, the aircraft 85 used also this code letters.
?		1 or 2/44	31	RL+P? also MR+N, W/o accident
?		1 or 2/44	32	RL+Q? also MR+L, W/o accident
?		1 or 2/44	33	MR+P?
BM 176	F. Vb	1 or 2/44	34	MR+Q?
BM 594	LF.Vb	29/4/47	35	MR+R?
AB 487	LF.Vb	22/4/47	36	MR+S
AA 728	LF.Vb	6/5/47	37	
AD 294	LF.Vb	28/4/47	38	
EP 452	LF.Vb	6/5/47	39	W/o accident
AR 366	LF.Vb	17/4/47	40	
AB 862	LF.Vb	28/4/47	41	
AD 499	LF.Vb	6/5/47	42	
AA 862	LF.Vb	28/4/47	43	

A three-quarters front view of a Supermarine Spitfire LF Mk V in the last "olive green/light grey" colour scheme. Again the absence of the National insignia under the left wing is notable, perhaps awaiting the implementation of the new Air Force Standards(?). (FAP/AHFA)

BL 646	LF.Vb	14/4/47	44	??+K, W/o accident
BL 850	LF.Vb	9/4/47	45	??+M
BM 298	LF.Vb	22/4/47	46	??+DD
AA 729	LF.Vb	6/5/47	47	
AB 203	LF.Vb	6/5/47	48	W/o accident
???	LF.Vb	???	49	MR+GG
BL 496	LF.Vb	20/5/47	50	
EP 767	LF.Vb	3/6/47	51	
AR 404	LF.Vb	12/6/47	52	
EN 903	LF.Vb	9/6/47	53	W/o accident
BM 343	LF.Vb	9/6/47	54	
EN 928	LF.Vb	24/6/47	55	W/o accident
AA 979	LF.Vb	17/7/47	56	RL+U
AD 464	LF.Vb	14/7/47	57	
W 3518	LF.Vb	14/7/47	58	
W 3180	LF.Vb	17/4/47	59	
EN 800	LF.Vb	3/7/47	60	
EP 244	LF.Vb	3/7/47	61	
BL 374	LF.Vb	24/6/47	62	W/o accident
BL 981	LF.Vb	23/7/47	63	
BM 514	LF.Vb	25/7/47	64	
BL 433	LF.Vb	8/47	65	
AD 191	LF.Vb	18/4/47	66	
W 3641	LF.Vb	25/8/47	67	
W 3128	LF.Vb	17/9/47	68	
AR 438	LF.Vb	22/9/47	69	
W 3431	LF.Vb	22/9/47	70	
EP 560	LF.Vb	1/8/47	71	ZE+A
BL 970	LF.Vb	8/8/47	72	ZE+B?
P 8788	LF.Vb	22/8/47	73	ZE+C?
W 3519	LF.Vb	22/8/47	74	ZE+D?
EP 785	LF.Vb	24/9/47	75	ZE+E?
W 3248	LF.Vb	15/10/47	76	ZE+F?
AA 967	LF.Vb	4/11/47	77	ZE+G?
BM 131	LF.Vb	23/10/47	78	ZE+H?

The first Portuguese Supermarine Spitfire LF Mk V, bearing code RL+A, serial number 1. Note that the wing-leading edge had the yellow identification strip painted immediately outside the cannon barrel, longer than established by the British standards. In the background is it "stable mate" the Hawker Hurricane Mk IIc code GL+D serial number 603. (Coll. Sarg. Ajud. Pacheco)

P 8791	LF.Vb	22/11/47	79	ZE+I?
EP 605	LF.Vb	26/11/47	80	ZE+J?
BL 671	LF.Vb	8/12/47	81	ZE+K
EP 242	LF.Vb	17/12/47	82	
EN 775	LF.Vb	16/12/47	83	
AB 988	LF.Vb	21/10/47	84	
EP 411	LF.Vb	23/12/47	85	MR+O
BL 368	LF.Vb	23/12/47	86	W/o accident
W 3902	LF.Vb	8/1/48	87	
AA 881	LF.Vb	3/1/48	88	
?	LF.Vb		89	

This sequence of three photos shows a number of Supermarine Spitfires Mk V, with some LF included, at the Ota Air Base, probably during October 1950. The leading aircraft bears the code letter MR+O and serial number serial 85. (Coll. MusAr)

Supermarine Spitfire LF Mk V RL+U, serial number 56 again at Ota Air Base. (Coll. MusAr)

This Spitfire LF Mk V presents a fine example of a double letter id code, MR+GG serial number 49. (Coll MusAr)

?	LF.Vb		90	
?	LF.Vb		91	
?	LF.Vb		92	MR+L
?	LF.Vb		93	

Notes:

1 – The following aircraft were also delivered to Portugal, but the correlation between RAF and A.M. serials is not known: BL890, BM311, W3951, AB895, AR367, BL449, BM300, BM479, AD383, EN928, BM131, BL976, BL821, AA756, BL898 and EP766.

2 – As can be seen from the above list the same aircraft sometimes used more than one code during their operational life with the A.M., probably as a consequence of movements between Flights.

Camouflage & markings

When delivered, the Spitfire Mk Vs wore the RAF Day Fighter Scheme of Dark Green/Ocean Grey disruptive camouflage over Medium Sea Grey under surfaces. In the Portuguese service they maintained this camouflage at least until 1952 when the *Força Aérea Portuguesa* (F.A.P.) was formed, replacing the *Aeronáutica Militar*. The red *Cruz de Cristo* over a white disc was placed above and below the wings and a simplified flag was painted on the fin, made up of two rectangles, one dark green forming 2/5 of the total flag and the other red, covering the remaining 3/5.

The serial numbers were painted in white on both sides of the fuselage, aft of the identification colour band. The colour of this band, together with the colour of the spinner identified the Flight. A three-letter code identified the Flight and the aircraft, the first two letters identifying the Flight and the third identifying the individual aircraft. These letters were also painted white and placed both sides of the fuselage *Cruz de Cristo*, in the style typical of RAF aircraft, i.e. the two code letters were painted always ahead of the Cross, with the aircraft letter on the other side of the national marking. Exceptionally, as explained above, some aircraft carried two aircraft identification letters.

The Flights and the respective colours were as follows:

Flight RL	Blue
Flight MR	Yellow
Flight ZE	Red

In 1952, with the formation of the F.A.P., the remaining Spitfires began to receive a new colour scheme of Olive Green upper surfaces and Light Grey under surfaces. The red *Cruz de Cristo* on a white disc was painted above the left wing and beneath the right wing. The white serial number, showing only the two last digits of the full serial, was painted above the Portuguese flag on the fin, which maintained its position and proportions from the previous scheme. Flight codes were abandoned, due to a change in the basic structure of the aircraft unit to the *Esquadra* (Squadron) from the *Esquadrilha* (Flight).

Although the Spitfires were intended to be included in the new serial block of 43** (where 41** was attributed to remaining Gladiators and the 42** to Hurricanes), according to the new F.A.P. regulations, as far as it is known, these were never applied to the airframes still flying after 1952, the old serial being maintained.

Unlike the Hurricanes, the Spitfires are not thought to have worn any unit insignia. However, a photograph of unknown origin depicts a Portuguese Spitfire (Mk I or Mk V) with an inscription on the left side of the cowling, assumed to be a personal insignia or nose-art. The drawing, probably in white only, shows what could be a chicken or other bird surrounded by an oval inscription stating above 'Onde tu Chegares', and below, 'Eu Chego' ('Where you Reach ... I will reach'). Unfortunately, it was not possible to obtain permission for the use of the photograph in this book

Supermarine Spitfire Mk V serial number 19, coded MR+D. (Coll MusAr)

Aircraft characteristics Supermarine Spitfire Mk V (*)	
Quantity used:	93
Crew:	One
Years of Service:	1943–1955
Span:	36' 10" (11.23 m)
Length:	32' 2" (9.80 m)
Height:	8' 2.25" (2.50 m)
Wing Area:	242 sq ft (22.48 m^2 **(Va)**
Engine:	*RR Merlin* 45, 45M, 46, 50, 50M, 55, 55M or 56, of 1,440hp. and 1,470hp.
Empty weight:	4,981 lb (2,259 kg) **(Va)**
Maximum take-off weight:	6,070 lb (2,753 kg) **(Va)**
Maximum speed:	at 20,000 ft 328 knots (593 km/h)
Service ceiling:	37,500 ft (11,430 m)
Armament:	8 machine guns with *Type A* wing **(Va)**, 4 machine guns and, 2 x 20 mm cannon, with *Type B* wing **(Vb)**, 8 machine guns or 4 machine guns plus 2 cannons or 4 cannons with *Type C* wing **(Vc)**
(*) Supermarine Spitfire Mk V, Va, Vb and Vc	

Supermarine Spitfire Mk Va, serial number 31, late '40s. Standard RAF Day Fighter Scheme. Received in January or February 1944 and supposed, without confirmation, of a "double identity case" as RL+P, this Spitfire Mk Va was one of the nineteen aircraft lost in accidents during the ten years period of the type service under Portuguese colours. As stated elsewhere in this book and contrary to what happened to the Hurricane fleet, apparently no serials of retired or destroyed aircraft were used in new airframes.

The Supermarine Spitfire serial number 31, MR+N being finally retrieved from its crash site. Although the date and place of this accident are unknown, the official records shown that aircraft s/n 31 was on active duty in March 1947 at Ota Air Base. (FAP/AHFA)

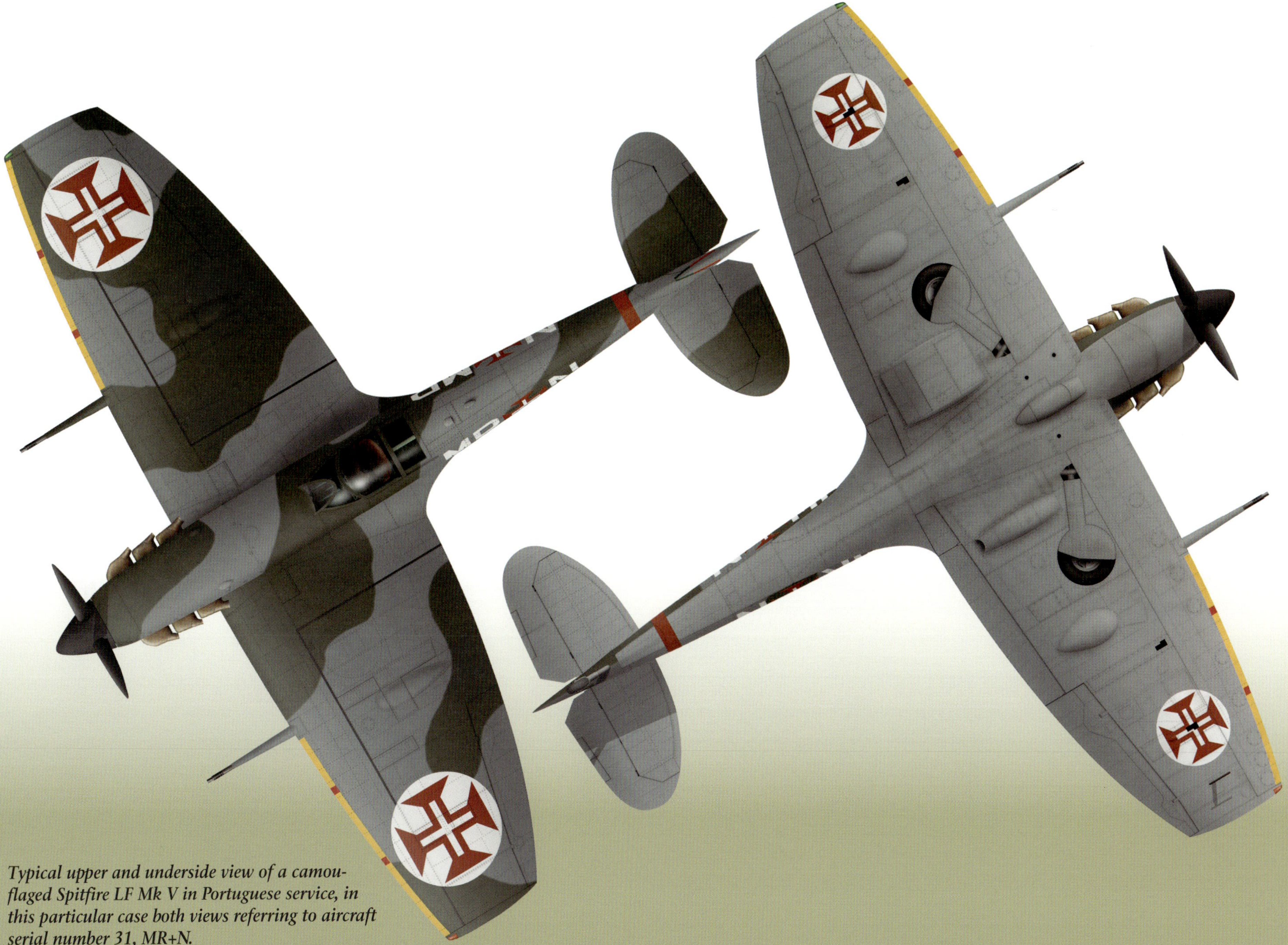

Typical upper and underside view of a camouflaged Spitfire LF Mk V in Portuguese service, in this particular case both views referring to aircraft serial number 31, MR+N.

Supermarine Spitfire Mk Va, serial number 92, 1947/1948. Standard RAF Day Fighter Scheme. The most plausible reason for the non-compliance of the colours of spinner and rear fuselage band with the Flight code (MR Flight should have those elements painted yellow) it is possible this particular aircraft was transferred from one Flight to another without the necessary changes. This aircraft was also equipped with eight Browning machine-guns.

Supermarine Spitfire Mk V serial 92, MR+L, after an accident, serving as a podium for a family photo. To an attentive observer, when comparing this photo with the one of another accident as shown elsewhere (Spit "31 / N+MR"), it is apparent that this aircraft (s/n 92) should not bear this code letter (L). The possible explanation for this fact is that the same aircraft was used by different flights. (FAP/AHFA)

Supermarine Spitfire LF Mk V, "clipped wing", serial number 81, December 1947. Standard RAF Day Fighter Scheme. Belonging to the last lot of aircraft received by the Arma de Aeronautica *between April 1947 and January 1948, this Spitfire LF Mk V shows to advantage the right correspondence of colours, red spinner and rear fuselage band, with the Flight code letters. Please notice the unpainted (natural metal) canopy frame.*

Supermarine Spitfire LF.V serial number 81, code letter ZE+K. (FAP/AHFA)

Supermarine Spitfire LF Mk V, "clipped wing", serial number 15, 1944. Standard RAF Day Fighter Scheme. Showing the RL Flight distinctive blue band around the rear fuselage and the same colour covering its spinner, this typical "clipped wing" Mk V does not differ from the British equivalent concerning the camouflage colours. Until very late during their service with the Aeronautica Militar, the Portuguese Spitfires maintained their original "RAF standard day fighter A scheme" colours, introduced in mid-May 1942.

Supermarine Spitfire LF Mk V Serial number 15, RL+O. This photo clearly shows all the elements of the Flight identification, spinner and rear fuselage band in blue. (FAP/AHFA)

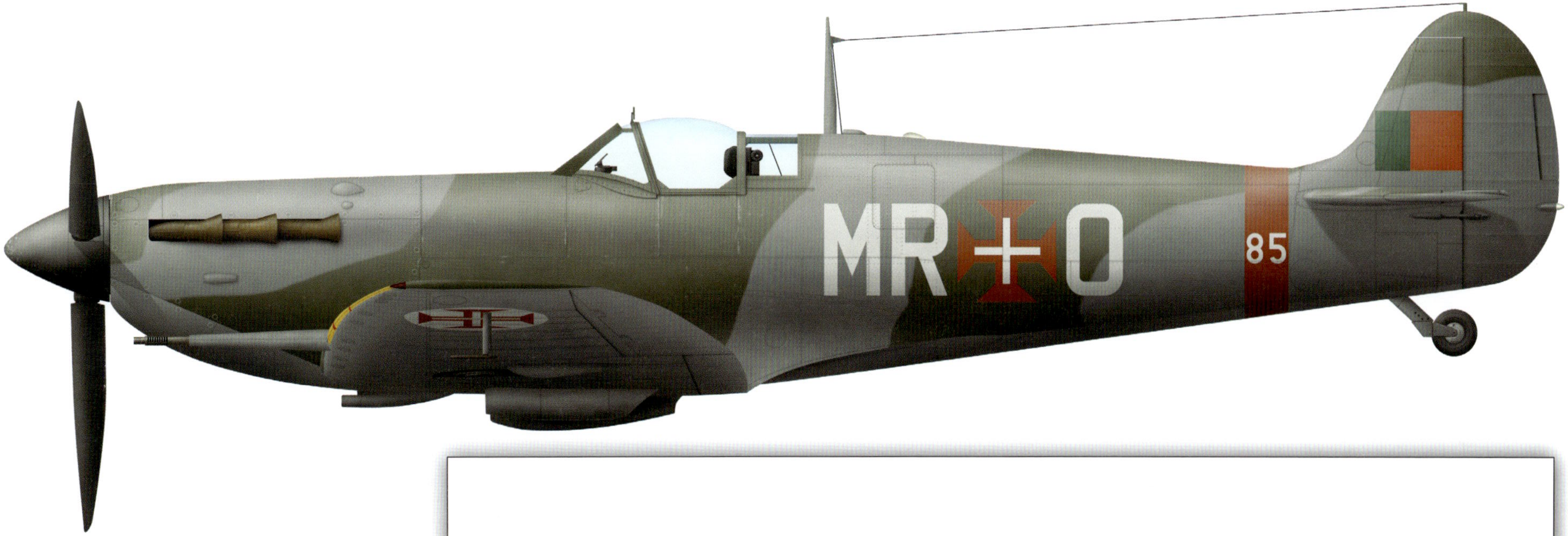

Supermarine Spitfire LF Mk V, "clipped wing", serial number "85", 1947. Standard RAF Day Fighter Scheme. As stated before, aircraft from MR Flight should display a yellow spinner and rear fuselage band. However a certain number of Spitfires exhibited coloured elements that were in complete disagreement with the established rules. See profile of Spitfire LF Mk. V, serial number "49".

Supermarine Spitfires Mk V, with some LF included, at the Ota Air Base, probably during October 1950. The leading aircraft bears the code letter MR+O and serial number 85. (Coll. MusAr)

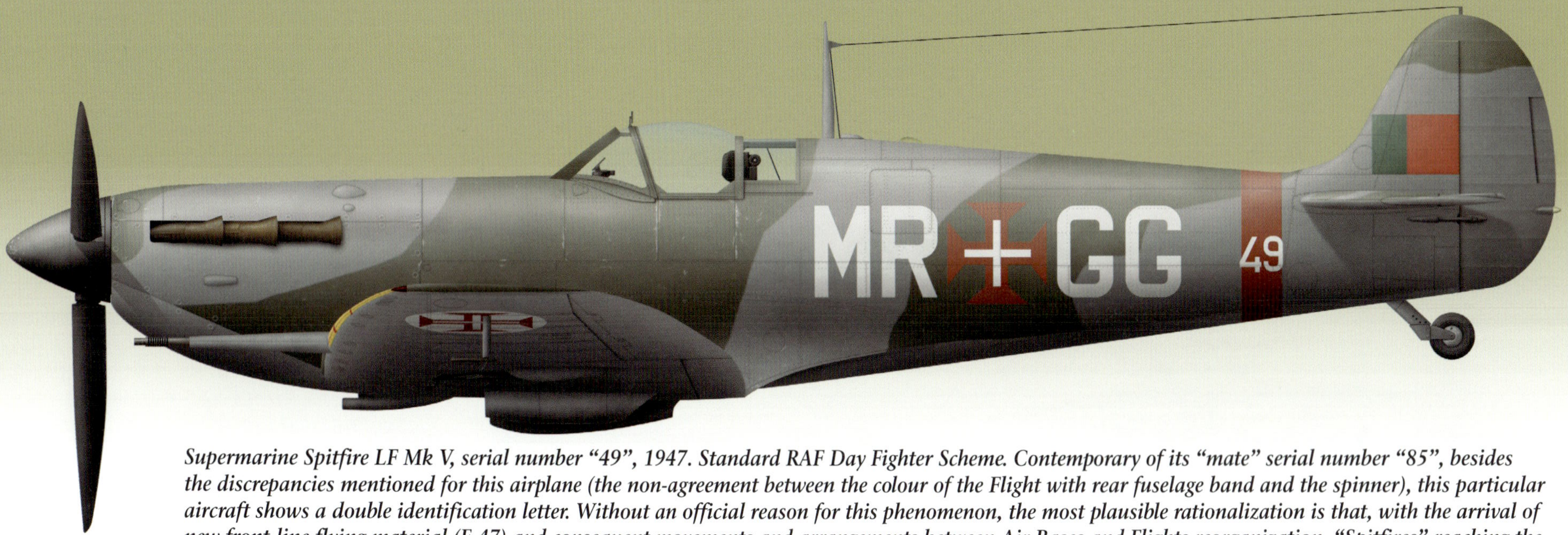

Supermarine Spitfire LF Mk V, serial number "49", 1947. Standard RAF Day Fighter Scheme. Contemporary of its "mate" serial number "85", besides the discrepancies mentioned for this airplane (the non-agreement between the colour of the Flight with rear fuselage band and the spinner), this particular aircraft shows a double identification letter. Without an official reason for this phenomenon, the most plausible rationalization is that, with the arrival of new front-line flying material (F-47) and consequent movements and arrangements between Air Bases and Flights reorganization, "Spitfires" reaching the end of their service life were gathered on the same Air Base (Tancos). The presence of such a large number of aircraft obliged, to a certain extent, the duplication of characters, creating another oddity in the Aeronautica Militar *identification system!*

Supermarine Spitfire LF Mk V, serial number "25", 1947. Standard RAF Day Fighter Scheme. A "veteran" bought by Portugal in January or February 1944 and previously coded "MR+J", Spitfire s/n 25 is an example of the necessity of giving a double identity letter during the movements and arrangements between Air Bases and Flights reorganization. As explained elsewhere, these movements and arrangements occurred in the prevision of the reception of a large quantity of new materials under the Mutual Defence Assistance Program.

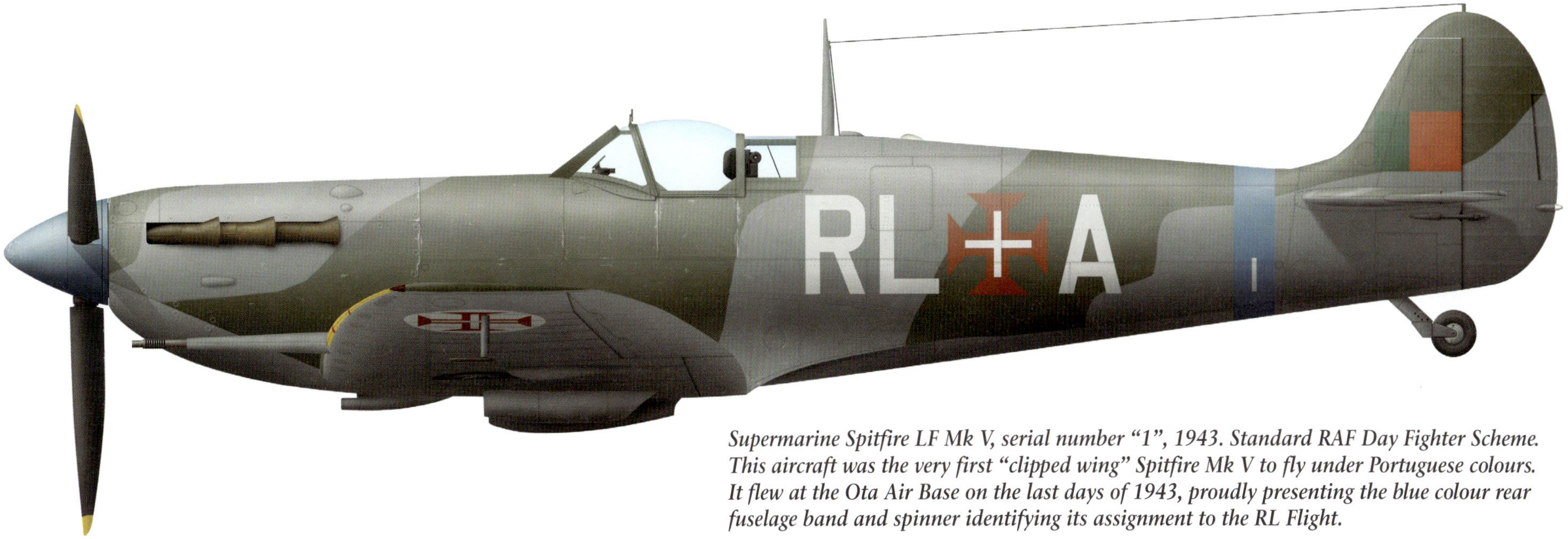

Supermarine Spitfire LF Mk V, serial number "1", 1943. Standard RAF Day Fighter Scheme. This aircraft was the very first "clipped wing" Spitfire Mk V to fly under Portuguese colours. It flew at the Ota Air Base on the last days of 1943, proudly presenting the blue colour rear fuselage band and spinner identifying its assignment to the RL Flight.

Supermarine Spitfire Mk V, serial number "2". Standard RAF Day Fighter Scheme. According to the established rules for the identification of the aircraft within the different Flights, this aircraft correctly displays the blue fuselage band and spinner identifying it as part of the RL Flight. Of notice in this aircraft is the different style of design used for the code letters identification. So much for standardisation...

Supermarine Spitfire LF Mk V, serial number "26", 1952. On the beginning of the '50s, with the merging of the Army and Navy Aviation in sight to form the future Força Aérea Portuguesa *that same year, the remaining "Spitfires" went throughout a cosmetic process to bring them to the new colours. This way, a small number of the remaining aircraft flew with an Olive Green upper and Light Grey under-surfaces colour scheme until their retirement in 1955 (last flight on 1st March). Unfortunately, and as with many other aircraft in service within the* Aeronautica Militar, *no Spitfire airframe survived to occupy its place of honour in a Museum today.*

Supermarine Spitfire V serial number 26 in the last "upper surface olive green over light grey undersurface" colour scheme used as described in the text. Of note is the absence of the under-wing National Insignia. (FAP/AHFA)

Supermarine Spitfire LF Mk Vb, RAF serial number "EP 785". Future serial number "75", code "ZE+E", this Spitfire Mk V shows the colour scheme of its arrival, displaying at the same time the Portuguese national colours and insignias and its original British serial number. For a very short period of time it flew in this configuration.

Enlargement of the photo showing the recently arrived Spitfires Mk V at the Ota Air Base, as mentioned before without fuselage markings and Portuguese serials, but with their ex-RAF serials still present. Looking carefully at the photo it is apparent that the second aircraft from the front row is equipped with a dH propeller. (FAP/AHFA)

Hawker Hurricane Mk IIB and Mk IIC

Background

The legendary Hawker Hurricane had its genesis in research carried on by Sir Sydney Camm stemming from his preceding design, the Fury. The latter aircraft had already represented a break in the usual concept of the fighter of the day, in being a fast-climbing interceptor. Camm began to develop a monoplane design to the same specification, initially to compare the benefits of the new layout with the biplane format, and then as research tool into high-speed flight with a view to a future fighter design, with the encouragement of the Air Ministry. As it developed, the design adopted retractable landing gear and an enclosed cockpit, while the initial choice for power fell on the steam-cooled Rolls-Royce (RR) Goshawk engine. Soon it became apparent that a better option would be the new Rolls Royce P.V.12 engine, later better known as the Merlin. As the design progressed, Camm also incorporated the new requirement for eight forward-firing machine-guns as set out in the conteporary specification F.5/34. Hawker Aircraft Limited received a contract to build one prototype, which would be completed during 1935 with the serial number K5083, and first flew on 6 November 1935. The prototype was powered by a Rolls Royce Merlin C engine of 1,025hp, driving a two-bladed wooden propeller and armed with eight Colt-Browning 0.3 in. machine guns, adapted to the British 0.303 calibre. It attained 270 mph (434 km/h) at sea level and 253 mph (407 km/hr) at 30 000 ft (9144 m), climbing to 20 000 ft (6096 m) in 12 min. The end of the biplane era was at hand.

Hawker Hurricanes from SU, TY and GL Flights at Tancos Air Base, date unknown but most probably 1944, the date on which these Flights started operating from this Air Base. Nearer to the camera are aircraft coded SU+O serial number 539, TY+I serial number 518, SU+P serial number 580. (FAP/AHFA)

Hurricane Mk I

Hurricanes in maintenance at Sintra Air Base. Note the id code letter "L" immediately below the spinner on the aircraft at the right. The green spinner with white spiral and the insignia of a peasant handling a cudgel identify this aircraft as belonging to the MP Flight, being the MP+L, based at the same airfield. The aircraft behind is coded MP+M. (FAP/AHFA)

In the face of the prototype's behaviour and performance, in June 1936 the Air Ministry ordered 600 aircraft and christened the new machine the 'Hurricane'. The first production variant, the Hurricane Mk I, made its maiden flight on 12 October 1937, and, within ten weeks the first operational Hurricane unit, 111 Squadron at Northolt, received its first aircraft. In the meantime a number of squadrons began also to exchange their Gauntlets and Gladiators for the new monoplanes. By the autumn of 1938 when the first Spitfires arrived at frontline RAF squadrons, six Hurricane squadrons were already operational.

This activity did not prevent the continuous development of the original design and by 1939 the Merlin III engine was adopted. This engine could accommodate the ROTOL constant-speed or de Havilland (DH) variable pitch 3-blade propellers. At the same time the wing was redesigned to introduce a metal stressed skin structure.

In the meantime Hawker was producing more aircraft than the RAF could absorb, and was therefore able to take advantage of export opportunities to countries that would oppose Germany in any war. Consequently, twelve Hurricane Mk Is were sold to Yugoslavia in 1938 followed by another twelve in 1940. A production licence was also granted to this country, with Hurricanes being manufactured there as from 1941, just before the German invasion.

Seven Hurricanes were also delivered to South Africa in November 1938, and an order for 12 more aircraft was put forward by Romania also this same year. Persia placed an order for 18 aircraft, and the Belgian Government bought 20 in 1939. In addition, the Belgian manufacturer Avions Fairey obtained a licence to produce 80 Hurricanes, having just started to equip its facilities to manufacture them, when Germany occupied Belgium. Poland received one Hurricane before being invaded by Germany and the fifteen examples requested by Turkey were only delivered after the start of the war.

Another important episode in the history of the Hurricane occurred at this time with the decision to build them in Canada. The Canadian Car and Foundry Co. Ltd built 1,451 examples between 1940 and 1942[1]. When war broke out there were already 497 Hurricanes equipping 13 RAF squadrons. The aircraft was employed in combat for the first time with the British Expeditionary force in France. Twelve Hurricanes were also sent to Finland in January and February 1940. In June, Hurricanes were employed in the Norway campaign, flying from frozen lakes. The Hurricane Mk

1 Some of these airframes were later to be delivered to Portugal.

I's finest hour, though, was the Battle of Britain from July 1940, when 527 Hurricanes and 321 Spitfires faced nearly 2,700 German aircraft. In other theatres, such as North Africa and resistance to the Italian and German invasion of Greece, Hurricanes also showed their value.

Hurricane Mk II

Hawker meanwhile continued the development and the improvement of their basic design. This would lead to the installation of the new Merlin XX engine, which initially delivered 1,185 bhp, with later models seeing their power increased to 1,280 bhp. The change of power unit require only minor modification to the general design.

The new version, named Hurricane Mk II, was divided into subvariants, and then into series, when developments in armament were brought forward. The first of these was identified as the Mk IIA Series 1, which retained the initial armament of eight machine-guns, while the Series 2 received modifications to accommodate new wings with a different armament arrangement. Early in 1941, additional Colt-Browning machine-guns were added, increasing its firepower first to 10 and then to 12 rifle-calibre machine guns and 6,000 rounds of ammunition. From this modification, the aircraft was now named Hurricane Mk IIB. (The Mk IIB could also receive a bomb rack under each wing to carry a 250 lb or 500 lb bomb on each).

The next variant addressed the increasing inadequacy of the 0.303 in. ammunition against ever more heavily armoured targets. By the end of 1940, 20 mm Oerlikon or Hispano cannon had been mounted and tested in a number of Hurricanes, resulting in a new model, the Hurricane Mk IIC, equipped with four Hispano 20 mm cannon, entering service in Spring, 1941. At the same time 44 gallon under wing drop tanks became available. The next important variant of the Hurricane, the Mk IID, was armed with a pair of Rolls-Royce BF or Vickers 'S' 40 mm anti-tank guns under the wings, retaining two 0.303 in. machine-guns firing tracer ammunition for aiming. This variant flew for the first time on 18 September 1941, the majority of this model being shipped to the Middle and Far East in 1942, being used for the first time in North Africa in May 1942.

Other variants

The next variant to be developed was initially to be known as the Mk IIE before being redesignated Hurricane Mk IV. It featured a 'universal' wing that allowed the mounting of Mk IIB, IIC or IID armament (including bombs and rockets), and a Merlin 24 or 27 engine developing 1,620 hp. A characteristic of this model was a deepened radiator with additional armour protection. The Mk IV was used both at home and abroad as from 1942.

Hawker Hurricanes code SU+S and GL+D serve as background for this typical airfield activity in preparation for a flight. (FAP/AHFA)

Hawker Hurricane Mk IIc, code SU+O serial number 539 from Tancos Air Base, 1944. On this enlargement of a previous photo the most notable elements are the underwing fuel tanks equipping this aircraft, most likely in preparation for a long distance flight. Behind, Hurricane code TY+I, s/n 518 is discernible. (FAP/AHFA)

The Hurricane Mk V was the last variant developed in the UK and was equipped with a Merlin 32 engine, boosted in order to develop 1,700 hp at sea level. This version never went into production or squadron service.

Canada was to play an important role in the production of the Hurricane, initially with forty aircraft being assembled from Mark I components shipped from the UK, before the full production of a specific indigenous model, the Hurricane Mk X, would follow. Using the 1,300 hp Packard-built Merlin 28 engine, production of this model would reach a figure of 489 aircraft.

The Canadian Mk XI model, with IIB or IIC, wings came next on the production line, followed closely by the Mk XII and Sea-Hurricane Mk IIA[2], both equipped with 1,300 hp Packard Merlin 29 engines.

Hurricanes flew all over the world and fought on all fronts. When the North Africa campaign ended in 1943, there were 20 RAF Squadrons equipped with the Hurricane. Hurricanes were also used in the Far East and equipped seven squadrons of the Indian Air Force. Another important theatre of operation where Hurricanes were used was the Russian Front, with 2,952 Hurricanes being supplied to the Soviet Union. Turkey received fourteen Hurricane Mk IICs, while the Netherlands

2 The naval variant was also divided into several sub-variants, i.e., Sea Hurricane Mk IA, Sea Hurricane Mk IIA, Sea Hurricane Mk IB, Sea Hurricane Mk IC, 'Hooked Hurricane' Mk II, Sea Hurricane Mk II, and Sea Hurricane Mk XIIA.

Hawker Hurricane Mk IIC from Flight MP, showing the Flight insignia on the left side of the front fuselage, a peasant with the motto "Antes quebrar que torcer"*. See Camouflage and Markings paragraph for the description of this insignia. (FAP/AHFA)*

View of Hawker Hurricane Mk IIC s/n 517 code MP+A. This profile photo clearly shows the positioning and design of all the identifying elements used on the Portuguese Hurricanes. (FAP/AHFA)

East Indies, South Africa, Persia, Greece, France, Egypt, Eire and Iraq and Australia were also recipients to a greater or lesser degree. In July 1944 the production of the Hawker Hurricane ceased after a grand total of 14,533 had been built. Today, around 13 Hurricanes exist in the World in flying condition, and 21 others are on permanent static display.

Hurricane in Portuguese service

Portugal struggled to maintain its neutrality during World War II due to the strategic position of both the mainland and, to an even greater degree, its island territories of Madeira and the Azores, which were attractive to both sides. The Portuguese Government saw an opportunity along with the threat, that would allow the country to re-equip its armed forces to attempt to resist any invasion. To do so, Portugal did not hesitate to invoke its secular defence alliance, signed in the 14th century with the United Kingdom, a treaty still in strength today[3].

3 The Anglo-Portuguese Alliance, or Aliança Luso-Britânica, ratified at the Treaty of Windsor in 1386, is the oldest alliance in the world still in force today, with its roots in the even older treaty of 1373. Today, with

Hawker Hurricanes at Ota Air Base parade, May 1944. The first aircraft is a Canadian Hurricane Mk XII coded TY+B, serial number 511. (FAP/AHFA)

The complete Flight VX at Espinho Airfield. The Flight insignia, a goggled fighting mosquito, is visible on the left side of the front fuselage and is fully described in the Camouflage and Markings paragraph. (FAP/AHFA)

Many of the belligerents involved in the war, including the US, UK and Germany, considered invading the islands, but finally the United Kingdom decided to ask officially for use of facilities in the Azores, instead of an invasion and forced occupation with unpredictable consequences. Within the term facilities were included airfields and sea ports able to be used in the war effort, and, in particular, the Battle of the Atlantic, then being fought against Axis submarines raiding in the Northern Atlantic area.

After lengthy negotiations, it was agreed in August 1943 that, among other items, modern fighter aircraft would be supplied for the defence of the Portuguese territories, in sufficient number to equip six day fighter squadrons with 10+5 airplanes each, i.e., a total of 90 aircraft minimum.

One of the points of the agreement was that a small number of aircraft would be supplied immediately and ferried by air. This took the shape of a secret operation with the code name *Mildew*. On 6 August 1943, six Hurricane Mk IICs were flown from North Africa via Gibraltar, overflying Lisbon at 1100 before landing at Alverca. The RAF pilots wore civilian clothes and were to remain in Portugal, as instructors of the future Portuguese pilots. According to one witness to the arrival, the aeroplanes already wore the *Cruz de Cristo* on the fuselage, but no Portuguese flag on the fin, and the RAF serials were still showing. Confirming the identification of these first aircraft received is not easy. The records available from Ota Air Base flight logs identify them only by the last three digits of their RAF serial, which are recorded as 354, 358, 459, 488, 840 and 964.

From the end of August until December that same year a further 73 Hurricanes would be received by sea. The type and complete serials of these aircraft are recorded in official documents and their identities are shown in the list at the end of this chapter. However, two partial serial numbers found in the pilots' logbooks do not correspond to the aircraft recorded as being delivered by sea. These aircraft were given the serial numbers 499 and 599 and both were recorded as being flown to Ota Air Base in September 1943. This suggests that at least two more aircraft were received in 1943, leading to a total of 81 Hurricanes received before the end of the year. The aircraft were distributed across several shipments, with the 18 aircraft received from September to December to replace aircraft lost during the instruction period or on operations.

Deployment of the new aircraft

The British pilots stayed in Portugal until the end of August 1943, and the first Flight was formed at Ota with the six aircraft flown in, plus another 12 received by sea. This first Flight, in accordance with the practice started with the Airacobras, received the code letters 'VX' and was

both nations being members of N.A.T.O., the E.U. and U.N., relations between them are largely coordinated through those organisations rather than by the provisions of the treaties forming the Alliance.

A line up of Hawker Hurricanes, probably from Flight MP, at Sintra Air Base. The second aircraft on the row is Hawker Hurricane Mk IIC, serial 600, code MP+R, with the curiosity of being the very first of the serial number block. (FAP/AHFA)

designated *1ª Esquadrilha* (1st Flight)[4]. The 'VX' Flight was equipped with the Hurricane Mk IIC. Three other *Esquadrilhas* (Flights) began their formation at this time, in order to have two Flights equipped with the Hurricane Mk IIB and two with the Hurricane Mk IIC.

At the end of October a 'flag flying' demonstration took place, and the three Hurricane Flights then based at Ota ('TY', 'VX' and 'SU') flew overhead during Army manoeuvres near Pegões, 46 km East of Lisbon, in which 40,000 troops were involved. The table below shows the initial distribution of aircraft by Base and Flight:

Aeronautica Militar Hurricane Flights					
Flight Code	A/c Model	Air Base (*)	Quantity	A.M. Serial Number	Flight Colour i/d Spinner and Rear Fuselage Band
TY+... As from 22/01/44 (**)	Hurricane Mk IIC	Air Base 2 Ota	15 A/c	510 to 524	*TY – Red*
SU+... As from 15/02/44 (**)	Hurricane Mk IIC	Air Base 2 Ota	20 A/c	525 to 539 579 to 581 585 and 586	SU – White
RV+...	Hurricane Mk IIB	Air Base 1 Sintra	22 A/c	555 to 576	RV – Yellow
VX+... As from 21/12/43	Hurricane Mk IIC	Air Base 2 Ota	18 A/c	540 to 554 582, 583 and 584	VX – Green
GL+... As from January 1944(***)	Hurricane Mk IIC	Air Base 2 Ota	18 A/c	607 to 615 and. others	GL – Blue
MP+...	Hurricane Mk IIB and Mk IIC	Air Base 1 Sintra	?	Not in Blocks	MP – Spinner: Dark green only or green with white spiral.

(*) – Initial deployment Base
(**) – Date of Air Base *Ordem de Serviço* (Service Order)
(***) – Date of the shipment arrival

4 Officially, 'VX' flight was formed on 21 December 1943, by Service Order no.355 of Ota Air Base, which assigned serials from 540 to the 18 aircraft of the Flight (see table). The code letters A to P were also applied (VX+A to VX+P).

Hawker Hurricane Mk IIC Trop., s/n 633, code MP+C on Sintra runway. Despite the poor quality of the photo, the exhaust anti-dazzle guard is visible, denoting an aircraft with equipment for night-fighting. (FAP/AHFA)

The reorganization of 1944

At the beginning of 1944 a further 18 Hurricanes were delivered by sea. With the volume of materiel arriving almost simultaneously (99 Hurricanes, and a large number of Spitfires delivered more or less at same time), the Ota Base, despite being new and with large facilities, was overcrowded, so in May 1944, Hurricane Flights 'SU', 'TY' and 'GL' were sent to Tancos, with the Spitfire Flights staying at Ota. The other two Hurricane flights, 'VX' and 'RV', were also re-located, the former being sent to Lisbon on 1 May 1944, where it become the *Esquadrilha Independente de Aviação de Caça nº1*, or E.I.A.C.1 (Independent Fighter Flight no.1), its primary task being the defence of the capital. The last flight ('RV') relocated to Espinho, a small town South of Oporto, becoming *Esquadrilha Independente de Aviação de Caça nº2* (E.I.A.C.2), to provide air defence to the second largest city, Oporto. However the relocation of E.I.A.C.2 would take effect only from 1 March of 1945, when *Capitão* Duarte Silva presented himself at Espinho to command the Flight. (The Flight designations, E.I.A.C.1 and E.I.A.C.2, were officially created on 1 March 1945).

On 6 May 1944, a big exhibition of the newly acquired equipment of the *Arma de Aeronáutica* was held at Ota Air Base with a flypast of a large number of aircraft, including 'VX' Flight in the formation, and 'TY' Flight in the static display. The total number of aircraft presented on that occasion approached 200.

Interestingly, in August/September 1944, 18 Hurricanes flying at Tancos were still carrying their ex-RAF original serials, in the range LE***, as recorded in the Air Base flight logs.

Missions and employment

It was the intention of the *Arma de Aeronautica* to employ the Hurricane in a range of roles, including air superiority and bomber interception up to 6-7,000 meters, army support including bombing of land targets, and reconnaissance. The nominal strength of a Hurricane Flight was 18 aircraft, consisting of 12 operational aircraft plus six in maintenance or reserve, with the operational aircraft divided into three sections of four. The training in the various fields of operations started as soon as the first Flights were formed.

Training sorties frequently included large quantities of aircraft, as the Hurricanes joined with other fighter aircraft such as Spitfires and Airacobras. For example, over 24-28 October 1943, three Flights of Hurricanes, one Flight of Spitfires and one Flight of Airacobras were involved in support

Canadian-built Hawker Hurricane Mk XII serial number 511, code MP+N on the Sintra Air Base runway. This photo, as the previous one, is a partial enlargement of photo 0122 that shows both aircraft rolling together for take off. (FAP/AHFA)

operations to Army manoeuvres at Pegões, as mentioned above. At the same time they took the opportunity to 'fly the flag', passing over the city of Lisbon on 28 October in formation, impressing the inhabitants with the display of aerial power[5]. The availability of fuel and spare parts in the appropriate quantities allied to the eagerness of the pilots to fly the modern aircraft denied them until recently made such displays practicable for the first time.

By the summer of 1944, the night flying instruction started at Tancos, using three old Avro 626 biplane trainers. The initial stages of the training included take-offs and landings only, followed by more complex operations of night flight. During these primary exercises, an accident during the night of 17 October led to the destruction of two Avros, nos. 181 and 162, when the former aircraft, losing all electrical power, landed on top of the second Avro, while both were performing 'touch and go' landings on a moonless night.

This night instruction led to the certification of a number of Hurricanes for night flying, resulting, as in their British counterparts, in the installation of small metal shields on the fuselage, below and in front of the pilot, with the purpose of hiding the glare of the engine exhausts. This particular fixture is recognisable in several photographs and, to a degree, allows the identification of the aeroplanes as being certified for night fighting use, as it is visible in the photo of aircraft 624.

An interesting incident occurred on 3 May 1944 that justified the need for a nocturnal air fighting capability for the *Aeronautica Militar*. The interception of a German Junkers Ju 88H-1, the long-range reconnaissance version of the twin-engine combat aircraft, could not be found in Portuguese records but was related by one of the German officers that were directly involved.

On the late afternoon of 3 May, Ju 88 H-1 4U+AL of the 3rd Squadron of *Aufklarungsgeschwader 123* took off from the French airfield of Rennes, flew over the Bay of Biscay, then along the northern coast of Spain and the western coast of Portugal, to arrive over the Tagus estuary and a well-lit Lisbon as night was beginning to fall. The Ju 88 was then intercepted and chased by two fighters, and obliged to turn back over the sea. However the Ju 88 was eventually able to draw away from

5 The *Arma de Aeronautica* had never so many aircraft at its service as in 1943–44. The overflying of a large town or a small village, by a large number of airplanes was a rare event, especially in the days of global conflict.

Hawker Hurricane Mk IIC serial number 624 from the MP Flight, depicting its green spinner decorated with a white spiral. Note the damage to the tip of the starboard wing. (FAP/AHFA)

Hawker Hurricane Mk IIC, serial number 646 from Sintra Air Base MP Flight. The outer wing leading edge yellow painted strip can be clearly discerned as well as the exhaust anti-dazzle guard. As is well known, this simple device was usually installed on aircraft equipped for night-fighting, although the Aeronautica Militar *did not had a Flight exclusively dedicated to this mission. (FAP/AHFA)*

the fighters and finally left them behind. This event described in a book[6] published in 2006 by one of the German crewmembers, is the only encounter of German aircraft with Portuguese fighters during WWII in Europe known to the authors. The two fighters were probably Hurricanes from the Lisbon Flight. The German aircraft was able to return to Rennes where it landed at 01:41 on 4 May after flying 8 hrs and 20 minutes, covering 3,000 km. According to the author of the aforementioned book, this was also the first operational long range test flight of the Ju 88H-1.

Portuguese Hurricane pilots generally appreciated the aircraft and specifically features such as the high ceiling that allowed flight over the country at 10,000 m (33,990 ft), provoking the first vapour trails ever seen in Portugal's skies! Also, for the first time, they had modern fighter aircraft able to face any enemy on relatively equal terms. Even so, with the exception of the Ju 88 interception mentioned above, no other such encounters are known to have taken place.

6 The Easter Bunnies – Roman Gastager and Wendy von Well, 2006, Trafford Publishing. This event is also mentioned in Junkers Aircraft and Engines 1913-1945 by Anthony Kay-Putnam.

Hawker Hurricane Mk IIC serial number 517 of the MP Flight from the Sintra Air Base. (FAP/AHFA)

By the end of 1949, Hurricanes performed a number of long distance flights with the help of external long-range tanks, in missions destined to test the limit of the radius of action of the aircraft, check the navigational capabilities of the pilots and to prove the usefulness of several 'emergency airfields' dispersed around Portuguese territory. One such example was a flight concluded by four aircraft from the Tancos Air Base to Gibraltar, where they landed after 3 hrs 45 mins of flying time.

Additional deliveries, the serials used and the questions raised

To complete its fighter force, in 1945 Portugal ordered 45 additional Hurricane Mk IICs, that were delivered by air between April and December 1947, together with spare parts obtained from the dismantling of fifty other aeroplanes[7]. The Hurricane was, in this way, to become the aircraft used in largest numbers by the *Aeronáutica Militar Portuguesa* within the examined timeframe, reaching a grand total of 142 or 144 units, depending on the source consulted.

The newly arrived aircraft, which started reaching Tancos Air Base by 24 April, received serial numbers from 618 onwards, continuing the numbering sequence initiated previously, to reach the final serial of 652. There is, however, a gap between the 5** and 6** blocks of serial numbers. The first Hurricanes received were included on the 5** block, started their numbering sequence at 510

7 An interesting detail concerning the 1947 deliveries is that, among the aircraft received by the A.M. were four, LF422, PG538, PG543 and PG538, all Mk IIC, on which tests of tropical equipment and filters were conducted in November 1946-January 1947 in England before handover.

Hurricanes 633 MP+C and 511 MP+N of MP Flight. (FAP/AHFA)

The "peasant" insignia of the MP Flight is clearly seen here superimposed on a Hawker Hurricane Mk IIC. Date and location unknown as well as the identity of the pilot. (FAP/ AHFA)

and running to 588, representing 79 aircraft. The subsequent aircraft purchased were allocated serials starting with 600 and running up to 652 (according to official records), giving a total of 53 aircraft. Adding the total of both groups of airframes, they consequently present a grand total of 132 units.

It is well documented and registered that, between 1943 and December 1947, a total of 144 Hurricanes had been delivered to Portugal, mostly Mk IIB and IIC models but also other marks of Canadian origin. This total figures includes two 'extra' airframes that are not incorporated in the records, the origin of which has until now represented a mystery. Continuing the accounting and comparing the two figures reveals a difference of twelve aircraft, suggesting that older serials, in the 5** range and belonging to struck-off aircraft, were re-used in airframes delivered later, the most obvious example being aircraft no. 517. In fact, the existence of a photo showing a Hurricane Mk IIB and a Hurricane Mk IIC, with different codes but both with the serial 517 leads to this conclusion.

This explanation, however, has no basis in any concrete documentary evidence, though is is plausible given the considerable precedent of reusing serial numbers from destroyed or retired aircraft within the A.M. In fact, an identical phenomenon is observable in the Avro 626 and Tiger Moth fleets of the *Arma*, which complicates research and individual aircraft identification. Furthermore, the Hurricane fleet used also special identification or temporary serial numbers, demonstrated by 18 aircraft from Tancos Air Base in support of the 15-22 October 1945 Army manoeuvres, with ground attack, visual reconnaissance and bombing activities. To these aircraft were applied individual serial numbers 2-7, 10, 11 and 13-18. A photograph exists showing Hurricane 'GL-O'/ 614 displaying a small white 17 painted on the rudder.

The accidents / incidents

Up to 1947, 15 accidents were recorded with Hurricanes that led to the total loss of the aircraft. At least one of the aircraft belonging to the Espinho Flight was lost over the sea. From 1948 until their retirement another 21 accidents were registered, raising the total number of accidents to 36 during the operational life of the aircraft, with the loss of 13 pilots and 26 airframes.

New reorganization

On 1 January of 1947 the *Grupo Independente de Aviação de Caça* (Independent Fighter Group) was formed in Espinho from the amalgamation of 'RV' and 'VX' Flights, the latter from Lisbon. The Group was to stay at the Espinho Base until the end of 1951 when, in November and December that year, their aeroplanes were transferred to Tancos and Sintra Air Bases.

Flight line of Hawker Hurricanes belonging to the VX Flight. Even though the location and date are unconfirmed, it is believed that this photo was taken at the Espinho Airfield, home base of the Flight. (FAP/AHFA)

The last unit to fly Hurricanes was the 'MP' Flight formed at Sintra in 1947 with twelve aircraft, three coming from the Espinho 'RV' Flight and nine from Tancos, Flights 'TY' and 'SU'. Later this number would be increased, but the overall number is unclear. To this new Flight was assigned the mission of advanced operational training for pilots that would be later posted to other Hurricane Flights.

From 1947, the use of a Flight emblem painted on the left side of the aircraft, with 'RV', 'VX' and 'MP' Flights having their own individual emblems on a circular background (see Camouflage and Markings below).

The flight to England in 1951

A relatively well known event connected to the Hurricane service in Portugal was the flight of five aeroplanes from Espinho to Kenley in England, where they were used in the filming of 'Angels One Five', a film with a plot centred around the Battle of Britain. The invitation for this trip came

Line up of the Hawker Hurricanes equipped with long-range tanks that were sent to England for the filming of "Angels One Five". For an account of this mission, refer to the text. (Coll. Machado de Barros)

Hawker Hurricane Mk IIC of VX Flight showing to advantage the respective Flight insignia, the description and meaning of which can be found under the Camouflage and Markings paragraph. (FAP/AHFA)

directly from the British government, not only for filming reasons but also "to promote the good relations between the military aviation of both countries".

To this effect two aircraft from the 'VX' Flight, 544 'VX-E' and 554 'VX-O', and three from the 'MP' Flight, 601 'MP-S', 624 'MP-B' and 600 'MP-?' were used, all being Hurricane Mk IIC aircraft. To complete the two-way trip, long-range under wing tanks had to be used. When the aircraft arrived at the filming location, cannons and long-range tanks were removed in order to make them resemble, as closely as possible, Hurricane Mk I aircraft of the Battle of Britain era. The Hurricanes left Espinho on the 13 of July 1951, accompanied by an Avro Anson as a support airplane, with stops at Logroño, Spain, and Bordeaux, France, arriving at Tangmere three days later. The filming sequences took place from the 20 to 27 of July. (Some sources stated that the shots including the Portuguese aircraft were not used in the final version of the film, because the director, George More O'Ferrall, did not like them!) On the return leg and after stopping at Tours, Bordeaux, Logroño and Salamanca they were back in Espinho on 17 August.

The last days – 1952 to 1954

By December 1950 at Tancos, Flights of seven aircraft from the 5** block serial number range were recorded, as well as eleven Hurricanes belonging to the 6** range. There were however many aircraft out of service, under, or awaiting, repair, both in Tancos and Sintra Bases.

With the official creation of the *Força Aérea Portuguesa* in July 1952, the Hurricanes were distributed between Tancos and Sintra, with the last three aircraft still at Espinho leaving for Sintra on 2 December 1952. In 1954 there were 23 Hurricanes still recorded at Sintra. The end of their career came in August that year with an order to stop any repair on the Hurricanes and Spitfires still extant. It seems that the last flight of a Portuguese Hurricane took place in June 1954 at Sintra, by Hurricane Mk IIC 614. Finally, on 31 August 1954 came the final order: all Hurricanes were to be scrapped. Unfortunately, none were preserved.

Individual Aircraft Histories					
RAF Serial	Type	Date Arrival	A.M. Serial	Struck Of Charge	Codes & Remarks
JS 367	Canadian Mk XII	8/43	510		TY+A
JS 386	Canadian Mk XII	8/43	511		TY+B, MP+N, 511+B

Hawker Hurricane Mk IIC serial number 534 code MP+G, at unidentified location. (FAP/AHFA)

JS 400	Canadian Mk XII	8/43	512		TY+C
JS 308	Canadian Mk XII	8/43	513		TY+D
1360 (?)	??	8/43	514		TY+E
AM 294	Canadian Mk X	8/43	515		TY+F. Modified before del. to IIB or IIC
HV 879	Mk IIC	8/43	516		TY+G
JS 385	IIB. IIC	8/43	517		TY+H. This serial was apparently used by two different aircraft (see text). Code MP+A also used.
JS 390	Canadian Mk XII	8/43	518		TY+I
Z 3892	Mk II	8/43	519	22/4/44	TY+J
JS 347	Canadian Mk XII	8/43	520		TY+K
BX 128	Canadian Mk XIB	8/43	521		TY+L
HW 565	Mk II	8/43	522		TY+M
BE 668	Mk II	8/43	523		TY+N

Another Hawker Hurricane of the VX Flight at an unknown location, but probably Lisbon Airport. (FAP/AHFA)

Hawker Hurricane Mk IIC serial number 624 code MP+B. Oddly, this aircraft bears the VX Flight insignia below the exhaust stubs, the sole explanation for this being urgency to complete the MP flight. (FAP/AHFA)

JS 387	Canadian. Mk XII	8/43	524		TY+O
??'??	Mk IIC		525	4/11/46	SU+A Destroyed in accident 27/5/46
??'??	Mk IIC		526		SU+B
??'??	Mk II		527		SU+C
??'??	Mk II		528		SU+D
??'??	Mk II		529		SU+E
??'??	Mk II		530		SU+F
??'??	Mk II		531		SU+G Forced landing 14/9/48
??'??	Mk II		532		SU+H Accident 20/5/48. Retired
??'??	Mk II		533		SU-I
??'??	Mk II		534		SU+J later MP+G
??'??	Mk II		535		SU-K
??'??	Mk II		536		SU-L
??'??	Mk II		537		SU-M later VX – (?)
??'??	Mk II		538		SU+N
??'??	Mk II		539		SU+O
??'??	Mk II		540		VX+A Accident 17/6/47. Repaired?
??'??	Mk II		541		VX+B Destroyed accident 1/4/49
??'??	Mk II		542		VX+C
??'??	Mk II		543		VX+D Crashed in River Lima 18/9/50

Hawker Hurricane Mk IIC. This interesting photo shows to advantage details such as the cannon recoil springs, bomb racks, landing light, boarding footstep and part of undercarriage, as well as the colour delimitation on the wing leading edges. (MAIS ALTO, Coll F. Costa Cabral)

?????	Mk II		544		VX+E
?????	Mk II		545		VX+F Destroyed accident 10/3/50
?????	Mk II		546		VX+G Accident in 1/5/50 in Spain. Repaired. Destroyed in accident (crashed on 622 in flight 30/8/51)
?????	Mk II		547		VX+H
?????	Mk II		548		VX+I
?????	Mk II		549		VX+J
?????	Mk II		550		VX+K Destroyed in accident 27/6/45.
?????	Mk II		551		VX+L
?????	Mk II		552		VX+M
?????	Mk II		553		VX+N
?????	Mk II		554		VX+O
?????	Mk II		555		RV+A
?????	Mk II		556		RV+B Destroyed in accident 4/10/51
?????	Mk II		557		RV+C
?????	Mk II		558		RV+D Destroyed in accident 24/10/46
?????	Mk II		559		RV+E
?????	Mk II		560		RV+F Destroyed in accident 16/2/50
?????	Mk II		561		RV+G
?????	Mk II		562		RV+H
?????	Mk II		563		RV+I Destroyed accident 2/5/44
?????	Mk II		564		RV+J
?????	Mk II		565		RV+K
?????	Mk II		566		RV+L Destroyed in accident 5/2/52
?????	Mk II		567		RV+M
?????	Mk II		568		RV+N Destroyed in accident 14/4/50
?????	Mk II		569		RV+O
?????	Mk II		570		RV+P
?????	Mk II		571		RV+Q
?????	Mk II		572	8/4/46	RV+R Destroyed in accident 14/2/46
?????	Mk II		573		RV+S
?????	Mk II		574		RV+T
AM 289	Canadian. Mk X		575		RV+U
Z 3426	Mk II		576		RV+X
?????	Mk II		577		??+?
?????	Mk II		578		SU+P Destroyed accident 23/11/44
?????	Mk II		579		SU+Q
?????	Mk II		580		SU+R Later 580+D
?????	Mk II		581		SU+S
?????	Mk II		582		VX+P
?????	Mk II		583		VX+Q
?????	Mk II		584		VX+R Destroyed accident 6/7/48
?????	Mk II		585	4/11/47	SU+T
?????	Mk II		586		SU+U
?????	Mk II		587		
?????	Mk II		588		
?????	Mk II		600		MP+...
?????	Mk II		601		MP+S
?????	Mk II		602		??+?
?????	Mk II		603		??+?

?????	Mk II		604		??+?
?????	Mk II		605		??+?
?????	Mk II		606		??+?
?????	Mk II		607		GL+?
?????	Mk II		608		GL+I
?????	Mk II		609		GL+J
?????	Mk II		610		GL+K
?????	Mk II		611		GL+L
?????	Mk II		612		GL+M 612+F,612. (see photos)
?????	Mk II		613		GL+N
?????	Mk II		614		GL+O
?????	Mk II		615		GL+P
?????	Mk II		616		??+?
?????	Mk II		617		??+?
LF 342	Mk IIB Trop	4/47	618		??+?
LF 360	Mk IIC Trop	4/47	619		??+?
LF 422	Mk IIC Trop	4/47	620		??+?
LF 699	Mk IIC Trop	4/47	621		??+?
PG 533	Mk II	4/47	622	29/10/51	TY+T destroyed in accident (crashed on 546 in flight 30/8/51)
PG 543	Mk IIC Trop	4/47	623		??+?
PZ 759	Mk IIC Trop	4/47	624		MP+B
LF 425	Mk IIC Trop	5/47	625		??+?
LF 428	Mk II	5/47	626		??+?
LF 514	Mk IIC Trop	5/47	627		??+?
LF 564	Mk IIC Trop	5/47	628		??+?
LF 565	Mk IIC Trop	5/47	629		SU+E
LF 568	Mk IIC	5/47	630		??+?
LF 570	Mk IIC Trop	5/47	631		??+?
LF 586	Mk IIC Trop	5/47	632		??+?
PG 599	Mk IIC Trop	5/47	633		MP+C
LF 706	Mk II	5/47	634		By 1949/50 was SU+B
LF 717	Mk IIC Trop	5/47	635		By 1949/50 was SU+H
PG 521	Mk IIC Trop	5/47	636		By 1949/50 was SU+M
PG 538	Mk IIC Trop	4/47	637		??+?
PZ 735	Mk IIC Trop	5/47	638		??+? This Hurricane belonged to the last production batch PZ730 to 865, like A.M. serials, 639, 640, 643 and 644. By 1949/50 was SU+R
PZ 738	Mk IIC Trop	5/47	639		??+?
PZ 745	Mk IIC Trop	5/47	640		??+?
LD 439	Mk IIC	7/47	641		??+?
MW 373	Mk IIC	6/47	642		??+?
PZ 742	Mk IIC	7/47	643		??+?
PZ 767	Mk IIC	6/47	644		??+?
BE 371	Mk IIC	7/47	645		MP+F
LF 620	Mk IIC Trop	7/47	646		MP+G
LF 757	Mk IIC Trop	7/47	647		??+?
LF 772	Mk IIC Trop	7/47	648		??+?
LF 133	Mk IIC Trop	8/47	649		??+?
LF 383	Mk IIC Trop	4/47	650		??+?

LF 530	Mk IIC	9/47	651		??+?
?????	Mk II		652		??+?

Notes:

1 – The ex-RAF serials numbers of aircraft from 510 to 524 were obtained from an official Ota Air Base document (*Ordem de Serviço*). The other ex-RAF serials were taken from an article in the French magazine '*AVIONS*', corrected as necessary and confirmed from other sources where available. Furthermore, the equivalent Portuguese serial and Flight code are presented only where official documents and photographs confirm them. When the type designation appears as 'Mk II' this means that the subvariant is not known.

2 –Correlation between RAF Serial and the A.M. Serial numbers of the following aircraft is unknown: Delivered in 1943 – **354, **358, **459, **488,**840,**964,**499, *599, LD243, LD255, LD259, LD301, LD302, LD389, LE458, LB885, LB904, LB906, LB911, LB930, LB943, LB960 (Mk IIC), Z3148, Z3171, Z3265, Z3275, Z3358, Z5072, Z5220, Z5258 (Mk IIB), AM533 (Mk XB), BE404, BE502 (Mk II), BP746 (Mk IIB), BW962, BW963 (Mk XIB), JS281, JS329, JS335, JS401(Mk XIIB), Z2673, LB896, LB900, LB901, LB905, LB973, LB987, LD200, LD202, LD203, LD205, LD207, LD247, LD250, LD253, LD258, LD296, LD297, LD298, LD307, LD310, LD334 (all Mk IIC). Delivered in 1944 – LE641, LE830, LE831, LE833, LE519, LE522, LE640, LE648, LE953, LE998, LF131, LE456, LE466, LE470, LE475, LE476, LE632 (all Mk IIC). Delivered in 1947 – MW352, MW353, PG535, PG437, PG450, PG610, PZ749, PZ761, PZ772, PZ776, PZ825 (Mk IIC).

3 – It has been suggested, without confirmation, that a number of aircraft not initially of Mk IIB or Mk IIC characteristics were modified to one of those standards before delivery.

4 – The above listing shows that the same aircraft used different code letters during its operational life, probably as a consequence of its movement between Flights. However, this should not be compared with the re-allocation resulting from aircraft re-using serial numbers left open by retired or crashed aircraft, e.g. the existence of two different 517 aircraft, as explained above.

Camouflage and Markings

According to eye witnesses, the first six aircraft arriving in Portugal directly from North Africa in August 1943 wore, as it would be expected, the Dark Earth and Middle Stone disruptive camouflage over Azure blue under surfaces. However, there is no consensus around national markings, as some sources refer to the *Cruz de Cristo* on the wings only while others suggest the emblem was only applied on the fuselage[8]. Without doubt, the aircraft carried their RAF serial numbers on arrival and the tail did not show either the British or Portuguese fin flash. The other Hurricane batches received in 1943, 1944 and 1947 were already painted in the standard E.T.O. Day Fighter scheme of Dark Green and Ocean Grey upper surfaces over Medium Sea Grey under surfaces.

In *Aeronautica Militar* service, Hurricanes received the *Cruz de Cristo* in the customary six positions on the wings and fuselage sides (the latter without white disk). The white serial was also applied on the rear fuselage on both sides, usually over the coloured tail band identifying the Flight. The simplified Portuguese flag without Coat of Arms was applied on the fin. The rectangle was divided in two unequal parts, being 2/5 green (leading) and 3/5 red.

The Flight code and the individual aircraft letter were applied, on each side of the fuselage *Cruz de Cristo*, in white. Following British practice, the Flight code was applied between the *Cruz de Cristo* and the cockpit, with the aircraft letter to the rear. Spinners were also painted in the Flight identification colour (see table). Several aircraft were reported to have their ID letter stencilled in a small size character below the spinner, only detectable from the front. A photo depicting aircraft 624 shows this clearly, as well as the anti-glare panels for night flying

The Hurricane Badges

8 The Portuguese Connection – The Secret History of the Azores Base – R.E. Vintras – Bachman & Turner, London.

By the end of the 1940s, the aircraft of 'VX', 'RV' and 'MP' Flights had an insignia and motto applied to the left side of the nose, under the exhausts. Several designs appear to have existed and have been published several times. However only one, the emblem of 'VX' Flight, is sufficiently well documented to confirm its shape and colours, allowing the graphic representation shown here. The other two mostly published emblems do not conform to the designs shown in photographs. Efforts to find a clean and clear picture that allowed a correct graphic representation of the 'RV' and 'MP' Flight emblems, including a description of the colours, proved unfruitful. It was therefore decided to present only the best images found in the archives, limited to black and white photographic evidence, without a detailed illustration, in the hope that, in the future, the 'genuine article' will surface.

One of the oldest Portuguese military aviation emblems, the Tancos greyhound, described above, was also used on Hurricanes, as photographs show, applied on the fuselage sides. However it is not known to what extent this emblem was used.

By the end of their active life a number of the aircraft displayed a new form of identification painted in the fuselage. These Hurricanes had their serial number painted in white replacing the flight code, but maintained the code letter in the same position (see photo of aircraft 511+ B). A final variant in the markings application was the replacement of the Flight letters by the serial in large white figures, without the aircraft code letter, as can be seen in the photo of aircraft 612. This is an oddity, as the same aircraft is shown in another photograph still carrying the code letter 'F'.

Finally, when the Portuguese Air Force was formed in 1952, amalgamating the military aviation branches of the Army and the Navy, a new serial system and markings was designed and approved. The serial block attributed was in the 42** range and the new markings were to be applied according to the drawing presented here. A new camouflage scheme was introduced at the same time, consisting of overall upper surfaces in dark green with light grey under surfaces. However, although Hurricanes were still in service when the new numbering, markings and new colour were introduced, they did not, it is believed, have these changes applied before their retirement.

Aircraft characteristics Hawker Hurricane Mk IIB and IIC	
Quantity used:	144
Crew:	One
Years of Service:	1943–1954
Span:	40' (12.19 m)
Length:	32′ 2" 1/4 (9.80 m)
Height:	13' 2" (4.01 m)
Wing Area:	258 sq ft (23.97 m^2)
Engine:	RR Merlin XX of 1,260 bhp at 11,750 ft
Empty weight:	5,467 lb (2,480 kg) **IIB**, 5,658 lb (2,566 kg) **IIC**
Normal loaded weight:	7,233 lb (3,281 kg) **IIB**, 7,544 lb (3,422 kg) **IIC**
Maximum speed:	at 20,000 ft 320 mph (515 km/h) **IIB**, at 20,000 ft 328 mph (528 km/h) **IIC**
Service ceiling:	34,500 ft (10,520 m) **IIB**, 32,400 ft (9,876 m) **IIC**

Accident with Hawker Hurricane MkIIC serial number 614, code GL+ O. This accident occurred as it was flying from Espinho Airfield during a shooting training session. (MAIS ALTO, Coll .Gen. Brochado de Miranda)

Accident of Hurricane s/n 612, a good example of the final type of identification markings – only the serial in large characters. (MAIS ALTO, Coll. Gen. Brochado de Miranda)

Accident of Hawker Hurricane Mk IIC serial number 540 VX+A in 17th June 1947, near the Rio Douro (Douro River). (MAIS ALTO, Coll. Gen. Galvão de Melo)

Accident with Hawker Hurricane Mk II serial number 614, code GL+O. For the meaning of figure 17 on the rudder please refer to text. Under the left wing a non-identified device is seen, presumably part of a long range fuel tank (the upper fairing?). (MAIS ALTO Coll. Gen. Brochado de Miranda)

Hawker Hurricanes flying over their stable mates companions during a ceremony at Espinho Airfield. (MAIS ALTO, Coll. Gen. Brochado de Miranda)

Hawker Hurricanes from VX and RV Flights at Espinho airfield during a ceremonial parade. The first aircraft on the left is a Mk IIC, serial number 547, code VH+X. The date of the event is unknown. (MAIS ALTO Coll. Gen. Brochado de Miranda)

Coloured photograph of a VX Flight aircraft. (MAIS ALTO, Coll. Loureiro Peixoto)

VX Flight pilots posing in front of one of their aircraft in a rare, for the date, colour photo. General (Ret.) Brochado de Miranda in his early days as a pilot is second individual from the left. Behind him can be discerned the yellow id strip of the wing leading edge. Note also the exhaust anti-dazzle guard fitted either side of the aircraft nose. (MAIS ALTO Coll. Gen. Brochado de Miranda)

VX Flight – Ou vai ou racha – *(It's make or break) – A grey uniformed goggled mosquito in big red-brown boots, handling or shooting with a cannon.*

One of the original photos depicting the "Fighting Mosquito".

RV Flight – "Agora canto eu" – (It's my turn (to sing)) – A colourful fighting cock in a challenging attitude.

MP Flight – "Antes quebrar que torcer" – (Better break than twist) – A peasant in white shirt and black hat, trousers and waistcoat in a defensive/offensive attitude with a cudgel.

Interesting photo of a line-up of Hurricanes on Sintra Air Base at the end of their service life, showing the serial numbers painted on the fuselages replacing the Flight code as explained in the text (Camouflage and Markings paragraph). (FAP/AHFA)

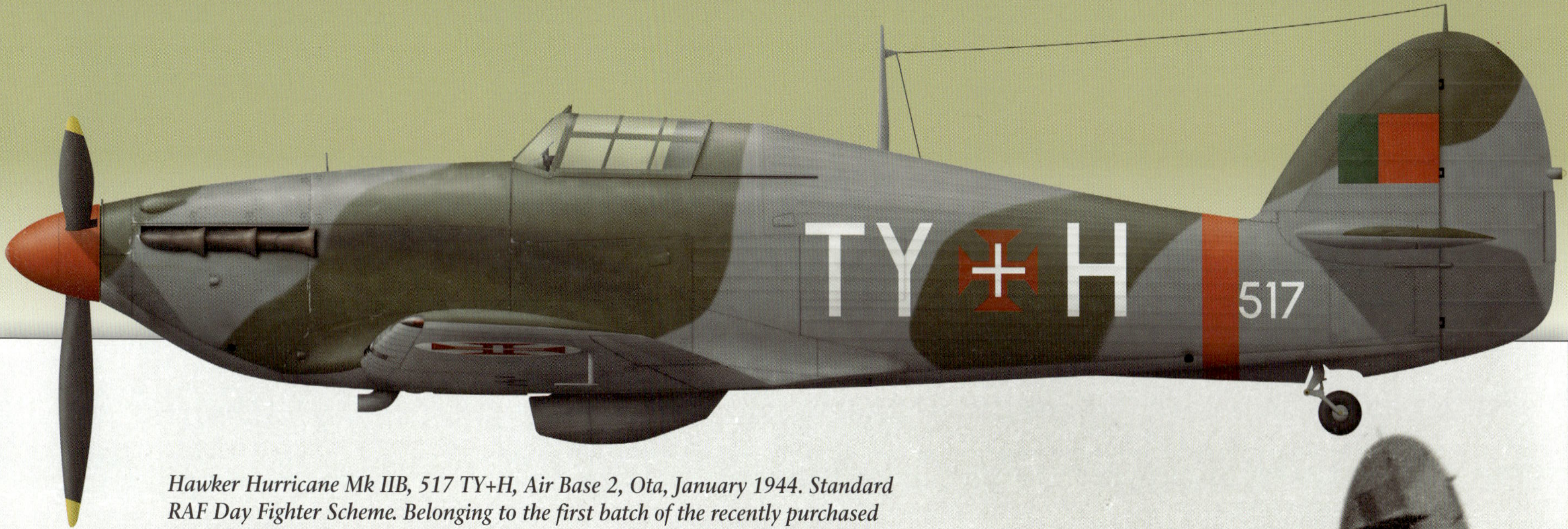

Hawker Hurricane Mk IIB, 517 TY+H, Air Base 2, Ota, January 1944. Standard RAF Day Fighter Scheme. Belonging to the first batch of the recently purchased aircraft, this new Hurricane s/n 517 is seen here displaying a serial number that later would to be used by a different aircraft. The red spinner and rear fuselage band allocated it to "Flight TY", then stationed at Base Aérea 2, Ota.

Hawker Hurricanes code TY+H, serial number 517 and TY+B s/n 511. This last aircraft is one of the Canadian-built Hurricane Mk XIIs received in August 1943. (FAP/AHFA)

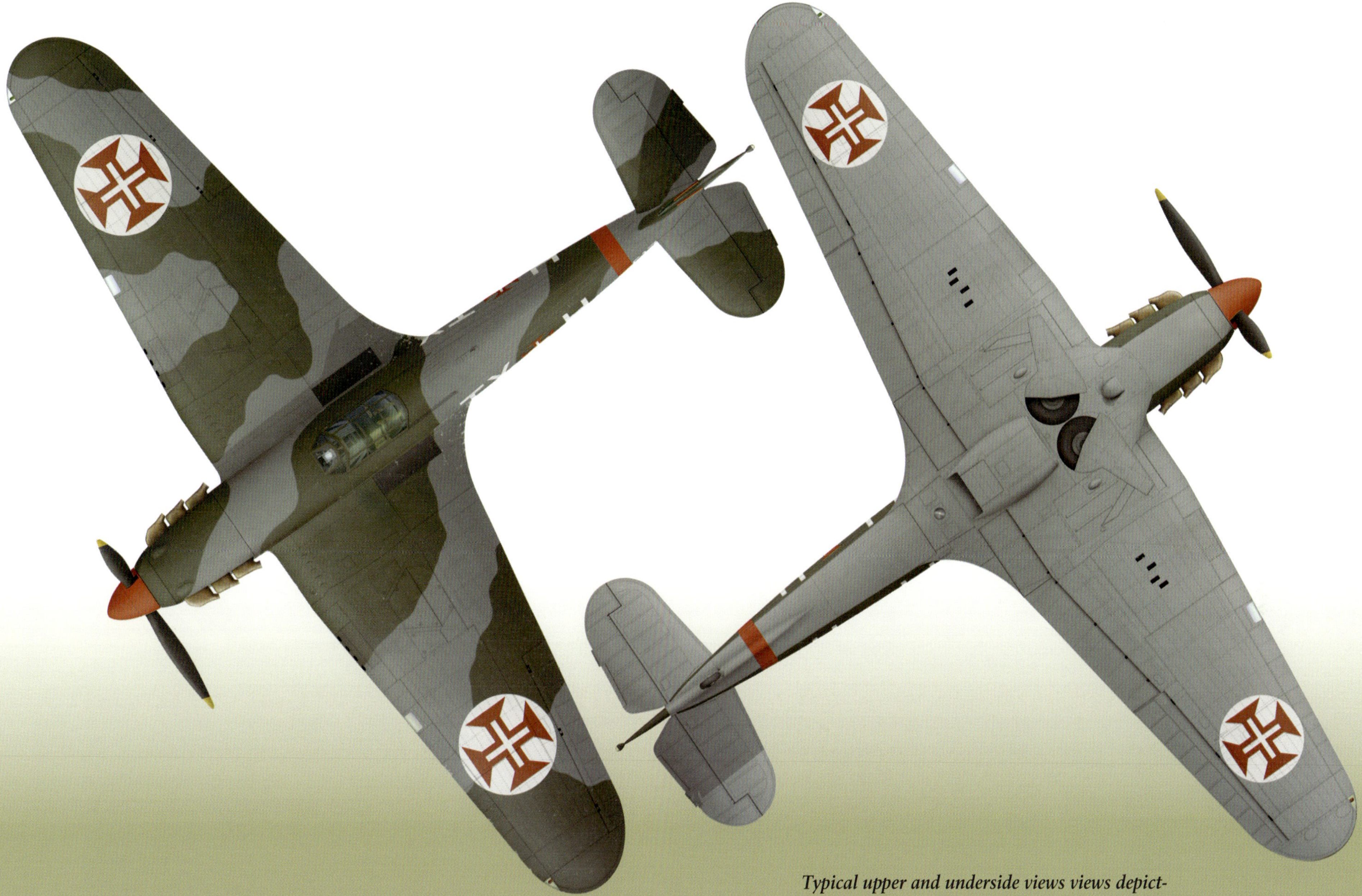

Typical upper and underside views views depicting the under surface colour and positioning of the National insignia, in this particular case on Hurricane TY+H, s/n 517.

Hawker Hurricane Mk IIC, 517 MP+A, Air Base 1, Sintra, late 1947(?). Standard RAF Day Fighter Scheme. As suggested in the text, the use of older serials belonging to struck-off aircraft is the only explanation for the employment of "serial 517", a former Hurricane Mk IIB, now in use on a Hurricane Mk IIC. This practice was, to a certain extent, a "common" exercise with the Aeronáutica Militar, *as happened before with the Avro 626 and Tiger Moth fleets.*

Hawker Hurricane Mk IIC serial 517 code MP+A. At the end of the Hurricane's career in the A.M. the Flight MP incorporated many aircraft used previously by other Flights, the identity of the aircraft being defined by the serial number. (FAP/AHFA)

Hawker Hurricane Mk IIC, 582 VX+P, Air Base 2, Ota, Date unknown. Standard RAF Day Fighter Scheme. Typical of one of the four Flights stationed at Base Aérea 2, Ota, Hurricane s/n 582 is seen here carrying the green spinner and rear fuselage band that identified Esquadrilha *(Flight) VX.*

Profile view of Hawker Hurricane Mk IIC serial number 582, coded VX+P. Of note is its well-worn appearance. (FAP/AHFA)

Hawker Hurricane Mk IIC, 535 SU+K, Air Base 3, Tancos, Summer 1944. Standard RAF Day Fighter Scheme. During May 1944 the "SU Flight" was diverted from Ota to be stationed in the Base Aérea nº 3, Tancos, Portugal's highly praised "Fighting Air Base". Hence Hurricane serial number 535 proudly displays the many times mentioned Galgo (Greyhound) motive, a very interesting and unique example of the use of the home-base emblem.

Hawker Hurricane Mk IIC, serial number 535, coded SU+K. Although not of a very good quality, this photo has the interest of showing the insignia of Tancos Air Base, the running greyhound, below the cockpit. This insignia has not identified before on Hurricanes until the recent surfacing of this photo. (FAP/AHFA)

Hawker Hurricane Mk IIC, 624 MP+B, Air Base 2, Ota, July 1951. Standard RAF Day Fighter Scheme. This particular aircraft was part of the group of five sent to Kenley in the UK, to participate in the filming of "Angels One Five", a British film centred on the Battle of Britain. Of note is the VX Flight emblem "Ou vai ou racha" painted on the left side only of the nose, from the previous allocation of the aircraft to this Esquadrilha.

Hurricane IIC serial 624 MP-B, but still with VX flight badge. (FAP/AHFA)

Hawker Hurricane Mk IIC, 608 GL+I, Air Base 3, Tancos, May 1944. Standard RAF Day Fighter Scheme. Located at Base Aérea 2, Ota, Esquadrilha (Flight) GL was soon obliged to move to Tancos Air Base, circa 64 km further up Northeast, owing to the original Base being quickly overcrowded, despite its new and large facilities, with the arrival of the recently acquired material, a large number of Hurricanes and Spitfires arriving almost at the same time.

Flight line of Hawker Hurricanes of the GL Flight with the aircraft serial number 608, code GL+ I closest to the camera in what appears to be a display. (FAP/AHFA)

Hawker Hurricane Mk IIC, 547 VX+H, Air Base 2, Ota, January 1944. Standard RAF Day Fighter Scheme. With the Allied victory in sight, Portugal was finally able to purchase a significant number of aircraft and other equipment to furnish its Armed Forces. Until the advent of the African Territories conflict in the '60s, the Hawker Hurricane with some 144 units was the aircraft used in largest numbers under Portuguese colours.

Hawker Hurricane Mk IIC serial number 547, code VX+H, showing to advantage the positioning of the underwing National Insignia as well as the respective Flight insignia. (FAP/AHFA)

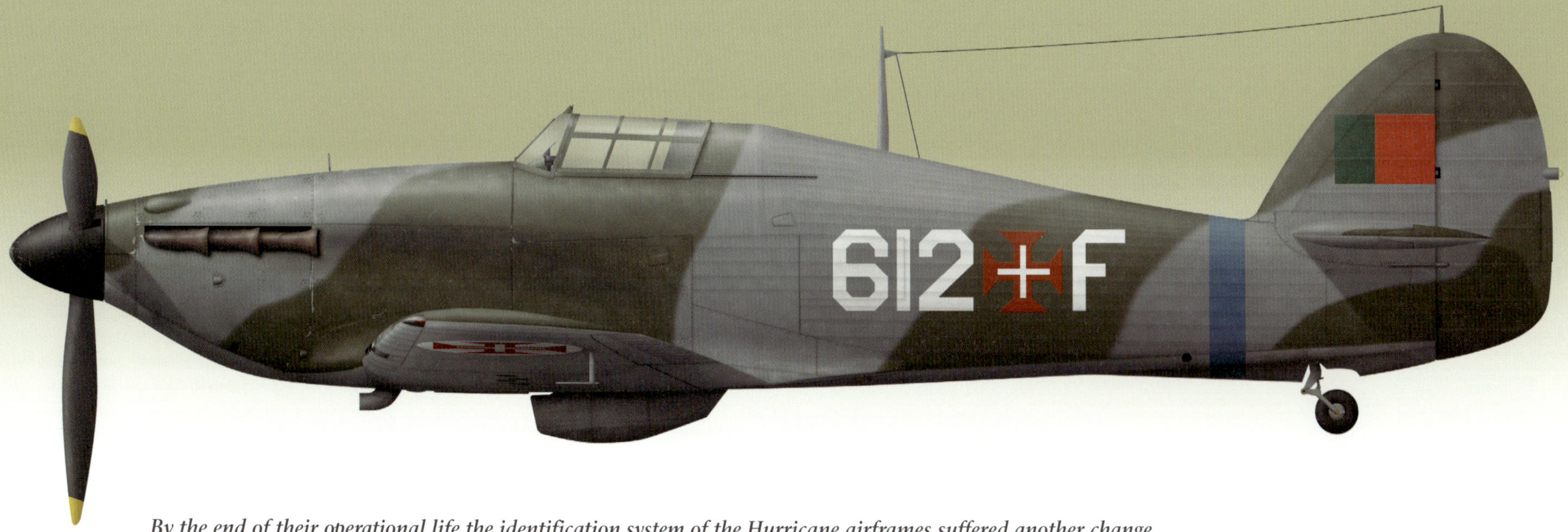

By the end of their operational life the identification system of the Hurricane airframes suffered another change. This time the serial number was painted in large white numerals followed by the individual letter. Two examples of this practice initiated in the early fifties was Hawker Hurricane Mk XII of Canadian origin former TY-B s/n 511 and its Flight companion Mk IIB, former GL-M s/n 612. Both aircraft in standard RAF Day Fighter Scheme.

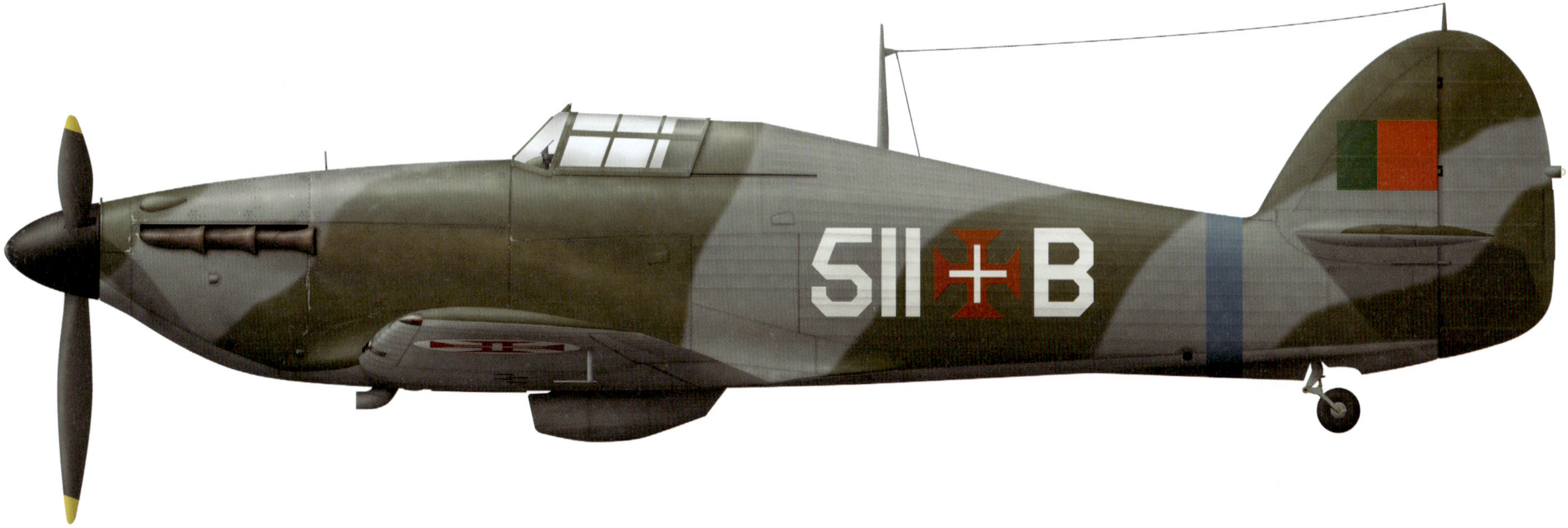

Hawker Hurricane Mk IIC, 612, Base?, Date unknown. Standard RAF Day Fighter Scheme. Apart from the fact that, again, we believe that we are in the presence of a duplicate use of a serial number, we cannot offer a coherent explanation to the light coloured zone (white? light grey? silver dope?...) of the fuselage deck just behind the canopy of this Hawker Hurricane Mk IIC and that is clearly seen on a number of photographs. Probably the outcome of some kind of repair, we can leave our imagination go wild and speculate on the size of the pigeons on the vicinity of this particular Air Base area...

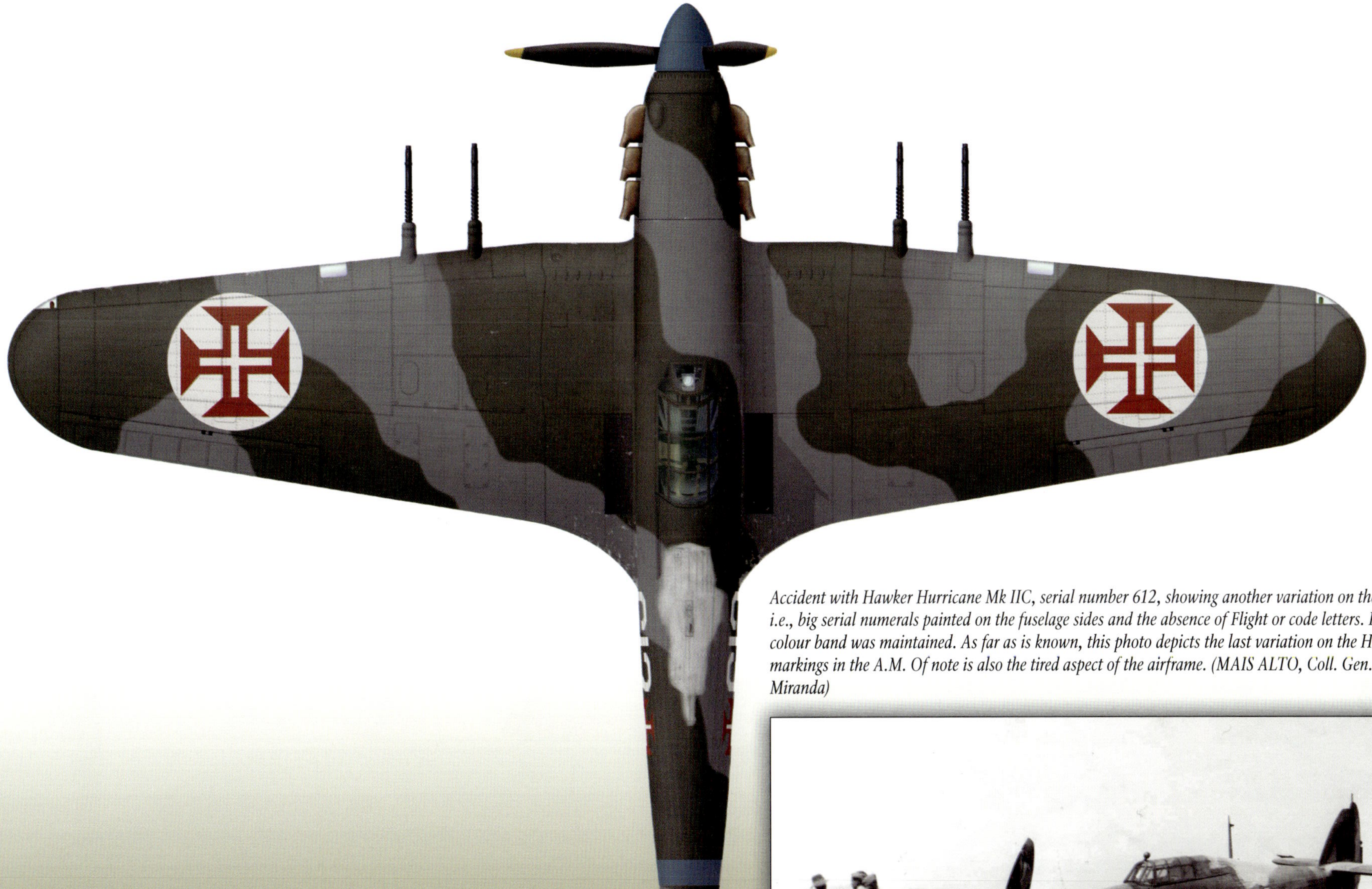

Accident with Hawker Hurricane Mk IIC, serial number 612, showing another variation on the markings, i.e., big serial numerals painted on the fuselage sides and the absence of Flight or code letters. However the colour band was maintained. As far as is known, this photo depicts the last variation on the Hurricanes markings in the A.M. Of note is also the tired aspect of the airframe. (MAIS ALTO, Coll. Gen. Brochado de Miranda)

And now, a "What if?..." Circa 1972 a draft drawing surfaced in what appears to be a document, probably attached to a sketchy version of the law from the early fifties, that would be implemented in the future Portuguese Air Force. This rough copy established that all surviving Hawker Hurricanes should be painted, as their Spitfire counterparts, in a uniform upper green colour over a light blue under surface. When the law was implemented in 1951, the drawing with the colour scheme had vanished and the existing Hurricanes spent the rest of their days in the WWII standard E.T.O. Ocean Grey/Dark Green over Medium Sea Grey delivery scheme.

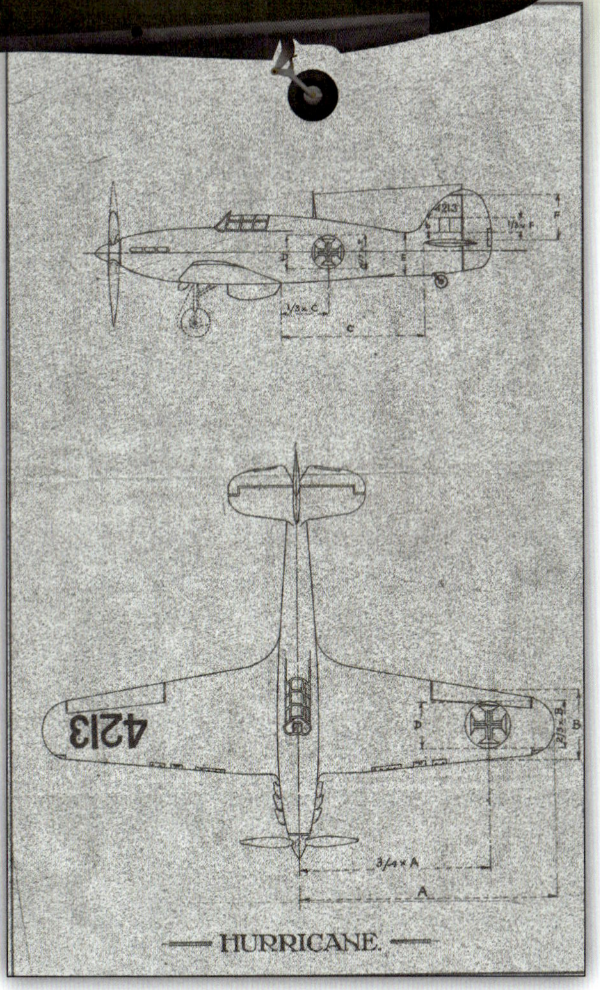

Drawing showing the proposed style of markings and its positioning for the surviving A.M. Hawker Hurricanes to serve within the new Força Aérea Portuguesa (FAP) – Portuguese Air Force (1952). As far as it is known, no such colour scheme was ever used even if the aircraft flew with FAP until 1954.

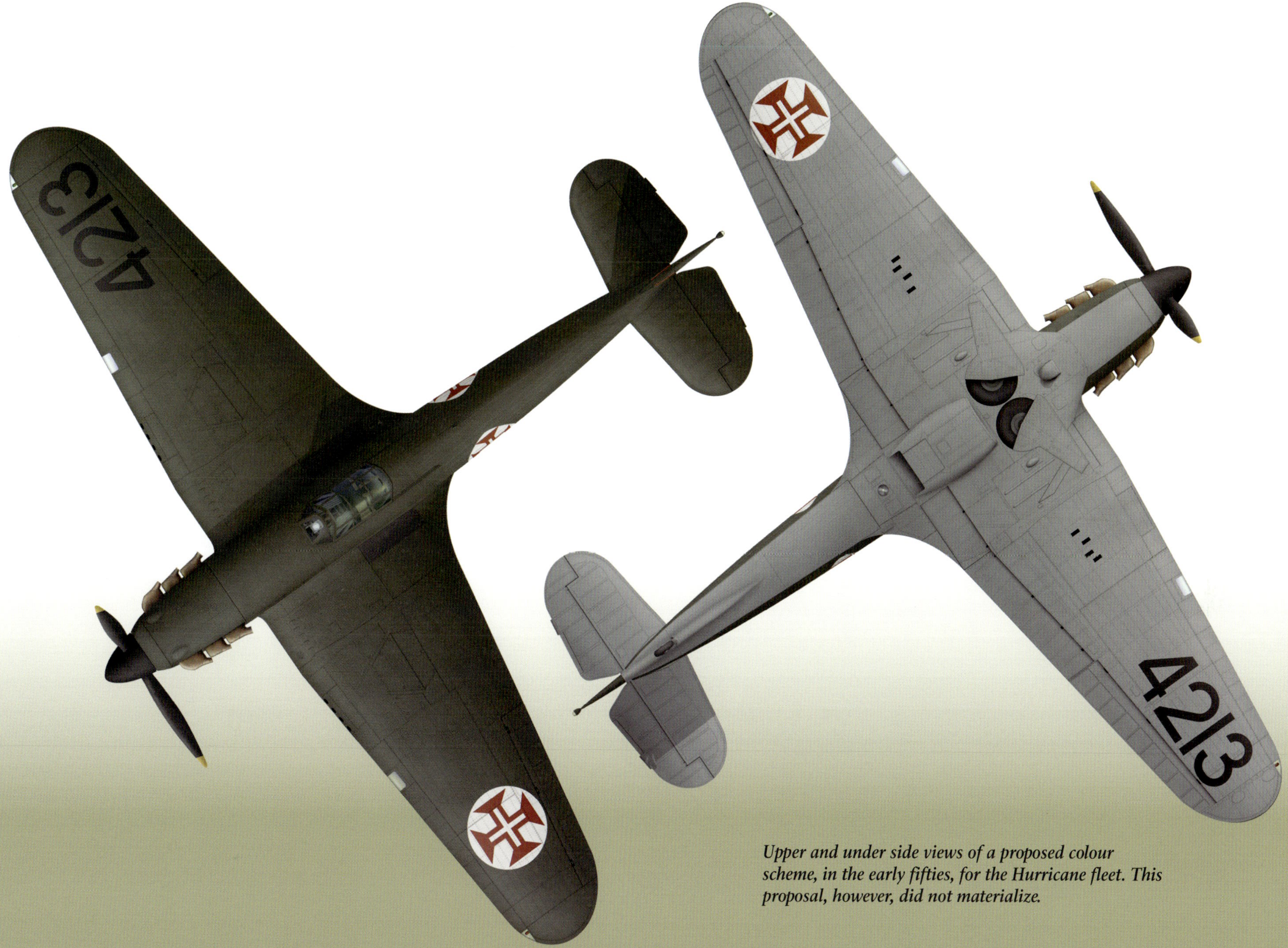

Upper and under side views of a proposed colour scheme, in the early fifties, for the Hurricane fleet. This proposal, however, did not materialize.

Bristol Beaufighter TF. X

Background

In the mid-1930s the concept of a twin-engined fighter, able to maintain long-range action, carrying heavy offensive and defensive armaments, was being developed or considered by countries including Germany, Italy and France. However, the British Authorities did not prioritise such an aircraft as highly as short-range, high-speed fighters.

It is often said that the best aircraft are conceived outside the scope of specifications drawn by government authorities. In the case of the Bristol Beaufighter, a private venture subsidised by the Bristol Aeroplane Company, this was the case. Bristol's designers foresaw a plausible need for a heavy twin-engined fighter, able to carry diverse weaponry and execute a variety of tasks. Using elements of the design of the Bristol Beaufort, a general-purpose torpedo-bomber for Coastal Command, the team headed by Leslie Frise, started the development of an aircraft initially called the "Beaufort Fighter". The planned aircraft would use components of the Beaufort, such as wings, undercarriage, and tail assembly, with more powerful engines (two Bristol Hercules radial engines instead of the Taurus engines used on Beaufort), and armed with four Hispano 20 mm cannons. Thus many existing Beaufort jigs could be employed on the new aircraft, allowing for speed of manufacture, economy and simplicity of production.

As the design of the new project included a majority of features requested in Specification F.11/37, a preliminary layout of the "Beaufort Fighter" was presented to the Air Ministry a few days after the Bristol Beaufort's first flight in October 1938. The response of the authorities was enthusiastic regarding the possibilities of the new design, the paramount interest being naturally the economy and speed with which the new aircraft could be made available. Four prototypes were ordered, and the first flight, on 17 July 1939, of the aircraft now named Beaufighter[1] took place a mere eight months after the beginning of its design.

Deliveries of the new fighter began one year later, on July 1940, the RAF receiving them in time to be involved in the Battle of Britain. It was soon realised that the Beaufighter was a suitable platform to carry one of the first airborne radar systems, the A.I. Mk IV, without compromising its firepower or endurance, thus making of it an effective night-fighter. This modification occurred firstly on a restricted number of airframes and was completed mostly in the field instead of on the

1 With the project for the "Beaufort fighter", well on the way, the name Beaufighter came to fruition quite easily, being a contraction of the two words.

Beaufighter BF 13 at Instituto Superior Técnico (I.S.T) (see text) 1963. (Photo Luis Tavares)

Beaufighter BF 10 at I.S.T. 1963. (Photo Luis Tavares)

production line. This adaptation did not happen without problems, the early radar presenting a number of challenges, notably the lack of range. As a result, in the first months of operation more successes were recorded without the aid of the A.I. Mk IV than with it. On 25 October 1940 the first confirmed Beaufighter 'kill' was accomplished by an aircraft belonging to 219 Squadron, the victim being a German Junkers Ju 88A.

To the first examples of the Bristol Beaufighter delivered in 1940, another 5,562 units[2] would follow, to serve in a diversity of roles including long-range escort fighter, torpedo-bomber, day or night intruder, strike-fighter or night-fighter, all over the globe in all theatres of war, and with around 19 variants built or planned. The last aircraft left the production line in 1946.

'Air Enthusiast International', March 1974 issue, states: "...improvisation may well have been the keynote of the... concept, but in its capabilities it proved to be every inch a thoroughbred..." The Bristol Beaufighter proved during its career that it was a reliable and strong aircraft, able to sustain damage and return with its crews. However, besides the RAF and Commonwealth Air Forces, it did not attract the attention of many foreign customers, with only the Dominican Republic, Israel, Portugal and Turkey purchasing a number of new or refurbished aeroplanes. France obtained around 17 Beaufighters in 1945-46 but these were used only for ground instruction. The United States (USAAF) also used the Beaufighter under the 'reverse lend-lease' programme as night-fighters in the E.T.O., until May 1945.

The last flight of a Bristol Beaufighter was recorded from the RAF Base in Seletar, Singapore, on 16 May 1960.

A (very) Brief History of the Portuguese *Aviação Naval*

This Bristol Beaufighter was the sole fully operational fighter operated by the Portuguese Navy, and therefore a brief history of the *Aviação Naval Portuguesa* (Portuguese Naval Aviation) or *Aeronautica Naval* (Naval Aeronautics) is appropriate here.

The establishment of the first Military Aeronautical School in Portugal, at *Vila Nova da Rainha*, coincided with a period of turmoil across Europe, the work being initiated in April 1915 and the School being inaugurated one year later, in August 1916. Meanwhile, in 1915[3] a group of eleven Army and Navy Officers were sent to France by the Portuguese Government in order to obtain

2 Or 5,564 units according to other sources. Australia was the other producer of Beaufighters with a total of 364 aircraft completed by December 1945, the last Australian aircraft flying until the end of 1957.

3 As stated before in this book, see the "Introduction" Chapter, the involvement of Portugal in the Great War would not occur before March 1916.

Beaufighter BF 10 at I.S.T 1963. Photo Luis Tavares

their pilots' brevets. Upon their return, two of them, both Navy officers, *Primeiro-Tenente* Sacadura Cabral and *Segundo-Tenente* António Caseiro, were charged with finding a location for a future Naval Air Station.

The site they chose was on the (then) outskirts of Lisbon, near the Belém Tower, on the right bank of the Tagus River, on a place known as Bom Sucesso[4]. The first Portuguese Naval Air Station (*Estação Aeronaval do Bom Sucesso*) was thus born and with it the seeds for the *Aviação Naval* (Naval Aviation) were implanted. Governmental Decree nr 3395, dated September 1917, created the *Serviço e Escola de Aviação da Armada* (Fleet Aviation Service and School) and established it at the *Bom Sucesso* Naval Air Station. Meanwhile, other Naval Air Stations were created both in the continental territory of Portugal (São Jacinto, close to Aveiro) and on the Azores (Horta, in the Faial Island), in time to see action during the First World War, with Portuguese, American or French aeroplanes, mostly flying boats, patrolling the Atlantic in search of German submarines or other vessels. Another Naval Air Station was planned for Algarve.

The most notable achievement of the *Aviação Naval* began on 30 March 1922 at dawn, with a flight from Lisbon to Rio de Janeiro, Brazil, that would take seventy-nine days to cover the distance of 8,383 kilometres, with a flying time of only 62 hours and 26 minutes. The objectives of the First Crossing of the South Atlantic by air were twofold: the first political and diplomatic, celebrating the links between Portugal and Brazil, the other scientific, testing a navigational device invented by Admiral Gago Coutinho, the 'Portuguese Sextant'. The voyage was carried out with three aircraft, a Fairey IIID 'Transatlantic Load Carrier' seaplane, specially developed for the expedition, and two Fairey IIID seaplanes of standard configuration. The pilot was *Capitão de Fragata* (Commander) Sacadura Cabral and the Navigator *Capitão de Mar-e-Guerra* (Captain) Gago Coutinho[5]. The precision of Admiral Coutinho's invention was such that it was adopted and used by all international

4 According to historians, the name of Bom Sucesso ('Good Luck' or 'Good Fortune') is connected to the fact that at this place, a former beach, 15th century crowds used to gather to see off the vessels of the Age of Discovery departing to the unknown.

5 Admiral Carlos Viegas Gago Coutinho (Lisbon 17/02/1869–18/02/1959). An illustrious Navy Officer and respected scholar, holder of the most distinguished Portuguese and foreign decorations, his scientific and field works as a geographer, cartographer and historian are still valid and appreciated today.

Beaufighter BF 13 at I.S.T 1963. (Photo Luis Tavares)

aviators for navigational purposes almost until the advent of GPS. During the flight another of his inventions, developed with his companion Commander Cabral, was successfully tested, the *Plaqué of Drift* (later changed to 'Course Corrector').

Remarkably, Portuguese Naval Aviation never had any pure fighter aircraft until March 1945, when the Bristol Beaufighter came into service. Until then the majority of the aircraft types used were seaplanes or flying boats, devoted to ASW or SAR operations etc. Portugal had no aircraft-carrier in service and only a handful of its ships had the possibility of transporting their own armed scout planes. With the Naval Stations being located on land, defence of their air space fell under the *Aeronautica Militar*.

The Naval Air branch was resurrected in 1993 in the shape of a Navy Helicopter Flight (*Esquadrilha de Helicópteros da Marinha*) with Westland Lynx Mk 95 on board of Meko-Class frigates.

Bristol Beaufighter in Portugal

Some months before the defeat of Nazi Germany, but with victory now in sight, the British authorities finally assented to a Portuguese request dating from 1943 for Bristol Beaufighters to replace old and refurbished Blenheims of Navy Aviation 'B Flight' supplied after the Azores Agreement and stationed at Lisbon Airport, in Portela de Sacavém[6].

The aircraft were ferried to Portugal by the No.1 Ferry Unit in three batches: one of six aircraft on 13 March, the second of six aircraft on 18 March, and the final batch of four aircraft on 22 March 1945. These aircraft were newly made TF Mk X from the last Bristol-produced group of 500

6 In 1943 Portugal received 21 second-hand Blenheim Mk IV and V aircraft as an alternative to the requested Beaufighters, 14 of them being allocated to Naval Aviation. Stating that they were old and refurbished is kind to their almost dilapidated condition, all the airframes showing very high flying hours on their logbooks. An unknown number were equipped with the 4 machine-gun belly packs, which would automatically classify them, at least on paper, as long-range fighters. Besides, and due to the prevailing poor conditions of maintenance and storage during their entire service life in Portugal, mostly in the open air, the gun packs or at least the guns were taken from the aircraft to help to prevent damage to the armament. Although the Navy maintained a number of Bristol Blenheims flying until 1947 for training purposes, we opted for not consider them in our list of fighters.

Beaufighter BF 10 at Alverca 1977. (Photo Luis Tavares)

aircraft. As was the usual procedure with Navy aeroplanes at that time, sequential serial numbers were applied starting with the letters BF for Beaufighter and the numbers 1 to 16 (BF1 to BF16). With the first aeroplanes delivered, two British crews, pilots and navigators, stayed behind to serve as instructors to the Portuguese aviators. They returned to the UK within a couple of weeks, as the transition of the Portuguese crews to their new aircraft had proceeded smoothly.

The short service life of the Beaufighters within the Portuguese Navy was due more to a combination of events then anything else, and not due to any shortcomings of the aircraft. The period that immediately preceded the end of *Aviação Naval* in 1952, with the amalgamation of the Army branch to form the *Força Aérea Portuguesa* (Portuguese Air Force), was difficult for Navy Aviators. The transition was affected by old rivalries of the Navy versus the Army and aggravated by disagreements between politicians and the military. A number of officers and other ranks refused to join the new Air Force and either retired, or were transferred to other arms of the Navy, while a few left the forces to move into commercial aviation.

The turmoil of reorganisation led to a diminishing number of qualified personnel, notably mechanics, not helped by the lack of a suitable base. The new Montijo Air Base (the future B.A.6), on the Southern bank of the Tagus River near Lisbon, was earmarked to became an anti-submarine and air-sea rescue station but was not yet complete and would take some time to be inaugurated. The decision to maintain 'B' Flight at Lisbon Airport, also undergoing extension works and without proper shelters for maintenance, was not an ideal solution. The Flight aircraft spent more time gathered inside the few available hangars to avoid the dust and dirt, which badly affected their equipment and weapons, than in flight operations. At one point it was decided to remove some of the most vulnerable equipment and weapons from all aircraft and re-install it only when an airplane was to fly again. This did not help the efficient operation of the aircraft.

An accident on 22 October 1945 was also to hamper Beaufighter operations. Aircraft no. BF4, while on a low-level training sortie in the North of the country, suffered a sudden loss of power due to the shearing of the oil pump shaft of the port engine. The aircraft lost control and descended rapidly, hitting the sand dunes at Ovar beach, near Aveiro. In the accident and fire that followed the pilot, *Tenente* Félix Lobo, the mechanic, *Sargento* Antunes Nogueira and the radio operator, *Marinheiro* Luís Pacheco all died. Pacheco, while badly burned, survived long enough to pull the rest of the crew from the debris and then move up beach, looking for help. Unfortunately, he later died in the hospital from his wounds. A replacement aircraft was obtained in 1946 when the Bristol factory accepted to substitute the lost TF Mk X with a new Beaufighter Mk X, this time with a Mk VIII radar installed inside a nose 'thimble', for £10,000. The aircraft was flown directly

Beaufighter BF 10 at Alverca 1977. (Photo Luis Tavares)

from Filton by a Portuguese crew, being one of the last examples of an operational Beaufighter of *Esquadrilha B*.

Meanwhile the type's days under Portuguese colours were almost over. The situation in *Esquadrilha B* deteriorated day by day. The lack of pilots was more and more of a problem, and unlikely to be reversed. With personnel leaving or diverted to other services, the few operational Beaufighters were sporadically flown by the only pilot then left in the *Esquadrilha*, *2º Tenente* Manuel Beja. On 15 April 1946 this young Lieutenant almost suffered the same fate as his former colleagues when his Beaufighter, flying near the Spanish border, experienced a similar problem to the one that had caused BF4 to crash.

Contrary to the usual procedures that dictated an immediately bailout, he tried to return to Lisbon. With the oil temperature of his remaining engine reaching dangerous levels and badly smoking, on reaching the edge of the city he ordered his radio operator to bail out, and proceeded to approach the Portela runway. Beja was able to land, but on trying to leave the aircraft rapidly, found the radio operator clinging to the escape hatch, paralysed with fear to such a degree he had been unable to obey to the command to bail out.

By mid-1946 almost the entire 'B' Flight was grounded due to the lack of pilots. The C.O. of the S. Jacinto Naval Air Station, *Comandante* Cardoso de Oliveira, travelled to Lisbon every week with a couple of Navy pilots just to fly the surviving Beaufighters.

Tenente Beja carried out the last flight of a Beaufighter in Portuguese colours when, disregarding orders that had grounded all aircraft due to their state of airworthiness, he took off for a sortie over Lisbon. After a series of stunts, he landed and called his C.O., *Capitão-Tenente* (Lieutenant Commander) Paulo Viana to tell him of his deeds. The C.O., after listening what he did, simple told him "OK, you did your stunt and you must be happy. Now, ground the damn aircraft and forget we had this conversation"!

Finally, and ignominiously, Portela's 'B' Flight was disbanded in June 1949, the aircraft having already been struck off charge a year earlier. As a postscript, a note dated 8 June 1953 from the *Secretaria de Estado da Aeronáutica* issued an order to scrap the Beaufighter engine s/n 119398.

From Fighter to Tutor

The days of the Beaufighter in Portugal were not over, however. Around 1950 the Navy offered two of the best airframes (together with one surviving Blenheim) to the I.S.T., or *Instituto Superior Técnico* (Technical Institute of Engineering), in Lisbon, to serve as instructional airframes for future aeronautical engineers. The aircraft transferred were the ex-RD220 (BF10) and ex-RD253 (BF13). The airframes were parked inside the *Instituto*, in an open space surrounded by the classes'

Beaufighter BF 17. (FAP/ AHFA/MAIS ALTO)

buildings, and were a constant subject of antagonism between two *Instituto* Professors, Varela Cid, Professor of Aeronautics and António da Silveira, Professor of Physics – every week, during the Physics professor's classes, the former insisted on carrying out engine running and tests. The noise of the Bristol Hercules engines at full throttle, with the buildings working as a reverberation box, presumably had a less than positive effect on the nearby teaching.

The airframes stayed at the I.S.T. until the mid-1960s, when following negotiations with the RAF Museum, one of them, RD253 (BF13), was returned to its country of origin. Today it can be seen, showing its initial identity, at the Museum in Hendon, London. The remaining Beaufighter, RD220 (BF10), was donated to the *Museu do Ar*, in Alverca, which decided to exchange it with the South African Air Force Museum of Swartkop, South Africa for a hybrid Spitfire Mk IX. In 2000, this airframe was traded again, this time between the SAAF Museum and the Museum of Flight at East Fortune, Scotland, which purchased the remains for around £100,000. According to the Museum site, this airframe is currently under restoration, but in any case represents another piece of Portugal's aviation history sadly lost to the country itself.

Camouflage & Markings

As usual with aircraft bought by Portugal, when purchased, the Bristol Beaufighters were painted with the colours they had worn in service with their previous owners. In this case, colours were Dark Green and Ocean Grey upper surfaces and Medium Sea Grey under surfaces, over which the Portuguese National markings were painted, the *Red Cruz de Cristo* on the wings, above and beneath, painted on a White disc, which concealed the British roundels. The Red and Green National Flag, without Coat of Arms, was painted on the fin over the British 'fin flash'. Above the flag, a Black anchor denoted its Naval Aviation role. On the fuselage, under the tail plane and roughly in line with its leading edge, the serial number was painted in black. This was composed of two letters and one or two digits (BF1 to BF16).

The single 'thimble nose' TF Mk X BF17, ex-RD862, also kept its original colours of Extra Dark Sea-Grey upper surfaces and Sky under surfaces, the only difference being that the National Flag now occupied the rudder completely, being, as usual, Green foremost and Red.

For a time it was supposed that the Portuguese Beaufighters supported a three-colour camouflage, composed of Dark Grey/Dark Green/Dark Earth upper surfaces over Light Grey under surfaces. Several profiles produced by prominent magazines and books showed them in this form. This assumption resulted from the last years of the existence of the Beaufighters in Portuguese hands, when they were already out of service and used as instructional airframes. By then, the aircraft were parked in the *Instituto Superior Técnico* yards, subject to the Portuguese weather, harsh conditions and dust, the covering paints faded away to partially show the original colours underneath, including British serial numbers. This suggests that when delivered to the Portuguese Navy, the aircraft had not been stripped and repainted, but the new paint simply applied over the existing scheme. This situation could plausibly explain the appearance of a three-colour camouflage.

Individual Aircraft Histories					
British Serial	**Type**	**Date Arrival**	**A.N. Serial**	**Struck Of Charge**	**Remarks**
RD134	TF MkX	March 1945	?	April 1948	
RD148	TF MkX	March 1945	?	April 1948	
RD173	TF MkX	March 1945	?	April 1948	
RD189	TF MkX	March 1945	BF-4	---	W/o 22/10/1945, Accident near Ovar, 3 killed
RD197	TF MkX	March 1945	?	April 1948	
RD199	TF MkX	March 1945	?	April 1948	
RD206	TF MkX	March 1945	?	April 1948	
RD209	TF MkX	March 1945	?	April 1948	
RD216	TF MkX	March 1945	?	April 1948	
RD220	TF MkX	March 1945	BF-10	April 1948	I.S.T. (*), SAAF Museum, Swartkop, South Africa
RD250	TF MkX	March 1945	?	April 1948	
RD252	TF MkX	March 1945	?	April 1948	
RD253	TF MkX	March 1945	BF-13	April 1948	I.S.T. (*), RAF Museum, Hendon Restored as the original RD253
RD261	TF MkX	March 1945	?	April 1948	
RD319	TF MkX	March 1945	?	April 1948	
RD320	TF MkX	March 1945	?	April 1948	
RD862	TF MkX	April 1946	BF-17	April 1948	Externally different, with dorsal fin and radar dome ("thimble nose") (**)

(*) I.S.T. – Instituto Superior Técnico – Technical Institute of Engineering in Lisbon
(**) Bought as a replacement for BF-4. See text.

Aircraft Characteristics Bristol Beaufighter TF Mk X	
Quantity used:	16 (+1)
Crew:	Two or Three
Years of Service:	1945–1948
Span:	57' 10" (17.63 m)
Length:	42' 6" (12.94 m)
Height:	15' 10" (4.83 m)
Wing Area:	451 sq ft (41.90 m^2)
Engine:	2 x *Bristol Hercules VI* or *VII*, fourteen cylinder, two row, 1,770 hp, air-cooled radial engines
Empty weight:	15,600 lb (7,076 kg)
Maximum take-off weight:	25,200 lb (11,431 kg)
Maximum speed:	330 mph (531 km/h) at 1,300 ft (396 m)
Service ceiling:	15,000 ft (4,570 m)
Radar:	AI Mk III converted for ASV – work
Armament:	4 x 20 mm *Hispano* cannons on the nose, 6 x 0.303" (7.7mm) machineguns in wings (2 on left wing, 4 on right wing), 1 x 0.303" (7.7mm) machinegun (*Vickers* or *Browning*) manually operated in dorsal position, 1 x 18" (46 cm) Torpedo under fuselage *, 8 x 3" (75 mm) Unguided Rockets *
(*) Even if the aircraft were equipped with the possibility to carry torpedoes or under wing unguided rocket pallets the Portuguese "Beaus" never carried these weapons.	

Bristol Beaufighter TF Mk X "BF 2". Identified as being, in all probability, ex-RD148, this aircraft belonged to the first batch of six aircraft received by the Portuguese Aviação Naval *on the beginning of 1945 following a request for purchase by Portugal dated from two years before. As with all other aircraft bought by Portugal, it maintained during all its operational life the British Coastal Command camouflage of Dark Green and Ocean Grey over Medium Sea Grey, a Black anchor painted on the fin over the National Flag denoting its Naval Aviation origin.*

Beaufighter BF 2 at Portela (Lisbon Airport). (FAP/AHFA/MAIS ALTO)

Zygmunt Szeremeta '15

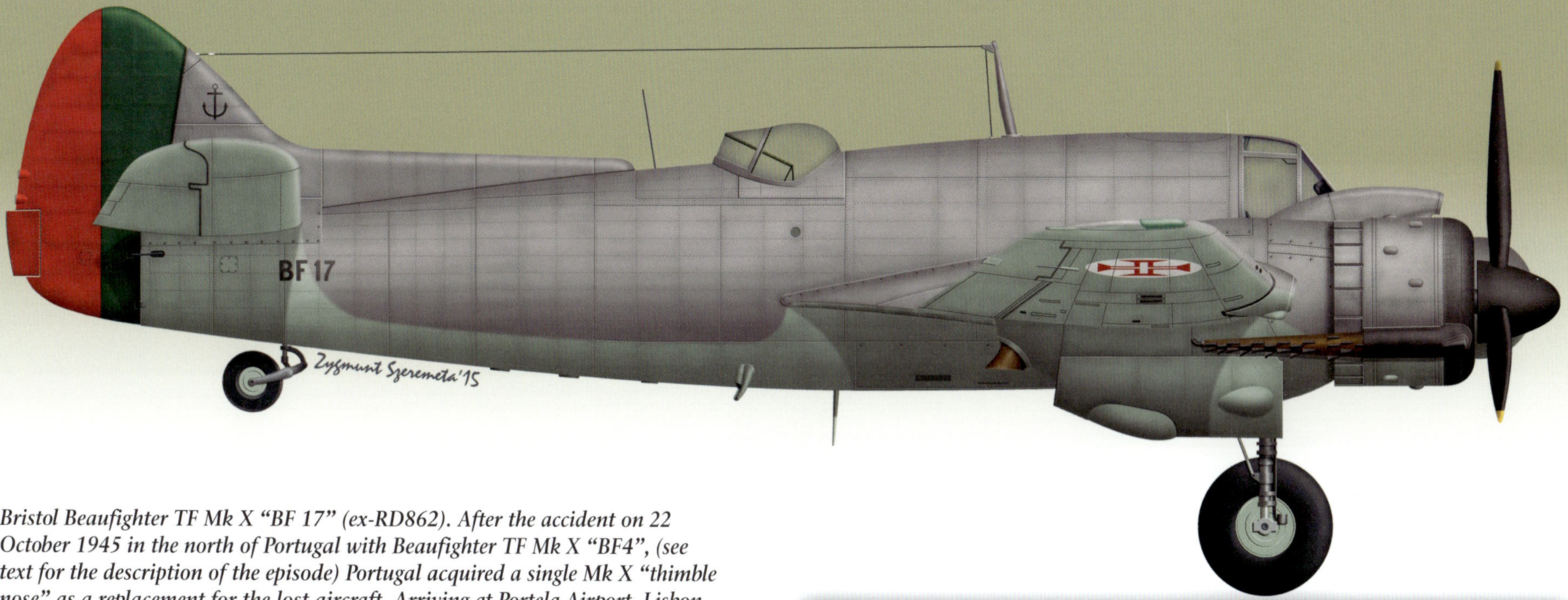

Bristol Beaufighter TF Mk X "BF 17" (ex-RD862). After the accident on 22 October 1945 in the north of Portugal with Beaufighter TF Mk X "BF4", (see text for the description of the episode) Portugal acquired a single Mk X "thimble nose" as a replacement for the lost aircraft. Arriving at Portela Airport, Lisbon, directly from Filton in 1946, it received the sequential serial number "BF 17" and maintained its original camouflage colours of Extra Dark Sea-Grey and Sky until the disbandment of "B Flight" in June 1949. Oddly, this particular aircraft carried the national colours on the entirety of its rudder instead of the more usual flag on the fin only.

Beaufighter BF 17 at S. Jacinto, date unknown.
FAP/AHFA/MAIS ALTO

Zygmunt Szeremeta '15

Republic F-47 Thunderbolt

Background

The Republic F-47 (formerly P-47), one of the biggest and heaviest single-seat fighters of the Second World War, became for many countries in the postwar years, the bridge to new trends in aircraft operation and maintenance, and, in many cases, the transition link between piston and jet aircraft.

The F-47 saga began with the founding of Seversky Aircraft Corporation by Alexander de Seversky in the United States in 1931, and with a proposal to a competition to supply the US Army Air Corps (USAAC) with a modern day fighter. The Seversky proposal secured an order in June 1936 for 77 aircraft under the designation of P-35.

The new aircraft drew also the attention of Sweden, which ordered 120 aircraft with a more powerful engine, the Pratt & Whitney R-1830-45 of 1,050 hp. In the meantime, Alexander de Seversky, the engineer behind the project, continued the development of the basic P-35 installing an even more powerful engine, equipped now with a turbosupercharger, a completely retractable landing gear and re-profiled rear fuselage. The new model received the designation XP-41 but was not ordered by the USAAC.

In October 1939 the Seversky Aircraft Corporation was transformed into the Republic Aircraft Corporation. Alexander de Seversky left the company and Alexander Kartveli became the new chief designer. From the XP-41, Kartveli developed the AP-4, which the USAAC designated YP-43 and ordered 13 pre-series aircraft in March 1939. The engine that propelled the new model was the P&W R-1830-35 of 1,200 hp.

Finally, the model AP-10 represented the progenitor of the Thunderbolt, under the USAAC designation of XP-47. The radial engine was replaced by the Allison V-1710 in-line engine in a search

Line up of Thunderbolts showing the yellow Tancos greyhound insignia over the Air Base motto "Res non verba" *in black. The last two digits of the serial are also shown on the cowling. This insignia was displayed on both sides. (FAP/AHFA)*

F-47 displaying the red Cross of Christ position under the right wing as well as the wing pylon. (FAP/AHFA)

for a better aerodynamic profile. In the meantime, reports from the battlefields in Europe regarding air combat convinced the USAAC that a radical design with more power and 'punch' was needed.

This reasoning led to a new fighter requirement employing a 2,000 hp engine with turbosupercharger, able to attain the speed of 400 mph in level flight and a higher dive speed than any fighter then in service. Furthermore, a ceiling of 40,000 ft was also required as well as an improved armour protection for the pilot, and a heavy armament. Kartveli rapidly understood that he should return to the radial engine and, chose the new P&W eighteen cylinders double-row XR-2800 of 2,000 hp. He enlarged the wing in order to install the requested heavier armament, proposing six or eight 12.7 mm (0.5 in.) machine-guns.

The new prototype received the designation of XP-47B from the USAAC, showing that a new kind of heavy fighter had been born. The height of 4.5 m., the length of 11 m. and a fully loaded weight of nearly six tonnes made the P-47 almost double the size of the Spitfire. The first flight occurred on 6 May 1941 and, with tests progressing well, an order from the USAAC was placed for 773 aircraft. A number of improvements, for example replacing the hinged canopy with a sliding one, were introduced, along with a more powerful engine. The first series of aircraft was officially accepted by the USAAC on 21 December 1941 and immediately reserved for official tests.

The next version to be built was the P-47C, with 602 aircraft completed. These had a longer fuselage and included a shackle for the connection of a long-range ferry tank to be installed. This version paved the way for the first variant that would be built in large numbers, the P-47D, of which 12,603 aircraft were built. During the manufacturing period, this version gave birth to a plethora of minor refinements and changes to equipment, reflected in the block numbers:

- P-47D-2 – RE: E.g. suppression of the compressor fairing
- P-47D-4 – RA: E.g. compressor GE C-1, water injection system
- P-47D-5 – RE: E.g. compressor GE C-1, water injection system and suspension points for a ventral external tank
- P-47D-25 – RE: E.g. a new 'bubble' canopy with all-round visibility, two additional oxygen bottles and increased internal fuel capacity[1]
- P-47D-40 – RA: E.g. dorsal fillet between the canopy and the tail, this modification also applied retroactively to practically all the bubble canopy D sub-models. Also received suspension points for eight rockets, a K-14 collimator and passive radar.

After the P-47D variant many others would appear, both as new prototypes or as operational aircraft as listed below:

- Prototypes: XP-47E, XP-47F, XP-47K, XP-47L and XP-72

1 The aircraft characteristics for this version is presented after the list of Portuguese aircraft.

F-47. (FAP/AHFA)

- Operational A/c: P-47G, P-47H, P-47J, P-47M and P-47N

Besides its extensive use by the USAAC (later USAAF) during WWII, the P-47 (renamed F-47 in 1947), served also with many other nations in the post-war years, among them Bolivia, Brazil, Chile, China, Colombia, Cuba, Dominican Republic, Equator, France, Guatemala, Italy, Nicaragua, Turkey, Venezuela, Yugoslavia and Portugal. In addition to the USAAC, the RAF, RAAF, the Soviet VVS, the Mexican Air Force and Brazilian Air Arm had used the aircraft during WW2 on different fronts.

Republic F-47D Thunderbolt in Portuguese Service

As a consequence of the founding of NATO[2] in 1949, a new era began for the Air Forces of the Alliance countries. Those countries still equipped with outdated WWII-era aircraft, as was the case with Portugal, were provided with interim machines that would prepare them for the arrival of jet aircraft.

2 The North Atlantic Treaty Organisation, NATO, was signed in Washington on 4 April 1949 involving twelve countries, two in North America, United States and Canada, and ten in Europe, Belgium, Denmark, France, Iceland, Italy, Luxembourg, Norway, Portugal, The Netherlands and the United Kingdom.

Twelve Thunderbolts in formation in flight. (FAP/AHFA)

Three F-47s in flight. (FAP/AHFA)

With this in mind, it was agreed early in 1951 that, under the Mutual Defence Assistance Program (MDAP), Portugal would receive 50 F-47 Thunderbolts to establish a bridge between the Spitfires and Hurricanes still in service and the T-33s and F-84 Thunderjets, to be delivered in the near future. This was not just to help adjust to the flight capabilities of newer fighters, but also to introduce the personnel of the recently formed Portuguese Air Force to the modern techniques in maintenance and support. At the same time, the United States proposed to the Portuguese authorities that pilots and technical personnel visit bases in the United States and Germany to be given the adequate preparation, an offer that was warmly accepted.

The personnel that would compose these first courses was taken mainly from the three Fighter Flights at Ota Air Base operating the old Spitfires, from the Espinho Base, and later from Sintra, where 'MP' Flight was still flying Hurricanes. By November 1951 some of the personnel earmarked

Eight Thunderbolts on the flight line. From front to back the following serials can be discerned in the original photo: 4401, 4417, 4420, 4405 and 4433. (FAP/AHFA)

to work on the new aircraft were already receiving theoretical training in Portugal when, in December 1951, the 50 aircraft arrived at Lisbon harbour on the deck of a US aircraft carrier. The aircraft were then transported to Lisbon Airport, where they were assembled in a military hangar and flight-tested almost immediately. The earliest known record of such a test flight dates from 19 December, probably being the first flight of a F-47 over Portuguese territory.

After being ferried to Ota Air Base, the F-47s began to receive Portuguese serials numbers in the 44** block range, under the new serial system of the Portuguese Air Force (FAP), that would officially be formed on 1 July 1952. The block ranges 41**, 42** and 43** were at that time applied respectively to the Gladiator, Hurricane and Spitfire, although as far as is known, they never used the new serials.

The first accidents soon happened, the first on 27 February 1952, leading to the death of the pilot. This was the start of a long list of accidents, resulting in the unfortunate death of six pilots up to November 1954.

The first reorganization of the Flight units

At the same time the re-organisation of the Flights into Squadrons began, introducing the *Esquadra*[3] of 25 aircraft, in place of the *Esquadrilha* of around 15 aircraft. In April 1952, the 1st and 2nd *Esquadras* were formed at Ota Air Base to incorporate the new aircraft. In the summer of 1952 the first FAP officers trained for instrument flight rules (IFR) in the United States returned to Ota as instructors to their fellow pilots. Then, again in April 1952, the new Squadrons were renamed *Esquadra 10* and *Esquadra 11*, in line with the new rule that directed FAP units to be designated by numbers instead of the old code letter system.

With the training picking up its pace, the last two aircraft (s/n 4447 and 4450) were delivered to operational units by the end of June 1952. Meanwhile, the lack of appropriate radio equipment installed at Portuguese airfields to instruct pilots was an important restriction to their training

3 In this new system each *Esquadra* was composed of four *Esquadrilhas*.

F-47 flight line at Tancos. On the first two aircraft the diagonal black strips on the top surface of the wing can be seen. They were used to assist in the control of the diving angle. (FAP/AHFA)

F-47 flight line at Tancos. (FAP/AHFA)

process. This constraint led to the initiative of performing flights to foreign airfields equipped with such a system and operated by fellow NATO nations.

An important operation for the 'young' FAP took six Portuguese F-47s from Ota Air Base to Zweibrucken, Germany, on 10 September 1952, to participate in the NATO Exercise 'Blue Alliance'. Here the F-47s would fly alongside their planned replacement, the F-84G Thunderjet. Meanwhile, in September 1952 *Esquadra de F-84G* (F-84G Squadron) was created at Ota alongside *Esquadras 10* and *11* operating F-47s. The first jet-trained pilots returned from Germany in October to man the Squadron, although the new jets wouldn't arrive at Ota before March 1953. In these conditions, they were obliged to continue to fly the F-47.

This situation, and the continuing series of accidents, demonstrate that the Portuguese Military Aviation should have had an aircraft like the F-47 earlier. This would have allowed a more satisfactory transition to a heavier and more modern fighter, before the arrival of the new generation jet fighters.

Those accidents continued to happen at a steady pace. Among them, the luckiest escape was seen with the collision of two aircraft, nos. 4429 and 4442, when flying over the village of Cartaxo, 58 km NNE of Lisbon, in October 1952. While the aircraft were heavily damaged, both pilots were able to made an emergency landing and escaped unscathed. By the end of 1952, with the further loss of four pilots, around 40 F-47 Thunderbolts remained – then, in an unrelated piece of bad luck, the Operations Officer was killed in a car accident on the last day of the year.

In the intervening time, in December 1952, the F-47s took part in exercises with Spitfires from Tancos Air Base and RAF Avro Lincoln bombers travelling from the UK for the purpose.

The second reorganization of the Flight units

In February 1953 a new Fighter Group arrangement was implemented at Ota Air Base, with the *10ª Esquadra* (now operating F-47 Thunderbolts, DH Vampires and North American T-6s as result of the amalgamation of the former 10th and 11th *Esquadras*), and a new 20th *Esquadra* exclusively flying F-84Gs. At around the same time, a number of pilots began to leave the F-47 unit to make their transition to the F-84G Thunderjets.

The typical pilot training mission programme for the period included:

- Formation and navigation flights,
- Instrument and night flying,
- Aerobatics, air to air combat simulation (dogfights),
- Air to air, and air to ground gunnery,
- Dive and level bombing, including the use of napalm, and
- Interception up to and above 7,500 metres.

In early 1953, the US revealed a sudden and surprising inability to supply spare parts essential to maintain the F-47 fleet. This complicated the regular training and operations of the *Esquadra*. At that time, the USAF. had retired all its F-47s so the problem of spares provision was hard to comprehend. However, the lack of spares did not forbid the over-flight of Lisbon on 27 April 1953 by 20 Thunderbolts.

As an example of the activity level of the *10ª Esquadra*, in May 1953 the number of 368 flying hours was reached, involving 41 pilots, with an average aircraft flight readiness of 16.6. Between June and December 1953 the average of monthly hours flown increased to 376.24 hrs. This increase can at least partly be put down to the *Esquadra's* participation in the October 1953 Army manoeuvres, with circa 175 hrs of flight time associated with that activity.

In November and December 1953, eleven aircraft were struck off the inventory, with another F-47 lost in an accident in which the pilot perished. Also in November, the F-47 Squadron lost another 17 pilots, for happier reasons, as they were detached to attend a F-84 conversion course.

The year of 1954 would commence with 37 pilots in *Esquadra 10*, only to see the Squadron closed down in February and the surviving Thunderbolts passed to *Esquadra 22*, where they would join the remaining T-6 Harvards of *Esquadra 10*, two newly received DH Vampires, and Lockheed

Thunderbolt serial number 4447 in Sintra Air Base where it was used as a study subject for the maintenance school. Two other photos show its wings in a scrap yard in Lisbon in May 1968. Those were the sad remains of the last Thunderbolt in Portugal! (FAP/AHFA)

Aircraft 4405 showing distinctively the position of fuselage Cross of Christ and flag in the tail. On this aircraft the Tancos insignia, the greyhound, is absent. (FAP/AHFA)

Left side of the Thunderbolt 4437 with the Tancos insignia on the cowling. (FAP/AHFA)

T-33 trainers. This new *Esquadra 22* was to be destined to act, therefore, as an instruction unit to prepare future pilots for the F-84G Thunderjet.

By mid 1954 the total of F-47 aircraft available did not exceed 17 units, still struggling with a lack of spare parts, now affecting the engines, and the level of daily availability of aircraft fell steadily. The situation continued to deteriorate even more in the following months, as *Esquadra 22* with their F-47s, Harvards and the two Vampires, had to provide training for 50 pilots, without which they could not fly the new Thunderjets! (The Lockheed T-33 trainers had been transferred the new IFR Training Flight.)

The new displacement to Tancos Air Base

A new home for the F-47s was envisaged at that point, in order to find better conditions than at Ota Air Base (B.A.2), where a large number of aircraft were now active. The decision to transfer the F-47 Squadron to Tancos Air Base (B.A.3) was taken in December and the movement of aircraft, men and equipment began immediately. At the end of January 1955 the remaining 14 aircraft available arrived at Tancos to form the so-called *Esquadra de F-47. Esquadra 22* had, in the meantime, been disbanded at Ota.

However, conditions at Tancos turned out to be much worse that those at Ota, mainly concerning personnel accommodation, maintenance facilities, auxiliary installations and the always-present problem of the spare parts. In March 1955 there were only 13 aircraft available,

Aircraft 4401 showing the position of the serial on the left wing. (FAP/AHFA)

suffering now from a more serious problem, the non-availability of engines due to maintenance problems and the general ageing of components. Nevertheless, with the hard work of all the personnel involved, it was possible to maintain the activity of the *Esquadra* although by February 1956 the number of available aircraft was no greater than seven or eight.

Around the end of 1956, the era of the F-47 Thunderbolt in Portugal was coming to its end, as more and more Lockheed T-33 were becoming available and the instructors becoming qualified in Germany and the USA The number of flights diminished until the end of that year when, it seems the final flights in F-47s were completed.

Unfortunately, once again no examples of the type were preserved for posterity. One F-47 airframe was used longer than any other, aircraft no. 4447, which was moved to Air Base no.1 at Sintra after retirement to serve as an instructional airframe for the mechanics' school operating at that base. However this aircraft was also later scrapped, as one of the authors saw its wings in a scrapyard in Lisbon in 1968. A picture of its wing is one of the photos illustrating this chapter.

Individual Aircraft Histories

USAF Serial no.	Type	Date Arrival	A.M. Serial no.	Struck Of Charge	Remarks
44-20588	F-47D-30-RE	1951	4401	6/56	
44-20848	F-47D-30-RE	1951	4402	11/56	
44-32677	F-47D-30-RE	1951	4403	11/56	
44-32693	F-47D-30-RE	1951	4404		Destroyed accident 2/52
44-32822	F-47D-30-RE	1951	4405	11/56	
44-32846	F-47D-30-RE	1951	4406	3/54	
44-32864	F-47D-30-RE	1951	4407	5/52	
44-32873	F-47D-30-RE	1951	4408	9/54	
44-32889	F-47D-30-RE	1951	4409	11/56	
44-32893	F-47D-30-RE	1951	4410	10/53	
44-32897	F-47D-30-RE	1951	4411	10/53	
44-32917	F-47D-30-RE	1951	4412		Destroyed accident 5/52
44-33275	F-47D-30-RE	1951	4413	7/54	
44-20835	F-47D-30-RE	1951	4414	11/56	
44-32675	F-47D-30-RE	1951	4415		Destroyed accident 8/54
44-32690	F-47D-30-RE	1951	4416	10/53	
44-32701	F-47D-30-RE	1951	4417	11/56	
44-32825	F-47D-30-RE	1951	4418	10/53	
44-32860	F-47D-30-RE	1951	4419		
44-32871	F-47D-30-RE	1951	4420	11/56	

F-47 4447 at Sintra Air Base used for the mechanics students instruction. (FAP/AHFA)

44-32874	F-47D-30-RE	1951	4421	10/53	
44-32890	F-47D-30-RE	1951	4422		Destroyed accident 5/52
44-32895	F-47D-30-RE	1951	4423		Destroyed accident 11/53
44-32904	F-47D-30-RE	1951	4424		Destroyed accident 11/52
44-33817	F-47D-30-RE	1951	4425	7/52	
44-33187	F-47D-30-RE	1951	4426		Destroyed accident 9/52
44-33790	F-47D-30-RE	1951	4427	10/53	
44-90122	F-47D-30-RE	1951	4428	6/56	
44-90125	F-47D-30-RE	1951	4429	11/52	
44-90133	F-47D-30-RE	1951	4430	7/52	

Right wing of 4447 in a scrap yard in Lisbon by May 1968. (Luis Tavares)

44-90137	F-47D-30-RE	1951	4431	11/53	
44-90152	F-47D-30-RE	1951	4432		Destroyed accident 5/54
44-90207	F-47D-30-RE	1951	4433	11/56	
44-90251	F-47D-30-RE	1951	4434	11/56	
44-90257	F-47D-30-RE	1951	4435	11/56	
44-90263	F-47D-30-RE	1951	4436	11/56	
44-90268	F-47D-30-RE	1951	4437	6/56	
44-90273	F-47D-30-RE	1951	4438	6/56	
44-90275	F-47D-30-RE	1951	4439		Destroyed accident 5/52
44-89991	F-47D-30-RE	1951	4440	11/53	
44-90124	F-47D-30-RE	1951	4441	11/53	
44-90128	F-47D-30-RE	1951	4442	11/52	
44-90136	F-47D-30-RE	1951	4443	2/56	
44-90146	F-47D-30-RE	1951	4444	10/53	
44-90200	F-47D-30-RE	1951	4445	10/53	
44-90212	F-47D-30-RE	1951	4446	10/53	
44-90261	F-47D-30-RE	1951	4447		To Air Base 1, Sintra, in 1953 for Maintenance instruction
44-90266	F-47D-30-RE	1951	4448		Destroyed accident 2/54
44-90271	F-47D-30-RE	1951	4449	9/56	
44-90283	F-47D-30-RE	1951	4450		Destroyed accident 4/53

Note: The USAF serial numbers and their correspondence to the FAP serials are taken from the book '*Aviões Militares Portugueses*', by Major Adelino Cardoso.

Camouflage and Markings

The F-47 Thunderbolts were delivered in natural metal, the new FAP markings being applied according to the newly issued regulations, i.e. the red *Cruz de Cristo* over a white roundel without border in four positions, on both sides of the rear fuselage, on top of the left wing and beneath the right wing. The serial number was applied in black under the left wing and over the right wing. On each side of the rudder was painted the simplified green and red Portuguese flag, and above it the serial number in small, black digits.

On a number of aircraft, four black guidance lines for the determination of dive angle were painted on the top surface of each wing (see photo). It is not certain whether these guides were already painted on the airframes when received or if they were added later on when assigned to the dive-bombing task in the *Esquadras*.

When the F-47 Thunderbolt entered service within the *Força Aérea Portuguesa*, the system of designating Flights or Squadrons by letters painted in the aircraft had been abandoned. Furthermore, in the particular case of the F-47, no Squadron insignia was painted on the airframe. The only concession to such a symbol was the Tancos *Galgo* painted in yellow on both sides of the cowling, with the Air Base motto '*Res Non Verba*' (Deeds Not Words) painted black underneath the greyhound in a semi-circle, and the last two digits of the serial number above it, also in black, close to the olive-drab anti-glare panel. This occurred solely when the aircraft operated from Tancos.

The other known emblem displayed by a Portuguese F-47 was to be seen on the sole survivor after the retirement at Sintra Air Base, aircraft serial number 4447. Painted in the cowling, apparently on the left side only, was a light-blue roundel with the letters E.I.M. (*Escola de Instrução de Mecânicos* – Mechanics Training School) in black.

Top view of aircraft 4416 showing the position of serial and national insignia. Note the absence of the dive guidance lines. (MAIS ALTO/AHFA)

Aircraft Characteristics Republic F-47D-28 Thunderbolt	
Quantity used:	50
Crew:	One
Years of Service:	1952–1956
Span:	39.37' (12.43 m)
Length:	36.08' (11.02 m)
Height:	13.12' (4.47 m)
Wing Area:	290.63 sq.ft. (27.87 m²)
Engine:	One *Pratt & Whitney R-2800-59* of 2,300 hp
Empty weight:	10,000lb (4,536 kg)
Normal loaded weight:	14,502 lb (6,578 kg)
Maximum speed:	426 mph (686 km/h) at 30,000 ft (9,150 m)
Service ceiling:	42,000 ft (12,800 m)
Armament:	8 *Browning* 12.7 mm machine-guns, 1250 kg externally suspended.

Pilots arriving after a mission. (Mais Alto/AHFA)

Flight line at Tancos. (Collection Alberto Covas)

Detail of machine guns. The tips of the dive angle black stripes are just visible over the leading edge of the wing. (Collection Alberto Covas)

The remains of the 4447 wing in the scrap yard in May 1968. (Luis Tavares)

Republic F-47D-30-RE Thunderbolt s/n 4434, (ex-USAF 44-90251), Tancos Air Base (BA 3), 1955. After WWII and under the MADP, as with other US allied countries Portugal received a significant number (50) of Thunderbolts as temporary fighters, destined to bridge the transition between the piston engine fighters still in service and the jet fighters already on the horizon. The F-47s maintained for the entirety of their operational life the original "natural metal" appearance to which only the national colours were added and, after their movement to BA 3 (Tancos) in 1954, the Galgo, *the Air Base motto "Res Non Verba" (Deeds No Words) and the "last two digits" were painted on both sides of the cowling.*

Aircraft 4334 and Tancos insignia. (MAIS ALTO/AHFA)

Republic F-47D-30-RE Thunderbolt s/n 4423, (ex-USAF 44-32895), Ota Air Base (BA 2), 1952. Destroyed in an accident in November 1953, this aircraft can be considered an example of the difficulties that the Portuguese Air Force faced in the transition for the "jet age". Counting nevertheless with excellent and very competent pilots and ground crews, the conversion from much lighter aircraft as the Hurricanes and Spitfires, took a heavy toll in human lives from its ranks and the loss of fifteen aircraft.

Side view of F-47 s/n 4423. (FAP/AHFA)

Republic F-47D-30-RE Thunderbolt s/n 4423, upper surface view – The painting regulations for the new FAP – Força Aérea Portuguesa *(Portuguese Air Force) established that the* Cruz de Cristo *should be painted over a white roundel without border over the left wing and under the right one. Correspondingly, the full serial number should be painted in black on the opposite surfaces. In a number of aircraft, four black guidance lines for the determination of the dive angle were painted on the top surface of each wing. It is not certain that such markings were already painted on the airframes when the aircraft were received or if they were added later on when assigned to dive-bombing task within the* Esquadras. *It is also uncertain whether those lines stretched from the leading edges of the wings to the fuselage or if they were always truncated as shown.*

Appendices

Appendix 1. Markings and Insignia 1919–1956

Although the first 'heavier than air' flight occurred in Portugal at the dawn of the 20th century, and the Army possessed an *aeroplano militar* (military aeroplane) in the shape of one Deperdussin[1], it was not until around 1914 that the need to clearly identify military aeroplanes became apparent. This necessity was connected to the events taking place in the Central European battlefields and the need to distinguish friends from foes.

The following types of insignia and markings along the years fulfilled this need:

- National markings
- Air Base insignia
- Unit insignia
- Personal insignia

National markings:

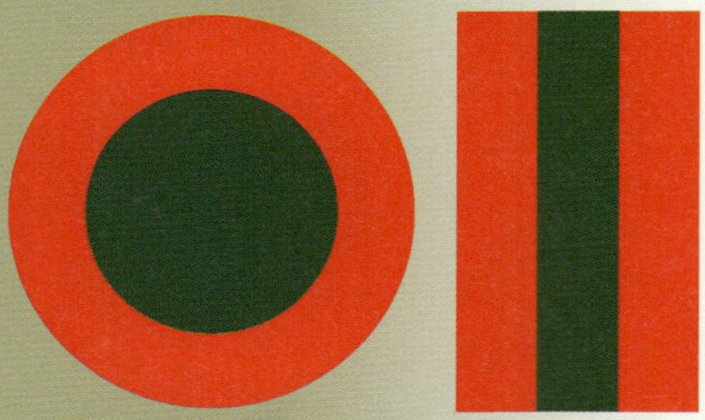

Wings. *Tail.*

Fig 1. Aeronautica Militar 1914–1919.

The first Portuguese National markings followed the most common form, the *cocarde*/cockade (roundel), consisting of a red circle surrounding a green (Fig.1.). From 1910, those were the colours of the Portuguese National Flag, introduced when the Republican regime was proclaimed on 5 October that year. The cockade was to be used on the wings in a four-position pattern while the rudder should show the colours as vertical stripes of red/green/red. This regulation was not followed strictly, and was applied randomly to the handful of military aeroplanes. In fact, there is no record of the tricolour rudder ever being used, as it was replaced almost immediately by the two shades of the National Flag, green and red, with the former always leading (at that time without the Coat of Arms superimposed).

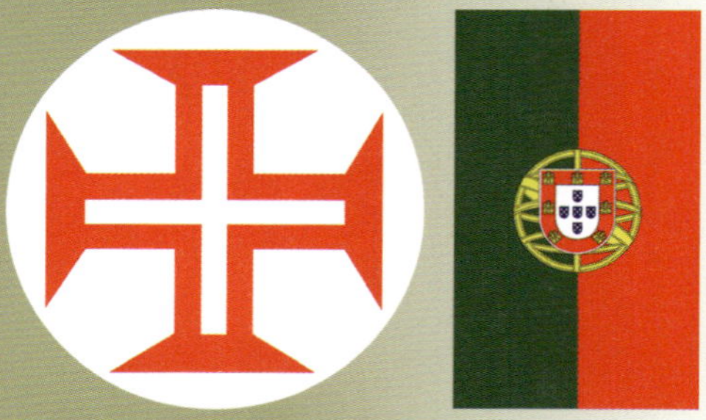

Wings. *Full rudder.*

Fig 2. Aeronautica Militar 1920–1940.

After the Great War, the arrival of updated equipment to the Armed Forces also brought the need for standardisation. The air component, the *Aeronautica Militar*, (A.M.), introduced a new national marking, consisting of the *Cruz de Cristo* (Christ's Cross) in red and white over a white disc (Fig.2) to be applied in four positions on the wings. Exceptions to this rule happened, however: Nieuport trainers had the insignia applied in six positions, i.e., above and below the upper wing, and on the under surface of the lower wing. The National Flag was now to include the State Coat of Arms, with an armillary sphere[2], and covering either all or part of the rudder.

Throughout this period, 1920 until 1940, at least two different types of crosses are recorded (Fig.3), with larger or smaller "arms". Period photos show that both styles were sometimes used at the same time on the same model of aeroplane. So much for standardisation!

Wings. *Rudder Flash.*

Fig 3. Aeronautica Militar 1920–1940.

Between 1920 and 1952 the *Aeronautica Militar* used a variety of fin or rudder flags (flashes), as per Fig. 4. These were to have the complete national Coat of Arms included. The convention for keeping the proportions of the flag roughly

1 Today the doubt still subsists on the type of the aircraft received, mostly due to the custom-made way that those aircraft were manufactured. The most common suggestion is that it was a Type B, but recent research points to a type *Militaire*, which characteristics, according to the firm's specifications, are closer to the one in Portuguese possession.

2 Armillary sphere – An nautical instrument used during the 15th Century Discovery era. Said to be a reference to Prince Henry the Navigator.

2/5 green to 3/5 red dates from this period. Photographic evidence shows that the partition of the flag did not always follow this rule The green part of the flag, as already mentioned, was (and still is) to be painted always leading on both sides of the fin, in the direction of flight.

Until the years of WWII the *Cruz de Cristo* is rarely observed on aeroplanes' fuselage sides. Exceptions were to be seen in the so-called 'flights to the Colonies', record-breaking attempts, test-flights of new routes (see the Morane chapter) or other 'flag flying' flights.

With the increasing number of interned aircraft on its territory during WWII, the need for the A.M. to camouflage the existing ones but provide rapid identification of any intruder into national air space grew. The national markings were painted more often on aircraft's sides, without the white background when in this position, the exceptions being the Mohawk and the Airacobra, which retained the white disc on the fuselage markings. In addition, letters identifying the Flight and the individual aeroplane were painted either side of the fuselage cross, apart from the case of the Gloster Gladiator.

Fig 4. Aeronautica Militar 1920–1952.

Fin flash with Coat of Arms.

Fin flash without Coat of Arms.

Air Base insignia

Air Base heraldry applied to aircraft within the *Arma de Aeronautica* was not practised until the formation of the *Força Aérea* in 1952. Even in 1940, during the reorganisation of the *Arma*, when the concept of the Air Base was implemented and they were numerically identified in the Portuguese Continental and Insular territories, no such form of recognition seems to have been contemplated. The naming of the Air Bases was related to the closest settlement, thus Air Base 1 being named after Sintra, a village five kilometres SW of it, Air Base 2 named after Ota, another village three kilometres away, etc.

Unit Insignia

The oldest unit insignia in the *Arma da Aeronautica*, and which identified not only Fighter Flights but also Training aircraft, is the *Galgo* (greyhound) (Fig.5) allegedly designed by the first C.O. of Tancos Airfield, *Capitão* Ribeiro da Fonseca, after his pet dog, a greyhound, that according also to legend, would invariably chase rabbits and hares that populated the airfield! Curiously, this Unit insignia became the Air Base no. 3 Tancos crest central motif when the Air Force Heraldry was established by mid to late 1950s, also retaining the motto devised then and included later beneath the dog design, *Res non Verba*, (Deeds not Words).

Fig 5.

During their assignment to the Azores Archipelago the two Gladiator Flights comprising the *Esquadrilhas Expedicionárias de Caça* (Expeditionary Fighter Flights) had their fuselage decorated with 'morale-boosting' insignia. The First Flight used a boxing mosquito and the Second Flight bore the aforementioned *Galgo* (see the Gloster Gladiator Chapter). Of the first design, three variants are known and included here (Fig.6).

When the Hawker Hurricanes Flights were formed in 1943-44, no specific insignia were envisaged to differentiate each Flight. Badges were only applied at the beginning of 1947 on the left side of the forward fuselage of the aircraft belonging to 'MP', 'RV' and 'VX' Flights. Their design is described in depth under the 'Camouflage and Markings' section of the relevant chapter. Again the legendary Tancos *Galgo* was painted on the fuselage side(s) of a number of aircraft, although it is not known to what extent this emblem was used.

Personal insignia

Personal insignia were not common in the *Arma da Aeronautica* or the Air Force, but were occasionally seen and were more or less tolerated by the authorities.

Fig 6. © Pedro Barbosa
The three different "Boxing Mosquito" emblems of the Gloster Gladiator. These elements, which as such are under copyright, were drawn by Mr. Pedro Barbosa from Oporto, for a decal sheet produced by Colorado and sponsored by IPMS Portugal. They are used here with his kind permission.

In general terms, the personal insignias were for the most part used during 'prestige' or 'flag-flying' flights, where a personal motto or an image of a loved-one alongside patriotic slogans would sometimes appear.

Personal insignia were seldom seen on service aircraft in the pre-independent air force days of the A.M. The most well-known and prevalent example is the sequence of aircraft named 'MITA', (with a new number for each new incarnation) by the Tancos C.O., *Tenente Coronel* Antonio Maya (then a *Major*). The name was the nickname of Maya's wife, Mrs. Maria Clotilde ('Mita') Dantas, and could usually be seen applied near the cockpit access of his personal aircraft (Fig.7). The last aircraft thus marked and identified was Hawker Fury no. 50, which was named 'MITA 9º'.

Another insignia, of unknown origin and meaning, is to be found on the left-hand side of the cowling of a Spitfire Mk V, this time a Hen's chick circled by the words "*Onde tu chegares eu chego*" ('Where you reach I will reach too'), probably painted in white.

A further example of individuality in markings, if not strictly a personal insignia, was the sentence *Não Faz Mal!* or *Não Faz...*, meaning "Doesn't matter...", often seen written on the forward fuselage of several interned but operational aircraft during WWII, such as B-24 Liberators and the sole Lockheed P-38 Lightning.

The Portuguese Air Force formation and new rules (1952)

It was necessary to wait until June 1952, with the formation of the *Força Aérea Portuguesa*, F.A.P. (Portuguese Air Force), for a standardised and regulated design of the cockade, fin flashes and letters or numbers to appear.

The Government's plan to create a new structure, merging the air components of the Army and Navy into an independent air force, was known for nearly a year before it happened, by means of a decree from the Ministry of Army, dated 11 July 1951. This stated that "... being necessary to normalise the identification marks and serial numbers of the aircraft... (confirming) the i.d. marks (to be) the *Cruz de Cristo* and National Flag without Coat of Arms...etc...". Furthermore, the need to conform to principles and regulations set down by N.A.T.O., of which Portugal was a founder member in 1949, contributed to the origin of these regulations. A translation of elements of this Decree is included in this section.

Fig 7.

Consequently, and from then on, the cross was to be painted on the upper surface of the left wing and under surface of the right wing only, instead of the previous four positions. Aircraft identification numbers of four digits would be displayed on the wings in the alternate positions, i.e. the upper surface of the right wing and under surface of the left, the top of them towards the front on both surfaces.

'The *Cruz de Cristo* (Fig.8) will be inscribed on a white roundel with the dimensions of 0.75 m, 1 metre or 1.50m. It will be selected the circumference closer to 4/5 of the distance measured from the leading edge of the wing to the leading edge of the aileron, with its centre distant 3/4 of the half-span. The same outlook will be applied to the block of four digits.

'Numbers are to be of "Arabic style" of 0.50m, 0.75m, 1 metre or 1.25m high and its design is very similar, if not the same, to the ones used by the RAF (Fig.9). For its display on the wings it will be chosen now a height closer to 1/2 of the length measured from the leading edge of the wing to the leading edge of the aileron, again with the centre (of the block) distant 3/4 of the half-span.

'Numbers will be equally displayed on the fin 10 cm. above the flag and will be either 15 cm. or 20 cm. high, depending on the dimension of the fin. The flag itself obeys as well to precise proportions, being its length 1.5 of the height (a= 1.5b), the green part equals 2/5 of the total length (c= 2/5 b) and the length itself will be 1/3 the height of the fin (Fig.8).'

Colours, in the absence of paint references, were just defined by their Portuguese names as *vermelho carregado* (dark red) for the cross, *branco* (white) for the background disc and inner cross and *escarlate* (scarlet) for the relevant part of the flag with *verde escuro* (dark green) for the rest of the flag. All paints were to be gloss enamel. By today standards we can consider the above-mentioned colours to be close to FS11136 (red), FS14109 (green) and FS17875 (white).

These regulations were to be maintained for more than a decade, until the beginning of the 1960s, when the need for a revision became apparent. Even so, with all the bureaucracy issuing and checking regulations, these were not always correctly implemented or followed.

Fig 8.

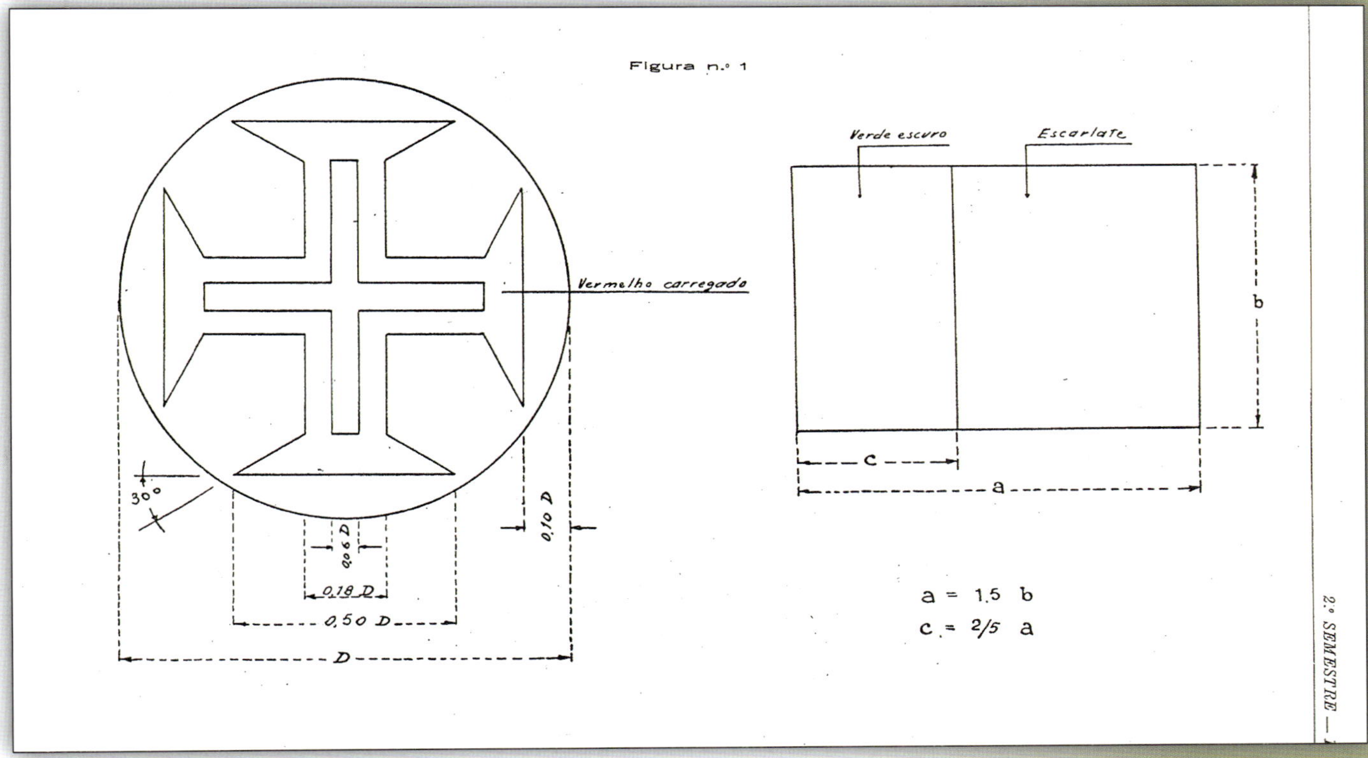

Fig 9.

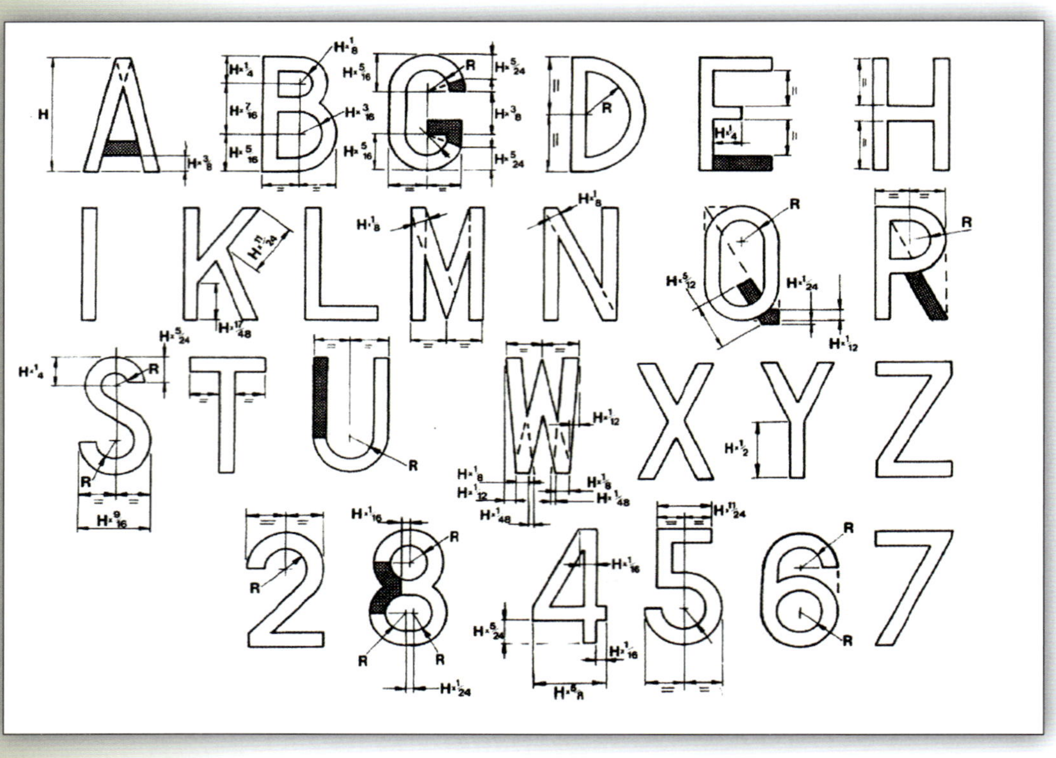

Appendix 2. Colours and Camouflage

Although the 'Colours and Camouflage' information on Portuguese Military Aviation's fighter aircraft has been covered in their respective chapters, it was felt that a word of explanation should also be included.

It was apparent to those who study the aircraft in service with the *Aeronautica Militar Portuguesa* (A.M.), that the original colour in which they arrived in Portugal, either brand new from the factory or second-hand from their previous owners, was maintained for the most if not all of their operational life.

In the mid-to-late 1920s, there were some timid experiments to develop homogeneity on the colours of the military equipment in the Portuguese Armed Forces, be it uniforms, vehicles, weapons and, obviously, aeroplanes. The chief priorities were by then camouflage and concealment, stemming from the lessons of WWI. In the case of Portugal, specifically Military Aviation, it is unknown if colour norms as such were established for newly received airframes and those already in service with the A.M. No evidence of such a move was discovered in official archives. One example is that of the four Martinsyde Buzzard aircraft, which, after being received with their original silver dope treatment, were painted in a tone of grey similar to the one used by the Army – of which the Military Aviation was part – a tone close to 'battleship grey', which could be identified recently, thanks to an original part of an aircraft of that era, to be close to Federal Standard 26132 (Fig. 1A). The Martinsyde Buzzard thus had the privilege of being the first fighter painted in "Portuguese colours"!

Fig. 1A. The name MITA 5º as applied to a fighter aircraft, of unknown type but contemporary of the Martynside F.4 Buzzard. For explanation refer to the chapter "Markings and Insignia".

Until the arrival of the first fighter that arrived wearing true camouflage, the Curtiss H75-A4 Mohawk, the A.M. fighters generally maintained the paint schemes with which they were received. When the Gloster Gladiators were purchased, the contract order stipulated that they should have the upper surfaces painted "green" and the under surfaces in "light blue". We can only speculate that, as this order was completed in the United Kingdom, the original colours would be the British Dark Green and Sky Blue in use at the time.

As during the existence of the *Aeronautica Militar* and after with the *Força Aérea Portuguesa*, it is unlikely that paint was an item included in the spare parts list when an aircraft was purchased. Minor repair 'touch ups' or overall repainting had to be completed with locally acquired supplies, resembling the original hues as closely as possible, but for which no specification was issued. This situation would change only in the 1980s, when a detailed Decree (*Portaria* 101/80) dated 12 March 1980, established painting norms based on Federal Standards 595 rules for colours, USAF. Technical Orders for camouflage patterns addressed to specific aircraft, and NATO STANAGs (standardisation agreements) for other internal and external markings, among other directives. This time, even if the paint supplies had to be purchased locally, the final result was obtained with a minimal margin for error.

Meanwhile and on the final stages of the existence of *Aeronautica Militar*, almost on the eve of the *Força Aérea* (1952), an attempt to standardize the A.M. aircraft markings was done with the issue of Decree (*Portaria* 13.602) dated 11 July 1951, which established dimensions for numbers, cockades, *Cruz de Cristo*, fin flags and their exact location, but omitted any reference to the airframe colours or camouflage[1]. Yet, also by then several Spitfires appeared painted in a lustreless upper surface dark green and light blue (or grey?) under surfaces, with markings already following the prescribed procedure (See photo on page 142) but without a colour specification. The above Portaria, rather than establishing rules for the existing and almost defunct *Aeronautica Militar*, was already preparing the way for the forthcoming *Força Aérea* inaugurated on 1 July 1952.

A drawing on which the Hurricane is specifically represented has emerged, implying that the same colour scheme would be applied to the surviving airframes. This type, however, appeared to maintain the disruptive grey/green over light grey initial scheme until the end of its operational life (See photograph on page 184).

Curiously, the *Aeronautica Militar* rigorously established painting standards for training aircraft since the mid 1930s. In effect, the purchase order to the de Havilland factory for the supply of DH 82 Tiger Moths in 1932 clearly specifies the colour painting of the entire airframe. This specification evolved from an initial 'overall dark green' (wings, fuselage, struts and landing gear) to a 'yellow Shell (?) wings, fin, rudder and stabilizer' with 'blue "Maria-Luiza"(?) fuselage, struts and landing gear'. This last specification is copied from the original "letter of understanding" dated 16 September 1937, with which the de Havilland factory authorised O.G.M.A. to manufacture the Tiger Moth after the purchase of eight airframes in the specified colouring.

Whatever those colours were, it has been possible to identify them today using the FS system on an Avro Tutor still bearing the original colours, the equivalence for the Yellow, FS 25190, and for the Blue, FS 23538. (Fig.2A). The dark green which started to be used in the 1930s as mentioned above, by 1973 was defined by the Robbialac colour 4/214/4 approximately equivalent to FS 595a 34079.

1 Although the *Portaria* 13.602 specifically indicates the colours to the *Cruz de Cristo* and the National Flag as being respectively *Vermelho Carregado* (Dark Red), *Verde Escuro* (Dark Green) and *Escarlate* (Scarlet), no other colour reference is given on writing. This being so, OGMA used for the fulfilment of this directive the local manufactured colours of Robiallac references. For instance, by 1972 the red of the flag and *Cruz de Cristo* was the *Titanine* TT10B colour, but was being replaced by the Robbialac synthetic enamel 31-26. However the green of the flag was a mix of the enamels Robbialac yellow 4/214/23 (equivalent to 31-24) and blue 4/214/22 (equivalent .to 31-20). Comparing with chips of those paints in our possession, we can assume that these colours corresponded to today's FS 11136 (red) and FS 14109 (green).

Fig. 4A. Avro Tutor in the FAP Air Museum showing the dark blue and yellow colour scheme mentioned in the text. (Coll A.J.Soares)

Appendix 3. Identification and numbering systems

This will, in all probability, be the very first time that such a complex subject has been explained in detail in a language other then Portuguese. It is important to describe it in this book, in order to enable the reader to understand the many and sometimes bizarre variations, revealed through the aircraft presented here.

The need to identify a particular aircraft in the Portuguese military aviation, as with many other air forces, arose with the increasing number of aircraft being used and the logistical requirements necessary to maintain them in airworthy condition whevever possible.

Army Aviation/Air Force

1 – General sequential system

In Portugal the first aircraft to be used by the military in the *Escola Militar de Aviação* were identified by a sequence of letters and numbers, starting with the number 1, for each type and model of aircraft.

This includes the Maurice Farmans MF-1, MF-2, and the Farman F.40s F3. These 'serials', attributed at unit level, may or may not include the type designation (MF, F.40, etc) and early on were not displayed on the aircraft.

Later, with the constitution of the *Grupo de Esquadrilhas de Aviação República* (see the SPAD chapter) and the sudden influx of 'new' aircraft, the need to apply the serial number or identification to the airframe of each aircraft arose.

From then on, sometimes confusingly, each aircraft was designated in written documents or colloquially as, for example, 'Breguet 15' or 'SPAD 8', referring to the fifteenth or eighth aircraft in the fleet of each type, and not the aircraft model. This meant of course that it was not sufficient to refer to one specific aircraft by its serial (as is done today) but the type had also to be referenced. It should be mentioned that, in several cases when there was only one example of an aircraft type, or even just a few, serial numbers were not issued. The most glaring case in this respect is the Martynside F.4/F.4A Buzzard which, as far as is know, did not receive any serial numbers, although there were four examples received and flown operationally. At least three of them, though, were 'baptised' with individual names referencing Portuguese heroic figures in two cases, and a local river in the third case (see Chapter on the Buzzard). One explanation is that only one Buzzard was received in 1919, the three additional ones only being accepted several years later.

The year of 1924 saw another reorganisation of Army aviation with the publication of the Decree no. 10094 dated 16 September 1924, which created the *Arma de Aeronáutica* and established, as the basic unit, the *Esquadrilha* (Flight) consisting of 12-15 aircraft, and the *Grupo* (Group), being the gathering of a number of *Esquadrilhas*.

2 – Serials by blocks or groups (1935)

By 1935, a new system was adopted replacing the one mentioned above. Now, separated blocks of serial numbers were to be issued to different aircraft types, which meant that for each aircraft there might exist gaps in the serials, as is explained below with the blocks assigned to Tiger Moth and Moranes:

Tiger Moth aircraft assigned to Sintra:

- Serials before the new rule: 1 – 2 – 3 – 4 …
- Serials after new rule applied: 100 – 101 – 102 – 103 …

Tiger Moth aircraft assigned to Tancos:

- Serials before the new rule: 10 – 11 – 12 – 13 …
- Serials after new rule applied: 135 – 136 – 137 – 138 …

Morane-Saulnier aircraft assigned to Sintra:

- Serials before the new rule: 2 – 3 – 4 – 5 …
- Serials after new rule applied: 150 – 151 – 152 – 153 …

Morane-Saulnier aircraft assigned to Tancos:

- Serials before the new rule: 6 – 7 – 8 – 9 …
- Serials after new rule applied: 180 – 181 – 182 – 183 ….

Several conclusions can be drawn from the above example:

a) The blocks were issued intermittently, allowing for the identification of the aircraft base;

b) In principle there would not be duplication of serials.

The system was officially implemented through the Circular (Note) nº 172 dated 16/3/1935 (internal regulation) of the 3rd Section of *Arma de Aeronáutica*. However, its application was not carried out without some setbacks: it seems that one interpretation lead to the conclusion that the groups of serials were only connected to the air base and not to the aircraft, so the following bizarre episode took place: on 12 November 1935, when Moranes 151, 152, 192 and 194 were assigned to Tancos, the new serials 185, 186, 183 and 184 were issued to them and painted on the fuselage. At the same time, Moranes 183 and 184 were struck off from Tancos and delivered to Sintra where they maintained these serials…

As a consequence of this shift of aircraft, during two years, 1936-37, there were two Moranes numbered 183 and two Moranes numbered 184, flying at the same time, one at Tancos the other at Sintra!

It also happened that during a certain period of time a duplication of serial numbers existed as the same block of serials was applied to different aircraft at the same instance: e.g. Tiger Moths and Ju-52s using block 101-110, and Tiger Moths and Avro 626s using block 125-137.

A strange combination can be seen in this crashed Airspeed Oxford: the Naval Aviation serial O-1 on the fuselage and the "A.M. serial 505" on the wing! The plausible explanation for this anomaly would be an exchange of aircraft between services. However no Oxford ever received such serial number in A.M.! (FAP/AHFA)

Another view of the same accident and aircraft. The explanation for the presence of two serials in this particular aircraft is that part of the original Oxford RAF serial number (LX 505) was still visible in the lower surface of the wing! (FAP/AHFA)

On the other hand, the implementation of the new serial system did not progress as quickly as it should, as units used the aircraft's maintenance periods to comply with the new rules rather than immediately applying the new markings. This being so, different identification systems coexisted for a long period.

3 – Serials by blocks or groups (1938)

By 1937 another re-organisation of Army aviation was taking place, with the *Comando Geral de Aeronáutica Militar* created by the Decree-Law no. 28401 dated 31 December 1937. This coincided with the arrival of several new aircraft, making it necessary to revise the numbering system, to rectify several mistakes introduced in the meantime and to rationalise the system in view of new aircraft arriving.

Consequently, the publication of 'Circular' (Note) no. 642 of 3 June 1938 gave specific indications in that sense: the document did not mandate the implementation of a new serial system but rather to correct and clarify the existing one. This document applied to the eight main types of aircraft then in service, serials 101 to 451 in blocks of 50 aircraft, leaving block 501 to 549 free for 'various aircraft'.

The blocks and the corresponding aircraft were as follows:

- 101 to 150 – Tiger Moth
- 151 to 199 – Avro 626 and Morane-Saulnier
- 201 to 250 – Junkers Ju 52
- 251 to 299 – Junkers Ju 86
- 301 to 340 – Potez 25
- 351 to 380 – Vickers Valparaiso
- 401 to 420 – Hawker Fury and Hawker Hind
- 451 to 499 – Gloster Gladiator
- 501 to 549 – Various, miscellaneous mainly when there was an unique example of a certain type and model of aircraft, for instance Caproni Ca 113 no. 501, Junkers W34 L no. 502 etc.

A number of changes had, in the meantime, to be made to a number of existing serial numbers already assigned, in order to harmonise the new '1938 system' with the old '1935' one in service.

The changes were:

"..........

a) Avros 626 125 to 131 and 135 to 137 shall be renumbered 160 to 169;
b) Vickers Valparaiso 200 to 207, 209 to 214, 225 to 228, 235 and 236 shall became 351 to 370;
c) Ju 52 101 to 110 shall became 201 to 210;

d) Hawker Hind 275 to 278 shall became 404, 405, 406, 407;
e) Tiger Moth 100 becomes 120 and Avro 626 150 becomes 170;
f) Ju 86 250 becomes 260
g) Hawker Fury 400 becomes 403
h) All Tiger Moths, Moranes, Potez, Ju 86, Fury with the exception of those indicated above, as well as Avro aircraft not mentioned over, and the various aircraft (Dragon, Caproni) will maintain the serials that they already have.
i) These changes must be completed as soon as possible
j) The serials mentioned above will accompany the aircraft when they change unit

.........."

The Second World War and the influx of larger quantities of aircraft forced the assignment of new blocks. In 1943 Hawker Hurricane serial numbers were included in the blocks 510-599 and 600, while Spitfire Mk I aircraft received numerals in the 300 block. This would also to be used for Airacobras and the solitary Lightning P-38.

It is interesting to note that, before receiving serials in the block 370, Spitfire Mk Is received serials in the range of 420, this being confirmed by records at Lisbon Airport that show aerial movements at Lisbon of Spitfires 426, 427, 428 and 429.

From then on, care was taken not to have more than one aircraft with the same serial, as had happened before. Even so, this was not completely avoided, as although the blocks 800 and 900 were still free (the 700 block had been occupied in the meantime by the T-6 Harvard) Oxfords and DH 84s in the 500 block would find themselves sharing same serials in three instances. There was also an odd exception when in 1944 the serials 1 to 95 were assigned to the recently arrived Spitfire Mk Vs. One important detail to be mentioned in the context of the above system (Serials by block groups) is that records were found showing the re-use of serials that had been assigned to an aircraft that had been lost in an accident or withdrawn from service. Obviously, this practice complicates the correct listing of a certain type of aircraft, demanding the utmost care when researching and presenting the subject of aircraft serial lists and/or calculation of the exact numbers of aeroplanes received and used.

4 – Alpha-numeric system (1943)

During WWII a new system was applied to a number of aircraft interned in Portugal: Five Consolidated B-24D Liberators received the serials L1 to L5, while three Hudsons had serials H1 to H3, and one C-47, the serial D-1.

5 – The independent numbering system of Mozambique (1940)

Throughout WW II a number of aircraft used since 1940 by the *Quartel General de Moçambique* (Mozambique Army General Headquarters) received serials consisting of one or two digits, in a system completely independent of the one in use on Mainland Portugal: Tiger Moths – 1 to 9, Hornet Moth – 10, General Aircraft Monospar – 15, Avro Anson – 20 and 21, and Beechcraft Bonanza – 35.

In May 1952, the aircraft still in existence were re-numbered to fit in the new *Força Aérea Portuguesa* system, becoming then:

- Tiger Moth: 1180 to 1188
- Hornet Moth: 9201
- Beechcraft Bonanza: 9301

6 – The four-digit system of the Portuguese Air Force (1951)

This new system was implemented by *Portaria* (decree) *no. 13602* dated 11 July 1951, when planning was being carried out to establish the Portuguese Air Force. The new system was based on a four digit serial, specific to each type and model of aircraft, in which the first digit designated the main function of the aircraft, the second digit was particular to a type, and the last two marked the number of the aircraft within the fleet.

For example, Tiger Moth number 25 would have the serial number 1125, Miles Magister no. 14 would receive the serial number 1214 etc. Following the same criteria, Airspeed Oxford number 3 would be serial no. 2103. In some cases, serials were assigned but never used, mostly because the aircraft were soon to be retired. That was the case with the Hurricanes, to which serial numbers in the 42** range were allocated but, as far as it is known, never used. Also, a few serial blocks were applied more than once as the aircraft to which they were initially allocated were withdrawn. This was the case with block 71**, originally used by SA-16 Albatross and later by B-26 Invader when the former were retired.

An internal document dated 6 June 1951, a month before the above-mentioned *Portaria* was published, specified details of the aircraft the second digit should be assigned to. (The Decree itself did not specify that information). The following table features the aircraft types in use in the *Arma da Aeronautica* one year from the inauguration of *Força Aérea Portuguesa*, and which would be included in the new numbering system:

1 – Single-engine trainer aircraft	1 – DH. Tiger Moth 2 – Miles Magister 3 – DHC. Chipmunk 4 – 5 – Miles Martinet 6 – N.A. T-6 Harvard 7 – 8 – Reserved to single-engine jet trainer aircraft, UK origin 9 – Reserved to single-engine jet trainer aircraft, USA origin
2 – Multi-engine trainer aircraft	1 – Airspeed Oxford 2 – Avro Anson 3 – DH. Dragon Rapide 4 – Grumman Widgeon 5 – Beechcraft T-11 (D-18S, etc.) 6 – Reserved to Multi-engine jet engine trainer aircraft 7 – 8 – 9 –
3 – Liaison or observation aircraft	1 – Westland Lysander 2 – Piper Cub (F.A.C.) 3 – 4 – 5 – Reserved for Taylorcraft Auster 6 – Reserved for Taylorcraft Auster 7 – 8 – 9 –
4 – Single – and multi-engine fighter or ASW plane, piston engine	1 – Gloster Gladiator 2 – Hawker Hurricane 3 – Supermarine Spitfire 4 – Republic F-47 Thunderbolt 5 – Curtiss SB2C-5 Helldiver 6 – Lockheed PV-2 Harpoon 7 – 8 – 9 –
5 – Single – and multi – engine fighter plane, jet engine	1 – Reserved for single-engine fighter plane, jet engine 2 – Idem 3 – Idem 4 – Idem 5 – Idem 6 – Reserved for multi-engine fighter plane, jet engine 7 – Idem 8 – Idem 9 – Idem

6 –Transport aircraft, single or multi-engine, piston engine	1 – DHC. Otter – From 6101 to 6149. Slot reserved but aircraft never acquired. 1 – Douglas D.C. 3 Dakota. From 6150 onwards 2 – 3 – Junkers Ju 52-3mge 4 – 5 – 6 – Douglas C-54 Skymaster 7 – 8 – 9 –
7 – SAR aircraft or bomber, piston engine	1 – Grumman SA-16 Albatros 2 – 3 – 4 – Boeing B-17 5 – Douglas SC-54 Rescuemaster 6 – 7 – 8 – 9 –
8 – Multi-engine jet aircraft, except fighters	1 – 2 – 3 – 4 – 5 – 6 – 7 – 8 – 9 –
9 – Other aircraft	1 – Sikorsky H-19 Chickasaw 2 – 3 – 4 – Grumman G-21B Goose 5 – 6 – 7 – 8 – 9 –

Notes:

1 – The blank spaces apparent on the table were reserved for future acquisitions by the new Air Force.

2 – As stated in the text above, serial blocks 41**, 42**, 43** and 44** (in italic in the table) were allocated but not included in the document serving the basis for the elaboration of the table. Of those, only block 44** was used, for F-47 Thunderbolt serials.

7 – Revision of the 1951 system in 1993

By an internal order to the *Força Aérea* dated 7 September 1993, a revision was implemented to the 1951 system still in use, applying an extra digit to each aircraft, on a five-character serial. That extra digit would only be 1 or 0, depending on the aircraft being in active service or not. The remaining four figures were allocated as on the former system with slight variations. For instance, the ASK 21 gliders that previously had serials 1001 to 1004, saw them changed to 10101 to 10104. The Falcon 20 changed its serials sequence from 8101-8103 to 17101-17103.

Furthermore the newly received F-16A, to which serials numbers 6601 to 6617 had been initially assigned, were instead identified by serials 15101 to 15117, although in a demonstration flight in September 1994, aircraft 5106 and 15104 were seen flying in formation (a case of sticker peeling off?)

Naval Aviation

Naval Aviation (N.A.) created by *Decreto-Lei no. 3395* dated 28 September 1917 had the following systems in its history:

1 – Sequential system for each model of aircraft (1917)

This practice was only used on the FBA Type B and Donnet Denhaut 200ch flying boats. As the name suggests, a sequence of serials was assigned to each aircraft, always starting with 1.

2 – Unique sequential system (1918?)

Each aircraft, regardless of its type, received a number in a sequence from a unique list for all aircraft. For instance, the Fairey IIID fleet was given the serials 16 to 20, the Curtiss HS-2L, 21 to 24, etc.

The list of serials on this system went up to 136, this being apparently the last serial, allocated to an interned RAF Short Sunderland. However, without any further reference, a photograph of a Portuguese Sunderland exists, showing the serial number 120. No other references, written or photographic, confirm any further details in this case.

3 – Alpha-numeric system (1943)

From 1943, a new system was applied that lasted until the demise of the Naval Aviation service, the alpha-numeric system.

To each aircraft was given a serial consisting of a prefix of one or two letters, sometimes a hyphen, and the individual aircraft number. For instance, the Beech C-45 and AT-11 would receive serials BC-1 to BC-12, the SNJ-4, I-1 to I-8, the Beaufighters BF 1 to BF 17. When the aircraft were transferred to the Air Force, different practices appeared, in some cases both systems of serial numbers coexisting, with a number of aircraft maintaining the N.A. identification (Helldivers and Grumman G-21, for instance) while others received the Air Force serial. This happened, for instance, to the Grumman Widgeon, in the series 24**, and with the 18 Tiger Moths transferred in 1952 that saw their serial numbers changed from T-* to 11**. Examples are T-1, T-2 and T-3, which became, respectively, 1105, 1114 and 1116.

Appendix 4. Military Aviation Structure Evolution

This chapter intends, in a simplified way, present the Portuguese Military Aviation structure, its evolution during the period of time concerning the operational period of the aircraft presented in this book.

The beginning – 1914

Portuguese Military Aviation was officially born with the publication of Law no.162, dated 14 May 1914, which created the *Escola de Aeronáutica Militar* (Military Aeronautical School), the place chosen for the installation of its facilities being Vila Nova da Rainha, a hamlet not far from Lisbon. The infrastructure's construction works started in April 1915, with the first group of student-pilots entering in November 1916.

However only in 1918 was the *Serviço de Aviação Militar* (Aeronautical Military Service) formed, with the publication of Decree 4529 dated 29 June 1918, being then a dependent branch of the Army and including the following entities:

- *Direcção de Aeronáutica Militar* (Directorate of Military Aeronautics)
- *Comissão Técnica* (Technical Commission)
- *Escola Militar de Aviação* (Military Aviation School)
- *Escola Militar de Aerostação* (Military Ballooning School)
- *Parque de Material de Aviação* (Aviation Material Depot)
- *Tropas Aeronáuticas* (Aeronautical Troops).

The first operational military aviation flying units emerge as a result of that law, the *Esquadrilha Mista de Depósito* (Depot Mixed Flight) initially based in Alverca and later moved to Tancos airfield, and the *Grupo de Esquadrilhas de Aviação República* G.E.A.R. (Group of Aircraft Flights "Republica") at Amadora, near Lisbon. These units are mentioned in the chapters dedicated to the SPAD S.VII and Martinsyde F.4 Buzzard.

At this point it must be stressed that the Portuguese Navy was carefully paying attention to progress in the use of the aircraft by other navies, and although having Navy officers instructed at the *Escola de Aeronáutica Militar*, decided on the acquisition of its own aircraft, leading to the publication of Decree nr 3395 dated September 1917 which created the *Serviço e Escola de Aviação da Armada* (Service and School of Navy Aviation).

From then until the formation of the *Força Aérea Portuguesa* in 1952, the Navy maintained its own aviation service as in many other countries.

Returning to the new aviation branch of the Army, by 1920 the *Escola de Aeronáutica Militar*, now renamed *Escola Militar de Aviação*, was moved to a new location near the town of Sintra, again not far from Lisbon, becoming the embryo of the future Air Base no. 1. In 1928 it would change its name again, becoming *Escola Militar de Aeronáutica*, in practice reverting to its first name.

The first reorganization – 1924

The Decree-Law no.10094 dated 16 September 1924, created the *Arma de Aeronáutica* (Aeronautical Branch), and from October 1927 the flying and support units were re-organised as follows:

The flying units *Esquadrilhas* (Flights) were replaced by *Grupos* (Groups) that in turn contained the Flights deemed necessary for the Group mission, therefore creating:

- *The Grupo Independente de Aviação de Protecção e de Combate* (G.I.A.P.C.) (Independent Group of Protection and Combat Aviation) at Tancos replacing the Flight already located there.
- *Grupo de Aviação de Informação* (G.A.I.) (Group of Scouting Aviation) at Amadora, replacing the G.E.A.R. mentioned above.
- *Grupo Independente de Aviação de Bombardeamento* (G.I.A.B.) (Independent Group of Bombing Aviation) at Alverca.

In 1928 the *Parque de Material de Aviação* (Aviation Material Depot) located at Alverca was renamed *Oficinas Gerais de Material Aeronáutico* (General Aviation Works), and is still in existence today, as a modern aircraft maintenance and construction plant. Without doubt it must be one of the oldest aircraft plants in the world, having worked under the same name and maintained the same location since 1928!

The reorganization of 1937

With war approaching fast, the Decree-Law no. 28401, dated 31 December 1937, implemented a new organisation of the *Aeronautica*. Accordingly, in peacetime Portuguese Military Aviation would be composed of:

- One *Comando Geral de Aeronáutica* (General Aeronautic Command), congregating:
- *Comando da Defesa Terrestre contra Aeronaves* (Anti Aircraft Command).
- Air Bases and Airfields
- *Esquadrilhas de Aviação de Informação* (Scouting Aviation Flights), which would encompass reconnaissance and observation flights, independent or grouped.
- *Esquadrilhas de Aviação de Caça* (Fighter Flights), independent or grouped
- *Esquadrilhas de Aviação de Bombardeamento* (Bombing Flights), independent or grouped.
- *Companhia de Aerosteiros* (Balloon Company)
- *Escola Prática* (Practice School)
- *Depósito de Material de Aviação* (Aviation Material Depot)
- *Depósito de Material de Aerostação* (Balloon Material Depot)

Three Air bases were then established, in the vicinity of villages or small towns from where they would take their names, i.e., Sintra, Ota and Tancos. Equally, an aerodrome-base was installed at Lisbon Airport, while the Espinho airfield in the Northern country, close to the town of Porto in the dependence of the *Escola Prática*, located at Sintra. The existing flying units were then distributed across those locations.

The basic flying unit was the *Esquadrilha* (Flight), the number of aircraft for each unit being as follows:

- Fighter Flights – 15 aircraft
- Bomber Flights – 5 aircraft
- Reconnaissance Flights – 9 aircraft
- Observation Flights – 9 aircraft

In the fighter Flights, for example, 12 aircraft at least should be operational at any time. They could be divided in two sections of six, or four patrols of three aircraft each. The total number of aircraft would be:

- Four Bomber Flights – 20 aircraft at Ota
- Three Fighter Flights – 45 aircraft, one Flight at each of Ota, Tancos and Lisbon
- One Reconnaissance Flight – nine aircraft at Tancos
- Five Observation Flights – 45 aircraft, being two Flights at Sintra and three at Tancos
- One Flight of Instruction and Training at Sintra – Quantity not specified.

Amadora and Alverca airfields ceased their existence as home bases for operational Flights in 1938, Amadora being closed while Alverca maintained as mentioned above the aircraft maintenance and construction facilities.

In 1940 when the Ota Air Base was officially inaugurated, the decision to allocate numbers to the Air Bases was taken, thus Sintra became Air Base No. 1, Ota, Air Base No. 2 and Tancos, Air Base No. 3. With the establishment of the *Aeronautica Militar* in the Azores, the defence of the Islands was also substantially reinforced with men and machines, including aircraft as bombers/transports and fighters.

The Rabo de Peixe airfield, São Miguel Island, the first to be activated during the military movement to Azores would later become Air Base No.4. Lajes Airfield, Terceira Island, would become Air Base No. 5. Later, with the dismantling of Rabo de Peixe Air Base, Lajes would take its number as Air Base No. 4, which it has retained to this day.

During the Second World War, the basic framework of the *Aeronautica Militar* was maintained, although with new military airfields becoming operational on the front line, such as Lisbon, smaller and more remote airfields such as Espinho and also Santana, a small airfield in the Azores, disbanded afterwards.

The birth of the *Força Aérea Portuguesa* (Portuguese Air Force) – 1952

During the war years the *Aeronautica Militar* grew exponentially with the great influx of aircraft, not only with the direct acquisitions by the Portuguese Government but also with the incorporation of interned and/or reception of aircraft resulting from the Azores agreement.

One of the major factors that weighed in favour of the birth of *Força Aérea Portuguesa* – F.A.P. (Portuguese Air Force) was the creation of NATO in April 1949. The ensuing adhesion of Portugal to the Organisation, resulting in the need for the modernisation of the Portuguese Armed Forces, dictated the amalgamation into a unique force of the separate Army and Navy Air components.

The promulgation of Law Nr 2055 of 27th May 1952, followed by Decree-Law Nr 38805 of 28 June 1952 defined the new entity and its structure, stating at the same time that the date of 1 July was the date for execution of the above mentioned laws. This way the date became the anniversary date for F.A.P.

The basic structure of the F.A.P., as defined in the Decree-Law 39071 of 28 December 1952, was the following:

- One *Comando Geral das Forças Aéreas* (General Command of the Air Forces);
- One *Comando das Forças Aéreas Operacionais* (Command of the Operational Air Forces);
- One *Comando de Instrução e Treino* (Command of Instruction and Training);
- Six *Bases Aéreas* (Air Base No. 1, Sintra, Air Base No. 2, Ota, Air Base No. 3, Tancos, Air Base No. 4, Lajes [Azores], Air Base No. 5 S. Jacinto, later disbanded and moved south near the village of Monte Real, Air Base 6 Montijo);
- 4 Aeródromos-Base (Airfields);
- *Grupo de Esquadras de Caça* (Group of Fighter Squadrons);
- *Esquadras de Aviação de Cooperação com as Forças de Terra e Navais* (Army and Navy Cooperation Squadrons);
- *Unidades de Busca e Salvamento* (Search and Rescue Units);
- *Formações de Transporte* (Transport Formations)
- *Esquadras de Treino* (Training Squadrons)
- *Escolas* (Schools)
- *Unidades de Alerta* (Early Warning Units)
- *Eventualmente Tropas de Defesa Terrestre Contra Aeronaves* (Eventual Troops for Anti Aircraft Defence).

On the other hand the flying units were now re-defined:

- *Brigada Aérea* (Air Brigade) – The biggest unit composed of
- *Grupos* (Groups) – Composed of
- *Esquadras* (Squadrons), with 25 aircraft in the fighter squadrons. Squadrons could be divided into smaller units, the *Esquadrilhas* (Flights).

Within this framework, the central unit ceased to be the *Esquadrilha* (Flight) with a nominal strength of 15 aircraft (in the case of fighter units), and became the *Esquadra* (Squadron) with a nominal strength of 25 aircraft (again, where fighters are concerned).

Also, although not forbidden in the new structure, the practice of using letters to identify the *Esquadrilhas*, now *Esquadras*, was quietly dropped, and replaced by the last two or three digits of the serial number, even if not always used on the aircraft. As an example of this practice refer to the F-47 chapter.

Appendix 5. Belligerent Fighters in Portugal during WWII

For the sake of completeness, the belligerent fighters that landed in Portugal, but unlike the Airacobras and the Lightning, were not incorporated within Portuguese Military Aviation during the WWII period, are described here. Naturally, not all of them would be in an airworthy condition and safe to fly on their arrival – some had ditched in the sea or were destroyed during the attempted emergency landing. Even where aircraft were serviceable, the incorporation of a one-off model in the air arm was not appealing, due to maintenance or operational problems.

The story of these fighters 'falling from the skies' starts on 1 May 1941, when a Beaufighter Mk IC, T3229 of 252 Squadron RAF ditched off Lisbon, the crew being rescued. This aircraft was part of a flight of fifteen belonging to the Squadron en route to Gibraltar and then Malta. This event was not only the beginning of the long story of the 'falling fighters' but also the first of a series of no fewer than seven cases of Beaufighters landing or ditching in Portuguese waters.

Twenty-one days later, 22 May 1941, another Beaufighter Mk IC also from 252 Squadron, serial T3249, force landed during a flight from Gibraltar to St. Eval in Cornwall (UK), the crew surviving and being interned.

The next 'visitor' was a Fairey Fulmar Mk II, from 807 Squadron on board HMS *Argus*, this being the only recorded case of a Royal Navy aircraft landing in Portugal. The Fulmar had the serial X8700, and landed on an Algarve island, in the Southern part of the country. The crew survived and were safely returned to their ship.

Another Beaufighter, this time a Mk IF model, followed on 17 December 1941, when one of its engines stopped in flight, forcing the aircraft to perform an emergency landing 12 miles southwest of Tancos Air base. The aircraft was serial number X7647 and was being flown by an O.A.D.U. (Overseas Aircraft Delivery Unit).

On 2 April, Spitfire P.R.IV/V BP906 made an emergency landing near Alcácer do Sal, south of Lisbon, and the pilot set the fighter alight, thus preventing it from being of any further use to anyone.

At a certain point, possibly after this event, an agreement was reached between the Portuguese and British authorities by which it was decided that, where the force-landed aircraft did not carry any secret equipment, it should not be destroyed by its crew. In exchange, the repatriation of that

Beaufighter Mk X RAF serial JM337 after internment. In the original photo the serial number can clearly be seen, proving that it was JM337 and not JM377 as stated elsewhere. (FAP/AHFA/MAIS ALTO)

Beaufighter Mk X RAF serial JM337, most probably at Sintra Air Base before being sent to scrap. (FAP/AHFA/MAIS ALTO)

same crew would be processed as soon as possible, instead of being interned in Portugal until the end of the war. This would also allow the eventual incorporation of the aircraft by the Portuguese Military Aviation, which later happened several times with other types of aircraft. The subject of interned crews has already been addressed in the P-38 Lightning Chapter.

The next case, with the exception of the Airacobras and Lightnings which are dealt with in their own chapters, occurred again with a Spitfire, this time a PR Mk XI, serial EN419 of the 1st O.A.D.U., that landed on Furadouro Beach on the Portuguese central Atlantic coast, on 5 May 1943. As the unit under which it was flying implies, it was probably on a delivery flight. We know that this aircraft survived the war, but for an unknown reason it was not taken into service by the *Arma de Aeronáutica*, being scrapped at the end of its days.

Another Spitfire PR Mk XI was next, serial MB782, this time on a ferry flight from Portreath in the UK (Cornwall) to Gibraltar, forced to land at Monforte, a town deep in the interior of the country and very close to the Spanish border. Incidentally, this case as in many others raises the question of the air corridors that started or ended in the UK in direction to and from Gibraltar. As

Beaufighter Mk TFX RAF serial NV321/SNAKE after its crash in Alto do Cobre, Cascais, its wing serving as a sun shelter for its guardians. (J. Touzet)

Beaufighter Mk TFX RAF serial NV321/SNAKE after its crash in Alto do Cobre, Cascais. The word SNAKE painted in an aircraft fuselage signified that this same aircraft could not be retained for any reason and at any stop during its delivery flight. (J. Touzet)

it is obvious with this incident, the flight path instead going around the airspace of a neutral country passed directly over it. It is appropriate to ask if the purpose of the flight was only the delivery of an aircraft or if there was also some kind of reconnaissance involved. In any case and once again the aircraft was not used and was later scrapped[1].

Another Beaufighter, this time a Mk XI model, serial JL895 from 304 Flying Training Unit RAF, ditched in the sea near the Portuguese coast between the towns of Leiria and Pedrógão on 1 July 1943. Two weeks later, on 14 July, Beaufighter Mk X, serial JM337, 'G for George', from 248 Squadron RAF, made an emergency landing at Portela Lisbon Airport. The available photographs show an apparently intact airframe, which however was abandoned for many years, being finally broken up and scrapped.

The next Beaufighter, this time an Mk IIF, serial number T3423, belonging to 233 Squadron RAF, would be the next fighter to fall, this time as a result of an encounter with an Fw 200 Condor near the Portuguese West coast. The Beaufighter was forced to ditch in the vicinity of Cabo Sardão. This incident took place on 7 September 1943.

The next event took place in the second half of 1944. On 5 August 1944, Beaufighter T.F. Mk X serial NV321/SNAKE made an emergency landing at Alto do Cobre (Cascais), some 30 km West of Lisbon. Again, it had been on a delivery flight to Air Command Southeast Asia, the word SNAKE after the serial meaning that the aircraft could not be appropriated by any other RAF unit while en route to its destination. From the available photographs and in accordance with prior agreements with the British Authorities, it is clear that the aircraft was carrying sensitive equipment, being damaged beyond repair (DBR) by its crew. Therefore it was not feasible to recover it, its destiny being the scrap yard.

Finally and to conclude this chapter two German aircraft, one being a bomber prototype, also arrived in Portuguese territory by the end of the war, and this time deliberately, recalling the two French and one Belgian aircraft that fled to Portugal in the summer of 1940[2].

1 The fate of these two Spitfires is mentioned in a note dated 17 June 1946 from Comando Geral da Aeronautica Militar to the Ministério da Guerra, informing that the British Government, when requested to recover the interned RAF aircraft still in existence and in storage, declined to do so, concerning at least a group of eight aircraft, among them the above two mentioned aeroplanes.

2 Other aircraft than fighters were obliged to force-land or ditch in the Portuguese Continental territory or waters, but as they did not belong to the fighters' category, they were not considered in this chapter,

The first case, while not a fighter, is included here because belongs to the same family of the fighter that followed it. The aircraft was one of the prototypes of the Junkers Ju 188 series, coded CE+XA V63/I, *Werk Nummer* 140669 and which escaped from the Junkers plant on 6 April 1945, landing intact at Lisbon Airport at 12:52 that day. The two occupants told the Portuguese authorities that they intended to reach South America where one of them had family, but it has not been possible to find any references or to confirm what happened to them in reality. It is known that the Germans tried to recover the aircraft but as they were apparently unsuccessful, the airframe was finally scrapped.

Ju 88G6-c 4R+LR. Werk Nummer *621800 after the arrival in Portugal. (Coll. Carlos B. da Fonseca)*

The other landing of a German origin aircraft was this time a night fighter of a related type, a Junkers Ju 88G-6c from the 7./NJG 2, which landed at Oporto airport only a few days before V.E. day, 2 May 1945. It was coded 4R+LR and had the *Werk Nummer* 621800. Nothing is known of its occupants but as it is attested by the photographs, the aircraft appeared intact, being later removed to Espinho airfield, where it stayed, rotting away, once there was no more German Government or authorities to ask for its return, as happened with the previous Ju 188. (Interestingly, on 5 May 1945, another Junkers Ju 88G-6c, D5-GH landed at Gormanston aerodrome in Ireland, the crew seeking refuge.)

Of the thirteen aircraft presented in this chapter, the *Arma de Aeronáutica* did not recover or use any of them. Ironically, the Portuguese Naval Aviation branch would purchase and operate after the war examples of the most numerous of those, the Beaufighter, as related elsewhere in this book!

two hundred and four aircraft being accounted in these conditions. Approximately the same amount was also recorded in the Spanish territory.

Ju 88G6-c 4R+LR. Werk Nummer *621800. Before being scrapped, the final days of the Junkers were spent as background for souvenir shots... (Coll. Carlos B. da Fonseca)*

As a final note, we would like to stress that the elements for this chapter are based on information researched and gathered over a large period of time by the authors with the invaluable help of Lieutenant-General Mimoso e Carvalho, to whom we address our gratitude.

Tail of 4R+LR. The Werk Nummer *621800 can be clearly seen. Note what appear to be 12 grey (?) "Kill Markings" under the black swastika. By the time this photo was taken, the aircraft was abandoned and served as a children's playground until finally being scrapped. (Coll. Sarg. Pepe)*

Ju 88G-6c 4R+LR. Photo coll. Carlos B.da Fonseca

Ju 188 CE+XA Werk Nummer *140669 V63/I at Lisbon Airport. (Coll. Conceição Silva)*

Appendix 6. Map of Portugal

Appendix 7. Portuguese Aviation Ranks

RANK EQUIVALENTS – OFFICERS – Circa 1975								
Portugal			United Kingdom			United States		
Army	Navy	Air Force	Army	Navy	Air Force	Army	Navy	Air Force
General	Contra-Almirante	General		Vice Admiral	Air Marshall	Lieutenant General	Vice Admiral	Lieutenant General
Brigadeiro	Comodoro	Brigadeiro		Rear Admiral	Air Vice Marshal	Major General	Rear Admiral	Major General
No Equiv.	No Equiv.	No Equiv.		Commandant	Air Comodore	Brigadier General	Rear Admiral/ Commodore	Brigadier General
Coronel	Capitão de Mar e Guerra	Coronel		Captain	Group Captain	Colonel	Captain	Colonel
Tenente Coronel	Capitão de Fragata	Tenente Coronel		Commander	Wing Commander	Lieutenant Colonel	Commander	Lieutenant Colonel
Major	Capitão-Tenente	Major		Lieutenant Commander	Squadron Leader	Major	Lieutenant Commander	Major
Capitão	PrimeiroTenente	Capitão		Lieutenant	Flight Lieutenant	Captain	Lieutenant	Captain
Tenente/ Alferes	Segundo Tenente Guarda-Marinha e Sub-Tenente	Tenente/Alferes		Sub Lieutenant	Flying Officer/ Pilot Officer	First Lieutenant/ Second Lieutenant	Lieutenant Junior Grade/Ensign	First Lieutenant/ Second Lieutenant

RANK EQUIVALENTS – Other Ranks – Circa 1975								
Portugal			United Kingdom			United States		
Army	Navy	Air Force	Army	Navy	Air Force	Army	Navy	Air Force
Sargento Ajudante	Sargento Ajudante	Sargento Ajudante	Warrant Officer	Fleet Chief Petty Officer	Warrant Officer	Sergeant Major	Master Chief Petty Officer	Chief Master Sergeant
Primeiro Sargento	Primeiro Sargento	Primeiro Sargento	Warrant Officer II	No Equiv.	No Equiv.	Master Sergeant	Senior Chief Petty Officer	Senior Master Sergeant
Segundo Sargento	Segundo Sargento	Segundo Sargento	Staff Sergeant	Chief Petty Officer	Flight Sergeant Chief Technician	Sergeant 1st Class	Chief Petty Officer	Master Sergeant
Furriel	Sub-sargento	Furriel	Sergeant	Petty Officer	Sergeant	Staff Sergeant	Petty Officer 1st Class	Technical Sergeant
Segundo Furriel	Segundo Sub-sargento	Segundo Furriel	No Equiv.	No Equiv.	No Equiv.	Sergeant	Petty Officer 2nd Class	Staff Sergeant
Primeiro Cabo	Cabo	Primeiro Cabo	Corporal	Leading Rate	Corporal	Corporal	Petty Officer 3rd Class	Sergeant
No Equiv.	Marinheiro	No Equiv.	Lance Corporal	No Equiv.	No Equiv.	Private 1st Class	Seaman	Airman 1st Class
Segundo Cabo	Primeiro Grumete	Segundo Cabo	Private (Classes 1-3)	Able or Ordinary Rate	Leading Aircraftsman Senior Aircraftman	Private	Seaman Apprentice	Airman
Soldado	Segundo Grumete	Soldado	Private (Class 4)	Junior Rate	Aircraftsman	Private	Seaman Recruit	Basic Airman

Bibliography:

Hereunder we are including a list of books that have been published along the years, that we sense should always be considered "*The reference works*" when dealing with the History of the Portuguese Military Aviation. In what concerns books dealing with specific subjects they are already designated under each chapter.

Nonetheless, as the publishing dates of these books cover a large period of time, some care must be taken when one uses them, since the research concerning the History of Portuguese Military Aviation during the last 20 or 30 years developed enormously, the advent of new communication technologies being but one of the factors that helped bring to light many aspects and details unknown at the date of their first issuing.

A good example of this are the numerous research articles published along the last 25 years in *MAIS ALTO*, the official magazine of *FAP*, which is bringing almost in every issue new information aspects of the Military Aviation History, often contradicting and/or expand facts found in those books

Abecasis, José, Krus, *Bordo de Ataque*, Coimbra Editora, Coimbra 1985, Vols. I and II (in Portuguese only)

Aircraft cards, USAAF accident reports, several USAAF letters, and other official documents.

Alto, Mais, (Magazine of Portuguese Air Force), Several issues

Andrade, John, M., *Spanish and Portuguese Military Aviation*, Midland Counties Publications, Leicester, 1977

Author´s archives

Pilot's logbooks and Air Bases flight logs

Avions – No.139, October 2004

Bell P-39/63 Variant Briefing, Wings of Fame, Volume 10

Bell, Dana, *Air Force Colours - Vol.2 – ETO & MTO 1942–45*, Squadron-Signal Publications

Bowers, Peter, *Curtiss Aircraft 1907–1947*, Putnam

Bowyer, Michael, J.F., *Fighting Colours – RAF Fighter Camouflage and Markings*, 2nd Edition, P.S.Limited, 1975

British Aviation Colours of World War Two – RAF Museum Series Vol.3, Arms and Armour Press, 1976

Callaway, Tim, *Lockheed P-38 Lightning*, Aviation Classics nr 14

Camouflage and Markings nr 1 – Supermarine Spitfire RAF Northern Europe 1935–45 – Ducimus Publications

Cardoso, Adelino, *Aeronaves Militares Portuguesas no Século XX*, Essencial, Lisboa, 2000 (in Portuguese)

Cardoso, Adelino, *Aeronaves Militares Portuguesas – Cem anos de aviação em Portugal*, Essencial, 2009 (in Portuguese)

Cardoso, Edgar, *História da Força Aérea Portuguesa*, FAP Edition, 1984

Caruana, R.J., *Born With A Sting – The Hawker Fury*, Scale Aviation Modeller Vol.3, Nº 8, August 1997

Caruana, Richard J., *P-47 Thunderbolt – Famous Aircraft of the World*

Correia, J.M., *Os Gladiator da Cruz de Cristo*, Esq. 33, 2005

Correia, José, Manuel, Dr. *Mais Alto no. 364*, November/December 2006, (Portuguese only)

Correia, José, Manuel, Dr., *Asas da Cruz de Cristo – Spitfire Mk I em Portugal*, (Portuguese only)

Crawford, Alex, *Hawker Fury and Nimrod*, MMP Publications Nº 8105

Crawford, Alex, *Gloster Gladiator Vol.1*, MMP Publications, 2009

Cross, Roy, *Lockheed P-38 Lightning Described*, Kookaburra Technical Publications

Cuny, Jean, Beauchamp, Gerard. *Curtiss Hawk 75*, DOCAVIA

Davilla, and Soltan, *French Aircraft of the First World War*, Flying Machines Press 2002

de Barros, Machado, General (R), *Fury e Gladiator, Revista "Mais Alto"*, nº 243

Dez Décadas de Força Aérea – Comissão Histórico-Cultural da Força Aérea, Lisboa, 2015

Dorr, Robert F., Scutts, Jerry C. *Bell P-39 Airacobra*, Crowood Aviation Series, London

Ehrengardt, C.J., *Le P-47 Thunderbolt*, Aero-Journal HS no.5, Editions Caraktère, Mars-Avril, 2010

Franks, Richard A., *The Hawker Hurricane*, SAM Publications, 1999

Goulding, J., Ward, R., *Gladiator, Gauntlet, Fury, Demon, Ducimus Camouflage and Markings* Nº 5

Gracier, Vincent, *La Guerre du Desert – "Torch"*, Wing Masters Hors Serie nº 13

Green, W., Swanborough, G., *Barrier Breaking Fury*, Air Enthusiast Quarterly Nº Three

Hall, Allan, *Hawker Fury and Nimrod*, Scale Aircraft Modelling Vol.16, Nº 2, December 1993

Hall, Allan, *Lockheed P-38, F-4 & F-5 Lightning*, Camouflage and Markings nr 18, Ducimus Publications
História da Força Aérea Portuguesa 1952-1959 Volume I, FAP Edition, 2007
Humphreys, Robert, *The Supermarine Spitfire (Part 1: Merlin powered)*, SAM Publications, 2000
Illfrey, Jack, *Happy Jack's Go Buggy*, A Fighter Pilot's Story
James, Derek N., *Gloster Aircraft since 1917*, Putnam, 1971
Jerram, M., *The Best Flying Club In The World*, Scale Aviation Modeller Vol.12, N° 3, March 2006
Juszczak, Artur, Pęczkowski, Robert, *Bell P-39 Airacobra*, MMP Publications
Lapa, Albino, *Aviação Portuguesa*, Lisboa, 1928 (in Portuguese)
Le Moniteur de l'Aeronautique no. 5, Fevrier, 1978
Lochery, Neill, Lisbon, *War in the Shadows of the City of Light, 1939–1945*, 2012
Lockheed P-38 Lightning, Scale Aircraft Modelling Vol.11 No.2, Aircraft in Detail
Lopes, Mário, Canongia, Eng°, *Mohawks and Spitfires in Portugal*, Avions Magazine no. 92 and 93, (French only)
Lopes, Mario, Canongia, Costa, Rodrigues, José, Manuel, *Os Aviões da Cruz de Cristo*, 1st Edition, Dinalivro, Lisboa, 1989 (in Portuguese only)
Lopes, Mário, Canongia, *Os Aviões da Cruz de Cristo*, 2nd Edition, Dinalivro, Lisboa, 2000 (Bilingual, Portuguese and English)
Lopes, Mário, Canongia, Eng°, *Spitfires e Hurricanes em Portugal*, Dinalivro, Lisbon, 1992, Bilingual Portuguese/English version
MAIS ALTO, Issue no. 371, Jan-Fev., 2008
MAIS ALTO, Set/October 2001
Marchand, Patrick, Picard, Isabelle, *Les P-38 de la 33e Escadre*, Les Ailes de Gloire n° 16
Mason, Francis K., *Hawker Hurricane Described*, Kookaburra Technical Publications, 1971
Mason, Francis K., *The Hawker Hurricane*, Aston Publications, 1987
Mitchell, Rick, *Airacobra Advantage: The Flying Cannon*, Pictoral Histories Publishing Co., Missoula, Montana, USA
Persyn, Lionel, *Les Curtiss H-75 de l'Armée de l'Air*, Lela Press
Portaria 13602
Serejo, Carlos, *Subsidios para a história da Aviação Militar Portuguesa*, FAP, Lisboa, 2012 (in Portuguese)
Several articles in the Portuguese Air Force magazine MAIS ALTO
Spitfire 70 – Key Publishing
Swanborough, Gordon, Bowers, Peter, *United States Military Aircraft since 1908*, Putnam
Tadeu, Viriato, *Quando a Marinha tinha asas*, Edições Culturais da Marinha, Lisboa, 1984 (in Portuguese only)
Terbeck, Helmut, and others, *Spitfire International*, An Air-Britain publication
Vieira, Rui, Aballe, *1930–1934 Entre Varsóvia e Londres*, Revista "Mais Alto" n°s. 361 and 362.